HUMBER COLLEGE

Date Due		
OCT 1 1984		
SEP 21 1984		
JAN 23 1990		
JAN 15 1990		
DEC 21 1992		
NOV 24 1993		
NOV 24 1993		
NOV 18 1994		
NOV 18 1994		
NOV 14 1994		

Public Rights

and the

Private Press

Public Rights

and the

Private Press

Jerome A. Barron

BUTTERWORTHS
Toronto

Public Rights and the Private Press
© 1981 Butterworth & Co. (Canada) Ltd.

All rights reserved. No part of this publication may be reproduced, stored in a retrieval system, or transmitted, in any form or by any means, photocopying, electronic, mechanical, recording, or otherwise, without the prior written permission of the copyright holder.

Printed and bound in Canada

The Butterworth Group of Companies
Canada:
Butterworth & Co. (Canada) Ltd., Toronto and Vancouver
United Kingdom:
Butterworth & Co. (Publishers) Ltd., London
Australia:
Butterworths Pty. Ltd., Sydney
New Zealand:
Butterworths of New Zealand Ltd., Wellington
South Africa:
Butterworth & Co. (South Africa) Ltd., Durban
United States:
Butterworth (Publishers) Inc., Boston
Butterworth (Legal Publishers) Inc., Seattle
Mason Publishing Company, St. Paul

Canadian Cataloguing in Publication data

Barron, Jerome A.
  Public rights and the private press

Includes index.
ISBN 0-409-81295-1

1. Press law - United States. 2. Mass media - Law and legislation - United States. I. Title.

KF2750.B37   343.73'0998   C81-094370-0

Cover design by Brant Cowie

FOR MYRA

Contents

Preface, ix

1 Reflections on the *Tornillo* Case, 1
2 American Journalism and the First Amendment: An Access Perspective, 11
3 Access through Grace?, 21
4 Public Media and Editorial Autonomy: *The Reflector* and the Gay Alliance, 39
5 The Rise and Fall of a Doctrine of Editorial Privilege: Reflections on *Herbert* v. *Lando,* 53
6 Whose First?, 83
7 Access for Advertising in the Print Media and the Commercial Speech Boom, 89
8 How Fair Should Investigative Television Be?: Appraising the Alternatives, 121
9 The Cross-ownership Case and the Trouble with Judge Bazelon's Conversion, 137
10 Through an American Looking Glass: Law and Press in Britain, 159
11 The Future for Media Law in the 1980s, 173

Epilogue, 183
Table of Cases, 193
Index, 197

Preface

As a lawyer critic of the press, it is my purpose to bring about a new accommodation between individual rights and media freedom. Nothing here is designed to encourage or prefer government in any direct conflict it may have with the press. The essence of a free press is in its immunity from direct restraint by government. Nonetheless, law, and the legal institutions such as the courts, which an ordered society makes possible, can be used to resolve in a fair and reasoned manner conflicts within the private sector - conflicts between media and individuals.

In this post-Watergate phase of First Amendment history, we can rejoice that a free press was able to play a vital, critical investigative role in safeguarding constitutional democracy. But we should not let our enthusiasm for the heightened investigative and corrective role of the press in its contests with government deflect consideration of contests where the relative power of the combatants is far different. Such is the case in the fields of access, reply, protection of reputation, and entry into media ownership where powerless individuals and giant media occasionally collide. In short, in conflicts between the individual and the media I would write large the views expressed by Mr. Justice Harlan when he considered an individual's claim that his privacy had been invaded by a media defendant. 'The "freedom of the press" guaranteed by the First Amendment, and as reflected in the Fourteenth, cannot be thought to insulate all press conduct from review and responsibility for harm inflicted.' In recent years the Supreme Court has instructed us that the press is free and need not be fair. In this book, I make an extended argument that, in this unique and abundant land, the press can be both free and fair.

To my wife, Myra, and my children, Jonathan, David, and Jennifer, I express my gratitude for their constant encouragement to continue the task once begun. For Myra, my thanks and love for her constant faith that the future always gives hope to the battle. My thanks go also to my students, particularly those in the public policy and mass media course in the National Law Center, George Washington University. I first shared with them many of the ideas expressed here. Their intense and open-minded criticism perhaps made the final exposition a little more meaningful.

Finally, I would like to thank those lawyers and journalists in England who gave freely of their time and hospitality during my sabbatical in England in the fall of 1976. I would like to mention specifically the following lawyers and journalists: Lord Goodman, Anthony Howard, Brian Niell, Bernard Nossiter, Michael Rubinstein, Michael Scammell, John Whale, Michael Zander, and Graham Zellick. I would also like to thank J.A. Boxhall and his colleagues at the Institute of Advanced Legal Studies of the University of London for making a desk available to me in their handsome facilities in Russell Square. Finally, I would like to thank Miss LaMona Rivers of the National Law Center, George Washington University, who typed the entire manuscript. Her patience, skill, and enthusiasm for both work and ideas made this book possible.

Jerome A. Barron

Washington, DC
February 1981

THE FIRST AMENDMENT, UNITED STATES CONSTITUTION

Congress shall make no law . . . abridging the freedom of speech, or of the press. . . .

The Fairness Doctrine, Section 315(a), Federal Communications Act

Sect. 315. Candidates for public office; facilities; rules

(a) If any licensee shall permit any person who is a legally qualified candidate for any public office to use a broadcasting station, he shall afford equal opportunities to all other candidates for that office in the use of such broadcasting station: *Provided,* that such licensee shall have no power of censorship over the material broadcast under the provisions of this section. No obligation is imposed upon any licensee to allow the use of its station by any such candidate. Appearance by a legally qualified candidate on any -
    (1) bona fide newscast,
    (2) bona fide news interview,
    (3) bona fide news documentary (if the appearance of the candidate is incidental to the presentation of the subjects covered by the news documentary), or
    (4) on-the-spot coverage of bona fide news events (including but not limited to political conventions and activities incidental thereto), shall not be deemed to be use of a broadcasting station within the meaning of this subsection. *Nothing in the foregoing sentence shall be construed as relieving broadcasters, in connection with the presentation of newscasts, news interviews, news documentaries, and on the spot coverage of news events, from the obligation imposed upon them under this chapter to operate in the public interest and to afford reasonable opportunity for the discussion of conflicting views on issues of public importance.*

Public Rights

and the

Private Press

1

Reflections on the Tornillo Case

On June 25, 1974, the Supreme Court held that the Florida right of reply law was unconstitutional.* The decision was unanimous.[1] A right of access and reply had been advocated and debated in the United States as a major public issue for less than a decade. But the span of time culminating in the Court's massive rejection of a right of access to the press in June 1974 covers half a century in trauma and revolution in spirit and social attitude.

In the tumultuous days of the early and middle sixties, the excluded blacks and the outraged anti-war radicals were in the foreground of concern with respect to a need for a legitimized representation in the daily press. Better a right of access to the daily press than daily demonstrations in the streets.

Yet as the great access issue came to the court, its liberal background was obscured. Pat Tornillo, then head of the Classroom Teachers Association of Dade County, who brought the case seeking a right to reply against the *Miami Herald,* was thought of as just another aspiring politician, not as a labor leader. To what extent the *Zeitgeist* affected the *Tornillo* case is of course speculation. However, it is clear that the social climate had dramatically altered since another unanimous decision of the Supreme Court, the landmark opinion in *Red Lion*[2] in 1969, holding that the fairness doctrine in broadcast regulation was consistent with the First Amendment. *Red Lion* gave new momentum to citizen groups who used the claim of First Amendment access to break down the absolute control broadcasters and networks had over program content. The movement even encountered a new convert, Spiro Agnew. Agnew was a convert to the critique of the media offered by access proponents, if not a convert to the legal solutions offered by those proponents.

Access was striking responsive chords in all sections of the political

---

* This chapter is largely based on the text of an address which I delivered to the Association for Education in Journalism at their convention in San Diego, California, on Aug. 19, 1974. This address was prepared shortly after the decision of the Supreme Court in the Tornillo case earlier in the summer of 1974.

spectrum. On almost the very eve of the *Tornillo* case, President Nixon spoke warmly of a right of reply and the need for a federal law of libel. Senator McClellan spoke on the floor of the Senate on the desirability of a federal right of reply law. With such friends, the cause of a right of reply had less to fear from its enemies. The access movement had surely won converts far beyond the confines of its liberal origins. But the pace of change affected those origins as well. The ACLU, which had skirted sympathetically with access in 1968, by the time of the *Tornillo* case, had in the main turned its back on the doctrine. The anit-Vietnam war beginnings of the access movement involving suits seeking to compel publication of advertisements protesting involvement in the war had been dramatically co-opted by the adoption of the most famous and important newspapers in the land of the anti-war cause. The death of Martin Luther King and the shift of some sections of the civil rights movement from moral non-violence to violence eventually helped to blunt the moral intensity of the access claims of minority groups.

What is the significance of the transformation of the movement for a right of access and reply from a liberal and even radical cause to a cause with support among conservatives and the right? In a sense, it can be said that this development illustrates the neutrality of ideas of access and reply. If minority groups and Agnew both pleaded for access, was that not all right? Was that not what debate was all about? Nevertheless, the conservative endorsement of a right of reply is a factor in the social climate which must be considered. Important Supreme Court decisions are not arrived at in some juristic heaven but here on this troubled earth. The moral claims of the Negro civil rights movement, and the persecution of that movement through the vehicle of the Alabama libel law may have had much to do with the readiness of the Court to fashion a new law of libel in *New York Times* v. *Sullivan* in 1964.[3] Similarly, the travail of the executive branch and the disgrace of the resigned vice-president, when seen in the light of an unfettered press's vindicated exposure of executive scandal and wrongdoing, may have generated a reluctance to recognize in 1974 the constitutional validity of a statutory right of reply which if presented either at an earlier or later time might have won a different judicial response.

An idea like access which is of wide-ranging interest can be halted but not stilled by a single court decision. Portents of a new concern for property by the Burger Court (a concern which was hardly a dominant motif of the Warren Court) were apparent a year before the decision in *Columbia Broadcasting System* v. *Democratic National Committee*.[4] In that case, some of the justices went out of their way in what was, after all, a case involving the broadcast media and not the press to announce their distaste for a right of access to the press.

When Toby Simon[5] and I briefed, argued, and won the *Tornillo* case in the Supreme Court of Florida, we were hardly heartened by the *CBS* case, but we discounted it. *CBS* had called for the creation of a right of access on the basis of the First Amendment itself. The courts, in such a situation, would have the difficult task of establishing definitions and perimeters. *CBS* involved the difficult state action problem. *Tornillo* involved none of these things. The Florida right of reply statute could be narrowly read, the statutory definitions had been narrowed by the state supreme court,[6] and there was no state action problem.

In retrospect I see that *CBS* established a mood. It reflects a viewpoint which looks at the media as a species of property different from other property; the very existence of the First Amendment is thought, in this view, to confer on media ownership a unique immunity from legal obligation. Such a viewpoint would be bound to resist a First Amendment theory which required newspaper publishers to provide free space against their will. In the *CBS* case, the Court held that there was no First Amendment right to purchase broadcast time for the dissemination of social and political ideas. Advertising time was to be sold at the absolute discretion of the networks without passing on the question whether the First Amendment commanded a right of access to broadcasting. Four of the justices said that networks were private actors and that the commands of the First Amendment ran to the government and not to private parties.

In *CBS*, the court did emphasize that balanced presentation of ideas was not endangered by the result in the case because the existence of the fairness doctrine assured such balanced presentation. Although Chief Justice Burger gave a very robust definition to the fairness doctrine, the 1974 FCC report gave it a very modest scope.[7] In *Brandywine-Main Line Radio*,[8] the case in which Dr. McIntyre lost his license, Judge David Bazelon, previously one of the staunch defenders of the fairness doctrine, wrote a dissent full of doubts about the workings of that doctrine. The dissent was studded with approving quotations from prominent journalists about the folly of imposing any affirmative obligation on the broadcast media. The years since the *CBS* decision have, on the whole, seen a turning away from interpretations of the First Amendment which would impose affirmative obligations on the media.[9]

What of the *Tornillo* decision itself? It may be described as having two ends but no middle. The first part of the decision recites the arguments for access, including the whole of the text of that portion of the decision in *Rosenbloom* v. *Metromedia*[10] written by Mr. Justice Brennan and joined in by Mr. Justice Blackmun and Chief Justice Burger suggesting that the *New York Times* v. *Sullivan* doctrine had grown to swollen proportions. These passages challenged the assumption that the public official-public figure libel plaintiff would necessarily have a forum to respond to a defamation. This assumption was declared to be doubtful at best and surely absurd where the doctrine was extended to private plaintiffs of whom no one had ever heard but who were nonetheless involved in a public issue. If damages were not to be a remedy in such situations absent "actual malice," then perhaps right of reply legislation was the answer. It was, in my judgment, the powerful passages in the Court's 1971 plurality opinion in *Rosenbloom* that persuaded the Florida Supreme Court to sustain the state's right of reply statute.

Despite the fact that this material was faithfully spread on the pages of the Court's decision in *Tornillo*, there is not a word to explain why right of reply, which in theory had seemed the answer to implementing that concern for debate in the press which was so major a force in creating the new public law of libel, was actually cast aside.

In 1971, right of reply legislation had appeared to be constitutional to Blackmun, Burger, and Brennan. In fact, the states were urged to enact such statutes.[11] In 1974, statutes telling papers what to print were held to be intolerable governmental intrusion into editorial discretion. Why? We are not told.

Although Mr. Justice Brennan said nothing in *Tornillo* to explain his surprising willingness to invalidate right of reply legislation, in his dissent in *Gertz* v. *Welch*[12] he did cite, apparently with some continuing approval, the text and footnote from his plurality opinion for the Court in *Rosenbloom*, which was so heavily relied on by counsel for *Tornillo* in the courts.

Thus, in *Gertz*, Mr. Justice Brennan made the following remarks:[13]

> My brother White argues that the Court's view and mine will prevent a plaintiff - unable to demonstrate some degree of fault - from vindicating his reputation by securing a judgment that the publication was false. This argument overlooks the possible enactment of statutes, not requiring proof of fault, which provides for an action for retraction or for publication of a court's determination of falsity if the plaintiff is able to demonstrate that false statements have been published concerning his activities.

If I understand Mr. Justice Brennan correctly, what he is saying is this: the libel plaintiff is not going to be able to recover damages unless he can show lack of care on the part of the libel defendant. This need not mean that a libel plaintiff of whom something is printed that is in fact false will be without a remedy. What are the remedies available? Compulsory statutes not requiring proof of fault which would provide for retraction are apparently seen by Mr. Justice Brennan as one remedy. Similarly, statutes compelling publication of a court's determination of falsity if the plaintiff can show the false statement was in fact made are seen as another possibility.

Since *Gertz* and *Tornillo* were decided on the same day, these remarkable observations do prompt a question: isn't this where we came in? Are not statutes compelling newspapers to print that which they may not wish to print a violation of the First Amendment à la *Tornillo*? The only oblique reference in Mr. Justice Brennan's dissent in *Gertz* to the fact that *Tornillo* was decided on the same day as these remarks were announced is a cautious confession that some questions "could be raised concerning the constitutionality of such statutes."[14] Perhaps we would not give so much attention to Mr. Justice Brennan's abiding, if inconstant, affection for compulsory publication statutes were it not for the fact that some concern for rebuttal in defamation is found as well, in, of all places, the majority opinion for the Court in *Gertz* v. *Welch*.

Mr. Justice Powell's opinion for the Court in *Gertz* holds that a distinction between public figures and private figures must be maintained in the law of libel. One of the reasons he gives for retaining the distinction is that "private individuals" are more likely to "lack effective opportunities for rebuttal." Counsel for *Tornillo* had argued to the Court in that case that the extension of *New York Times* to private figures through the public interest concept was illogical because *New York Times* was rooted in a presumption of easy access to respond to defamation on the part of the public official-public figure plaintiffs covered by that rule.[15] That presumption was questionable when the plaintiff was an elected public official, as in the *New York Times* v. *Sullivan* case, and was simply foolish when applied to private figures. In his opinion for the Court in *Gertz*, Mr. Justice Powell suggests that the unavailability of the "self-help" remedy of rebuttal is important in evaluating the impact of the First Amendment on the traditional rules of the common law of defamation.

What are we to make of the decision of the Court in *Gertz*? One observation which I think would be fair is that the unanimity of the Court in *Tornillo* does not run very deep as a matter of First Amendment philosophy or approach. That which appears to be irrevocably clear in *Tornillo* appears to be left unsettled yet again in *Gertz*. Would a statutory right of reply remedy made available to a person not a political candidate permitting him to respond to editorial attack which constituted a defamation still be constitutional? The Court does not answer this question and it is true that there is nothing in *Tornillo* to suggest that right of reply statutes made available to persons other than political candidates would be constitutional. On the other hand, *Tornillo* was not a case involving a right of reply statute limited to response to defamation. With regard to such a limited statute, there is much that is implicit in Mr. Justice Powell's opinion in *Gertz* and much that is explicit in Mr. Justice Brennan's dissent which suggests that a carefully limited right of reply statute designed to provide a remedy for a proven defamatory falsehood might still be constitutional.

Perhaps one trying to fathom Supreme Court opinions should remember Plato's counsel concerning poetry: marvel at the result but do not ask the poet for an explanation. The *Tornillo* decision is a rather sphinx-like document. It is my conviction that the true indicator of ferment in the Court concerning matters such as attack by the press and reply by the victim is shown by the numerous, troubled, and discursive opinions in *Gertz* v. *Welch*, its more restless mate.

Tornillo is a far terser document. The decision centers almost entirely around two ideas. One is that there is no difference between a governmental requirement to add speech and a governmental requirement to delete it. The other idea is that editorial discretion embraces the true meaning of freedom of the press and editorial discretion must be untrammelled in deciding what is to be included in the paper and what is not.

There is little that is cautious or anticipatory of the future in the opinion. The only explicit indication that a different day may bring a different result is found in a couple of sentences from Mr. Justice Brennan to the effect that the opinion should not be thought to suggest the invalidity of retraction statutes. Whether the First Amendment merits of a statutory right of reply afforded to a private plaintiff suddenly catapulted into the arena of notoriety by means of a newspaper editorial attack would be treated differently from a right of reply statute availed of and limited to political candidates is not a distinction discussed in the opinion. Whether such a distinction would be a valid limitation on the scope of *Tornillo* in the future remains to be seen.

The problems of concentration of ownership conceded by the present Court to exist in *Tornillo,* and the resulting problem of the centralization of decision-making in the media continue to endure.[16] The justices of the present Court for different reasons - some out of an undeviating respect for property, some out of allegiance to a classic conception of freedom of expression - came to a 9-0 decision in *Tornillo*. I do not think it is a 9-0 issue. The problems are more intractable than that. The immediate proof of the intractability of the problem was demonstrated by the Court's decision in *Gertz*. In *Gertz* v. *Welch*, the rushing momentum of the *New York Times* doctrine was at last called to a halt. To my mind, many of the arguments pressed to the bar of the Court in *Tornillo* were accepted and applied in *Gertz*.

Looking at *Gertz* and *Tornillo* together, I suggest that the status approach to *New York Times* v. *Sullivan* is in the ascendancy once more. At least until 1971, the teaching of the cases extending the doctrine of *New York Times* v. *Sullivan* made the touchstone of the new and protective tests for the libel defendant the status of the libel plaintiff. The elected public official, the non-elected public official, and the public figure, were all successively forced to meet the rigors of the *New York Times* rule if they chose to sue as libel plaintiffs. In 1971, in *Rosenbloom* v. *Metromedia*, the rule was temporarily modified by a plurality of the Court. The new touchstone of the application of the *Times* test became not the status of the plaintiff but the content of the libel. Did the libel involve a public issue? If it did, no matter how obscure the libel plaintiff, the libel defendant could secure the benefits of the qualified privilege afforded by the *New York Times* v. *Sullivan* doctrine.

Because it is a rare defamation which is devoid of some public interest, the implications of this doctrine for the further devastation of libel law were clear. The "public issue" concept of *Rosenbloom*, insofar as that idea tended to constitutionalize completely the law of libel, was rejected in *Gertz* just as the use of a right of reply in *Rosenbloom* as an antidote to the inflation of *New York Times* was rejected in *Tornillo*. It had been argued on behalf of Pat Tornillo that the decline of the libel law threatened free debate and that right of reply was a necessary remedy. In *Gertz*, that argument was to some extent accepted. In *New York Times* v. *Sullivan* the Court had reasoned that whatever is left within the law of libel is taken from the domain of free debate.

As a result of *Gertz*, the domain of libel law has been somewhat enlarged, at least as contrasted with the Court's opinion in its 1971 decision in *Rosenbloom*. Does free debate have more to fear from heavy libel judgments than it does from a right of reply to editorial attack? To be sure, the Court tried to soften its retreat from the relentless and expanding logic of *New York Times* v. *Sullivan* by greatly restricting the availability of punitive damages. *Gertz* v. *Welch* has nevertheless sounded a retreat. The private plaintiff is now generally in a better position to recover in libel than is the public plaintiff. Whether right of reply statutes directed to the non-public plaintiff should attempt to build on this distinction is a question for the future.

As we reflect on *Gertz* and *Tornillo*, we see in the tension between them one of the consequences of *New York Times* v. *Sullivan*. The Court has gone very far with the idea that the citizen who enters public life has expected and should expect little in the way of legal recourse for unfair treatment, no matter how gross, by the media. This is still a young doctrine. It is too early to tell how, if at all, it will affect the quality of those who choose to enter public life in the future.

Fundamental and difficult questions, pressed at the bar of the Court in *Tornillo*, are still unanswered. Nathan Lewin, Washington lawyer and former law clerk to Mr. Justice Harlan, questions the soundness of the Court's "analogy between a prohibitory and mandatory inclusion." Lewin says: "Viewed from the vantage of the public, a 'right of reply' gives John Citizen two sides of a question, while suppression or prohibitions give him none.[17] Lewin suggests that the victory for freedom of the press in *Tornillo*, if that is what it is, had been won at the expense of freedom of speech.

I share this concern over the new legitimization of restraints on freedom of speech, but matters as restless and volatile as these cannot be resolved forever by a single court decision. The Court has changed its mind in the past. In a handful of years the pendulum has shifted first in favor of a right of access and then against it. Perhaps yet another day will show yet another somersault. In all this, one should be mindful of Mr. Justice Jackson's wise comments about the workings of the Supreme Court in cases involving First Amendment adjudication:[18]

> This Court never has announced what those [First Amendment] standards must be, it does not now say what they are, and it is not clear that any majority could agree on them. In no field are there more numerous individual opinions among the Justices. The Court as an institution not infrequently disagrees with its former self or relies on distinctions that are not very substantial.

For me, these words are an apt epilogue for the *Tornillo* decision.

Notes

1. *Miami Herald Publishing Co.* v. *Pat L. Tornillo, Jr* 418 U.S. 241 (1974).
2. *Red Lion Broadcasting* v. *FCC*, 395 U.S. 367 (1967).
3. *New York Times* v. *Sullivan*, 376 U.S. 254 (1964).
4. *Columbia Broadcasting System, Inc.* v. *Democratic National Committee*, 412 U.S. 94 (1973).
5. Toby Simon was, for a long time, lawyer to the head of the Dade County Teachers Union, Pat Tornillo of the Classroom Teachers Association. Simon had also been a long-time advocate of civil rights and ACLU causes in Florida. When Tornillo sought recourse to the *Miami Herald's* editorial attacks on his candidacy, it was Simon who saw the relationship to the 1913 Florida right-of-reply statute to the new claim for a First Amendment-based right of access and reply. It was Simon's enthusiasm, and infectious sense of fairness, that prompted me to accept his invitation to join him in the controversy about the First Amendment validity of the statute which the factual context of the *Tornillo* case necessarily aroused.
6. See *Tornillo* v. *Miami Herald*, 287 So.2d 78 (Fla. 1973).
7. See *Handling of Public Issues under the Fairness Doctrine and the Public Interest Standards of the Communications Act* (hereinafter the Fairness Report), 48 F.C.C. 2d 1 (1974). The FCC rejection of a petition for reconsideration is found in the Memorandum, Opinion and Order on Reconsideration of the Fairness Report, 58 F.C.C. 2d 691 (1976).
8. See *Brandywine-Main Line Radio, Inc.* v. *FCC*, 473 F.2d 16 (D.C. Cir. 1972); *cert. denied* 412 U.S. 922 (1973).

9. In retrospect, this pessimism with respect to the future vitality of the fairness doctrine appears to have been somewhat too severe. On Nov. 11, 1977, in a decision by the federal court of appeals in Washington, D.C., the FCC's 1974 Fairness Report, note 7, *supra,* was substantially affirmed but also reversed in part. The Court of Appeals directed the FCC to reconsider two proposals which had been made in the fairness inquiry but which it had rejected. One proposal involved a submission by the Commission for Open Media for specific access to broadcasting whereby, among other things, "a licensee would set aside one hour per week for spot announcements and lengthen programming which would be available for presentation of messages by members of the public." The Court of Appeals also asked the FCC to reconsider Henry Geller's suggestion that "the licensee list annually the ten controversial issues of public importance, local and national, which it chose for the most coverage in the prior year, set out the offers for response made; and note representative programming that was presented on each issue." See *N.C.C.B.* v. *FCC,* 567 F.2d 1095 (D.C. Cir. 1977). Whether the new Fairness Report decision portends a more committed approach on the part of the Court of Appeals to the fairness doctrine is, of course, unclear. It is interesting that the appeal panel who heard the fairness report appeal was composed of Judges Wright, McGowan, and Tamm. Significantly, Judge Bazelon was not a member of the panel and two of the panelists included were fairness doctrine stalwarts, Judges Tamm and McGowan. Does this Fairness Report appeal signify yet another swing of the pendulum, and a return to the idea of the First Amendment validity of imposing affirmative obligations on the media with respect to the encouragement of diversity? Or does it merely signify that the fairness report appeal happened to have been decided by a judicial panel whose membership was well disposed toward the fairness doctrine?

10. 403 U.S. 29 (1971).
11. *Id.* at p. 47 fn. 15.
12. 418 U.S. 323 (1974).
13. *Id.* at 368, fn. 3.
14. *Id.*
15. Brief for Appellee, Pat L. Tornillo, jr., *Miami Herald Publishing Co.* v. *Tornillo,* Supreme Court of the United States, No. 73-797, October Term 1973, pp. 27-39.
16. See especially Mr. Justice White's dissenting opinion in *Gertz* v. *Welch,* where he comments that he fails to see how "emasculation of state libel laws for the benefit of the news media" will aid public debate. He feared that this trend would prompt "a new and radical imbalance in the communication process" and he warned that unrestricted defamation of private citizens would "discourage them from speaking out and concerning themselves with social problems." See note 12, *supra,* p. 400.
17. See Lewin, "What's Happening to Free Speech?" *The New Republic,* July 27 and Aug. 3, 1974, p. 13.
18. See Mr. Justice Jackson's dissenting opinion in *Kunz* v. *New York,* 340 U.S. 290 at 308 (1951).

2

*American Journalism and the First Amendment: An Access Perspective**

The meaning of the First Amendment is almost as controversial as much of the speech which, it is hoped, it protects. In the process of First Amendment interpretation by judges, lawyers, and journalists, the human condition is at all times both vividly portrayed and betrayed. We are all astute enough to read the First Amendment with imagination and flexibility to protect interests we hold dear, just as we become strict constructionists to strike down interests that we fear. We have traveled a long way from the eighteenth-century world of John Peter Zenger and Thomas Paine to the media world of Henry Luce and S.I. Newhouse and our theory of free expression must necessarily be constantly reexamined. This latter third of the twentieth century in America presents the problem of First Amendment rights in conflict. Surely the First Amendment protects the publishers and journalists who operate our important media voices. What effective protection or opportunity does the First Amendment provide those excluded from those media voices?

In the famous *New York Times* v. *Sullivan* case in 1964 the Supreme Court read the First Amendment to provide new protection for journalists and pulishers against libel suits brought against them by public officials and public figures.[1] A process once begun is not easily stopped. Newsmen seized upon *Sullivan* to extend it to other areas. If the First Amendment provides a qualified privilege to journalists to defame public officials and figures, perhaps the same amendment could also provide an absolute or at least a qualified privilege for journalists to refuse to talk to

---

* Parts of this chapter were given as an address at the Rochester Institute of Technology in Oct. 1977 and at the Speech Communications convention in Washington, DC in Dec. 1977.

grand juries. In 1972 a majority of the Supreme Court held to the contrary.[2] Who was a journalist? How could such a privilege be kept from protecting criminals and at the same time protect bona fide journalists? That was the rub: if government could inquire into the *bona fides* of a journalist, perhaps there would be a reversion to that licensing of the press against which Milton had so eloquently railed more than three centuries ago. The newsman's privilege decision, decided adversely to the press, reveals that the Court will not always read the First Amendment to insulate journalism from legal obligation. Moreover, it should not be thought that the First Amendment is an exclusive charter for freedom for the journalist and no one else.

It occurred to others besides newsmen, such as citizen groups and dissenters generally, that the First Amendment might be read to provide them rights of self-expression. The *Sullivan* case had emphasized debate as a central First Amendment value, but the reality of debate is totally dependent on the pleasure of the owners of the dominant media. Perhaps a new view of the First Amendment was in order, a view which would see debate as a First Amendment right. Moreover, perhaps the First Amendment could be used as a sword as well as shield. If the First Amendment permitted, either by its own force or through Congressional legislation, establishment of a shield for journalists to refuse to testify before grand juries in order to protect their sources, did the First Amendment also permit, either through its own force or by legislation, recognition of a right of reply to media criticism? In the controversy about the 1974 Florida right of reply case,[3] some who thought that the press has an absolute privilege to refuse to testify before grand juries insisted that for the citizenry to talk of individual rights to respond to the press *in the press* was a violation of the First Amendment. Under such a view, the First Amendment becomes protectionism for journalism and little more.

Recently, Justice Stewart, a sitting member of the Supreme Court, in a lecture at Yale Law School gave impressive support for the view that the purpose of the First Amendment is to protect the press as an industry.[4] I prefer the view of the First Amendment taken by Mr. Justice White in 1969 in the case affirming the validity of broadcasting's fairness doctrine: "The right of free speech of a broadcaster, the user of a sound truck, or any other individual does not embrace the right to snuff out the free speech of others."[5]

The First Amendment's purpose is not to give an immunity from the law to the press enjoyed by no other business or industry in America. Nevertheless, some insulation from law for the press is a consequence of First Amendment protection. This is a consequence which most of us are prepared to both accept and to rejoice in, but we should rejoice only if the larger purposes for the creation of that protection are thoroughly understood.

The fundamental purpose of a constitutional guarantee of free expression is to enable the press to serve as the instrument of a free society. Press freedom is not an end in itself. Freedom of expression is a participatory as well as an elitist concept. In our society it is best understood as a process. Debate, dialogue, and criticism of both public and private institutions are both the means and the end of a free expression guarantee. As John Dewey might have put it, in the field of free expression there must be no separation between the ideal and the real.

Yet the fact is there is such a separation. In a nation of 200,000,000, participation in the dominant media is necessarily more restricted than any of us would like. The decline in number of big city daily newspapers, the rise of broadcast networks of great power and wealth, and the death of the general magazine, have, I am confident, not been welcomed by thoughtful journalists. New technology, rising labor costs, and the rise of chain newspapers have have all played a part in reducing the number of competitive daily newspapers in even our largest cities. Contrasted with the abundance of daily newspapers in New York in the early days of this century, the decline of daily newspaper competition in New York and other metropolitan areas is particularly marked. The decision of the Supreme Court that held that a state statute which provides that a right of reply for political candidates attacked in the press is unconstitutional further constricted the rights of expression of those outside the media.

The First Amendment is broad enough in its reach to provide for freedom of expression without governmental restraint and at the same time to provide rights of access and reply to the media. It is inconsistent and sad that many in the press who have no good word to say for a *laissez-faire*, or "trickle down," theory as a basis for insuring liberty and equality in any other area of American life find a *laissez-faire* appproach entirely acceptable in journalism. Such a view has its source in an *hubris* which it is no proper part of First Amendment theory either to stimulate or protect.

Currently, First Amendment law is very unsettled. Damages for libel have recently been specifically approved by the Supreme Court while a right of reply, for the moment, has been rejected.[6] In the Florida right of reply case, the Court reasoned that the Constitution had mandated a free press and not a fair one. This is a false conflict. Law certainly can lead to progress in the accomplishment of both goals even though in an absolute sense in an imperfect world neither goal may be capable of absolute achievement.

It should be permissible and desirable for the Court to find in the First Amendment a shield for journalists to justify a refusal to talk to grand juries so that journalism is not made against its will a spy for the state.[7] It should also be permissible for a state to give a right of reply to a citizen attacked by the press in a newspaper editorial in the same paper which attacks him. Censorship is not redeemed because its source is corporate rather than governmental.

Some journalists seek no help from government, whether benign or not. To them, all government assistance is malign. Two such journalists, Ben Bagdikian and Vermont Royster, have told me that the proper course for a newsman called to testify about his news sources before a grand jury is to go to jail. I respect the integrity of that approach more than I do that of those publishers who editorialized both for the Newspaper Preservation Act to give some newspapers immunity from the antitrust laws and against the Florida right of reply law. For such publishers, governmental intervention which serves the selfish interests of the press is unquestionably constitutional, but governmental intervention which seeks to remedy the inequality between a massive media assault on an individual or an idea is an impermissible intrusion by government into the affairs of the press. Bagdikian and Royster, who abjure government across the board, are on more honorable ground. Unhappily, they represent an individualism which for all its courage is inadequate to do battle with the new world of media conglomerates and newspaper chains.

For ordinary citizens who are not journalists, matters of reply, privacy, and reputation are of critical importance. For them, a view of press freedom which is entirely understood in terms of making the rights of free expression of society at large dependent on media managers and owners is simply too myopic a perception. Many of us have admired the courage of Alexander Solzhenitsyn. How many have actually pondered the meaning of the words he uttered on landing in the West after escaping from Russia? After a brief exposure to intrusion on his time and privacy by Western European journalists, he cried, "the Western press is worse than the KGB."

Of course, this not so, but this impatient burst of hyperbole should give us pause. Liberty exercised without responsibility by any power center becomes repressive. Absolute freedom for journalism is not necessarily the same thing as freedom of expression in an open society. Conglomerates now own distinguished publishing houses, newspapers own broadcast stations, newspaper-TV combinations own national news magazines. Do the wishes of the board of directors of these corporate combinations exhaust the meaning of freedom of the press in America in our time? This is the great question for the future of freedom of expression in this country.

Most members of the United Nations do not have what we would call a free press. Either their press is subservient to a military dictatorship or the press reflects the Marxist view, dominant in the Communist world, that the press is the instrument of government and that the indicator of a free press is not its divergence from government policy but its independence from bourgeois control.[8] I reject and distrust the view espoused by Herbert Marcuse and other Marxists that the media should serve the ends of progressive forces in society. (Suppose, alas, one were not progressive?) I am opposed to government ownership of the print media and I think the present mix we are developing between private and public broadcasting is to be welcomed. The recognition of some public rights in the media is a necessity if the marketplace of ideas metaphor is to have any continuing authenticity.

The press of the democratic West is in a unique position. Wedged between the reality of governmental constraint, on the one hand, and the reality of corporate restraint, on the other, it must struggle to make its relative immunity from law, at least as compared to other businesses and industries, socially justifiable beyond the justification that it is exhilarating to do exactly as one pleases and to step on toes, no matter how small or big, without fear of reprisal. The resolution of valid, noble, but conflicting claims between popular desires for self-expression and press freedom, between the rights of free expression and rights of property, is a great challenge of contemporary First Amendment interpretation.

I speak of a conflict between the rights of free expression and the rights of property. Many years ago, A.J. Liebling, a brilliant and caustic journalist, remarked: "Freedom of the press belongs to the man who owns one." With the development of newspaper chains and the demise of competitive newspaper situations across the country, this statement is unhappily even more descriptive today than it was when first stated. In a sense we have what might be called the plantation theory of the First Amendment. The newspaper publisher says of his paper, "This is my plantation and I may do with it what I choose." If there has been any dominating theme in the movement for access to the printed press, it has been centered around a rejection of this plantation concept. Readers in one-newspaper cities are now saying simply, "it is my plantation too."

When I say that the printed press is our plantation too, I want to be very careful not to be misunderstood. I am not suggesting that editorial discretion and editorial autonomy should not be given constitutional protection, nor am I suggesting that private ownership of the press should be reconsidered. What I am suggesting is that the reality of private ownership can be accommodated to the pressing demands of public obligation. First Amendment rights cannot be defined entirely in terms of property. Too few of us have title to the great vehicles of mass communication. If freedom of expression is limited only to those who own and manage the mass media, very few of us will be able to participate in freedom of expression.

If one reflects on the legal demands of the access movement, one cannot fail to be struck by their modesty. Essentially, access advocates have urged the adoption of two quite minor changes in the law. The first has been the enactment of statutes that would give those who are the subject of editorial attack an opportunity for reply. The second objective has been to establish a non-discriminatory right of access with respect to the publication of commercial advertising. At the moment, American law has not yet recognized either demand. The resistance of the journalistic establishment to these objectives has been bitter, relentless, and intense. Why? The answer does not lie in the enormity of what is being sought. In truth, there is no enormity in what is being sought. The controversy about the essentially limited demands of the access movement is at bottom a controversy about the scope of First Amendment protection. Are the readers, the ordinary citizenry, to be allowed to have any rights of participation in the daily press? The key word in this question is the word "rights." Whenever in history one asks any power center in society to share its power one can usually expect intense resistance. Therefore, the access controversy is really a controversy about symbolism. It is not so much the specific demands that are feared as access as a symbol, an idea that there can be public rights in private media.

No matter how thoroughgoing the claims of absolutism made in behalf of the press by even its more ardent advocates, one can still detect some evidence of guilty conscience. Increasingly, the American press has come to grant by way of grace what a few years back was granted neither by way of grace nor by way of right. Today we see new phenomena in the print media. We see press ombudsmen. We see op-ed pages which essentially encourage editorial points of view by those not on the editorial staff. Furthermore, there is a slightly less cavalier response to requests to purchase editorial advertising even when the subject of the advertising trespasses on the editorial stance of the newspaper involved. All these developments are consequences of the access movement. They should be applauded, but we should not be satisfied with them. Editorial freedom should not be a gift from the state. By the same token, public access, a right of reply, and an opportunity for expression of viewpoints opposed by the newspaper management should not be matters of editorial grace.

What new directions in the movement for a First Amendment right of access to the print media can be expected in the years ahead? In a formidable series of cases, the Supreme Court has given a new constitutional dimension to advertising. The right to advertise is protected today through limitations on state repression of advertising to a greater extent than ever before in our First Amendment history.[9] It is hard to believe that the same judicial distaste for state censorship of advertising will not eventually be extended to media censorship of advertising. In the long run, perhaps as a direct consequence of the new constitutional status of commercial speech, I believe that ultimately there will arise a First Amendment right of non-discriminatory access to publication advertising, whether commercial, editorial, or political, in our mass circulation daily newspaper press.

Furthermore, the mass media may be expected to continue the present pattern whereby ownership falls into the hands of an ever smaller group of corporate entities. Similarly, media assaults on individual privacy and reputation are likely to continue their present unabated and relentless pattern. In the light of these developments, it is likely that ultimately a right of reply as a remedy to libel at least with respect to public officials and public figures may yet be recognized. In the past several years, the attachment of the Supreme Court to the idea of relaxing the libel law in the interests of First Amendment debate has declined. The Court today is less ready to be generous in its definition of who is a public figure.[10] The Court is also less quick to make the assumption that any public figure who is defamed just by virtue of his status automatically will have an opportunity to secure access for his side of the controversy in the media. As a result, private plaintiffs are still able to secure heavy damages against the media if they can make out a case in libel.

The libel law is obviously designed to provide a measure of redress for injury to reputation. The libel law has another function as well. It is a mode of making the press accountable. In 1976, I spent several months in England interviewing English lawyers and journalists on their libel law, which is much tougher than our own. I did not encounter in England the same hostility to libel law that is so frequently encountered among journalists in the United States. Journalist after journalist told me: "We have no quarrel with the law of libel." After all, they said, the defense to libel is truth and, further, the existence of the libel law is a force for accuracy and integrity in journalism.

This is not to suggest that we should be converted by these English ideas. We should be skeptical about whether the libel law is the best vehicle for enforcing press accountability. Often the most heretical publications, which are therefore the most valuable contributors to the lively interplay of ideas, have the slenderest budgets. A heavy libel judgment for money damages is a measure to take against such a publication. Such a measure can all too easily put an economically marginal but intellectually valuable publication out of business. A well drafted and limited right of reply is far better equipped to serve the ends of the First Amendment - debate - and is at the same time far less likely to endanger the economic life of the media defendant.

A final question must be asked: what new directions for access may be expected in the electronic media? Right now, in communications law circles there is considerable discussion about the value of trading off access and fairness obligations as a matter of law for some obligation on the part of the electronic media to devote a specified part of the broadcast day to "free speech messages" and other public issue programming.[11] The idea behind this suggestion is that if some broadcast time is reserved for public access, then the rest of the broadcast day can be left in good conscience to the sole and unfettered discretion of the broadcaster. Access will have received its tithe. This is not a suggestion which appeals to me. A limited common carrier approach to public access is unlikely to be able to provide the viewing and listening audience with a balanced presentation of controversial ideas. Members of the public are not journalists. They lack both the skill and the resources which make journalism the powerful and valuable force in our society which it is. The fairness doctrine should not be functionally abandoned by providing broadcasters with transparently ineffective options. It is far more important to impose an obligation of fairness on broadcasters than it is to provide some small part of the broadcast day for a common carrier service.

The great appeal of the fairness principle is its ideological neutrality. The fairness doctrine is designed to provide a structure for discussion, not monologue. In a broad and loose way it requires debate about public issues on broadcasting. Despite constant efforts by the industry to repeal it, it has endured. Furthermore, the fairness doctrine is showing signs of new vitality. Lately it is developing an access component. Only recently, the FCC has held that a broadcaster has a duty to provide information on an issue vital to the community being served even though the broadcaster never in the past provided opportunities for an opposite viewpoint.[12] In other words, the fairness doctrine is being interpreted not only to provide a right of response to a particular viewpoint once the broadcaster chooses to present it; it is now being interpreted to impose on the broadcaster a duty to seek out and present particular public issues even though the broadcaster would not otherwise wish to present them.

Still another idea has developed with respect to the question of a right of access to the electronic media. This new idea is focused on the use of a policy of diversification of ownership to secure diversity of opinion. The theory seems to be that if the concentration of ownership with respect to newspapers, radio stations, and television stations all owned by the same corporate entity in a particular community can be broken up, greater diversity of opinion might well be the result. Furthermore, the judiciary is beginning to realize that diversity of ownership policy might not involve the same alleged trespass on broadcast journalism that the fairness doctrine or right of access are feared to involve.[13] Diversification of ownership, at least as that policy is presently being developed, is unlikely to lead to much more diversity of opinion than we have at present on broadcasting. Should we conclude that the greater the number of searchers after truth, the more likely the consequent enlightenment? The difficulty is that if we say that a particular newspaper cannot own a television station in its home town, all that will happen is that that newspaper will swap its television station for a television station in some distant community. The total number of "searchers after truth" is unlikely to be increased.

The centrifugal force represented by the tendency toward concentration of ownership in the media shows not the slightest sign of diminishing in intensity. It would be contrary to all human experience if the agglomeration of power, particularly communicating power, in ever fewer hands did not inspire some concomitant efforts to counteract these developments. Therefore, I believe that the movement for right of access to the media, both electronic and print, will become still stronger as we move toward the century's end. In the early twentieth century, in economic matters generally, before the rise of the labor movement, social critics used to deplore the inequality of bargaining power between employers and employees. Reminiscent of that inequality in our society today is the inequality in communicating power. The gulf between those who communicate and their audience grows ever greater. It will increasingly be the task of First Amendment theory to attempt to bridge that gulf.

Notes

1. *New York Times Co. v. Sullivan*, 376 U.S. 254 (1964).
2. *Branzburg v. Hayes*, 408 U.S. 665 (1972).
3. *Miami Herald Publishing Co. v. Tornillo*, 418 U.S. 241 (1974).
4. Stewart, "Or of the Press," 26 Hastings L.J. 631 (1975).
5. *Red Lion Broadcasting v. FCC*, 395 U.S. 367 at 387 (1969).
6. Cf. *Gertz v. Robert Welch, Inc.*, 418 U.S. 323 (1974) with *Miami Herald Publishing Co. v. Tornillo*, note 3, supra.
7. See Barron, "Does the Public have a Right to Everyman's Evidence - Or Should Newsmen Be Exempt?," Student Lawyer, Dec. 1972, pp. 62-3.
8. This is not to say that foreign and Third World concerns about American "media imperialism" do not raise difficult problems whose international resolution will be far from easy.
9. See *Bigelow v. Virginia*, 421 U.S. 809 (1975); *Virginia State Board of Pharmacy v. Virginia Citizens Consumer Council, Inc.*, 425 U.S. 748 (1976); *Bates v. State Bar of Arizona*, 433 U.S. 350 (1977). See discussion of these cases and their implications for the future of a non-discriminatory right of access to advertising in this book, Chap. 7.
10. *Time, Inc. v. Firestone*, 424 U.S. 448 (1976).
11. This specific suggestion sufficiently impressed the federal court of appeals to the point that it ordered the FCC to reconsider such a proposal. The FCC had earlier, in connection with its 1974 Fairness Report, rejected this proposal. See *National Citizens Committee for Broadcasting v. FCC*, 567 F.2d 1095 (D.C. Cir. 1977).
12. The new and leading case on the little used first part of the fairness doctrine, the duty to affirmatively present controversial public issue programming, is *Patsy Mink*, 59 FCC 987 (1976).
13. See *FCC v. National Citizens Committee for Broadcasting*, 436 U.S. 775 (1978) where the Supreme Court unanimously upheld the FCC's prospective ban on cross-ownership - the licensing or transfer of broadcast stations to those who own a newspaper in the same community.

3

Access through Grace?

PRESS PLANTATIONS AND INEFFECTIVE FREE SPEECH

Chief Justice Burger has said that "press responsibility is not mandated by the Constitution and like many other virtues it cannot be legislated."[1] The press is free but it is not required to be fair. If this is so, have we in the process forfeited not only a fair press but free speech as well? The contemporary understanding of the meaning of the phrase "freedom of the press" has increasingly been to limit the direct beneficiaries of that freedom. The primary beneficiaries of freedom of the press have become those who own and manage the press. The trouble with this new precision with respect to the identity of the ultimate beneficiary of freedom of the press is that its narrowness limits and restricts those who wish to exercise their rights of free speech. Free speech cannot mean much if one has no meaningful forum in which to exercise that right. If freedom of the press is intended to protect only the press itself, and if the freedom of the press is in the last analysis limited to those who own the press, we have not given free communication a new and deeper dimension. We have merely returned to a rigid unyielding conception of the rights of property. Are the media to be given property rights that are enjoyed by no other industry in our society? Absolute protection of the press as an industry, if it is understood in practice only as the exercise of a property right, denies all available terrain to those outside the media who would like to exercise their free speech rights. Enforced silence is still silence whether it is the result of government repression or of a view of media freedom that conditions all entry to the media solely on the consent of media owners and managers. If free speech is not perceived as an absolute but freedom of the press is,[2] what hope is there for making the right of free speech an effective rather than a theoretical right? One suggestion is through government funding. Perhaps government should subsidize efforts designed to enlarge the number of media outlets in order to expand the opportunities for expression of those seeking to assert their rights of free speech? The question involves the obligation of government to turn constitutional promise into reality. Recent developments bearing on the existence of such an obligation are not encouraging.

In the abortion field, the Supreme Court has made it clear that government is not bound to legislate to make a woman's right of privacy with respect to her body effective to the point of being bound to pay for an abortion she could not otherwise afford. The Supreme Court has not yet been asked to rule that First Amendment rights are meaningless for the indigent and the unpopular and that, therefore, it is legitimate for government to pay by subsidy for advertisements designed to win for such groups an entry they could not otherwise obtain. The precedent of the abortion decisions is not encouraging for those who would argue that government has an obligation to make the First Amendment effective for each citizen.

In 1980, in the much publicized abortion case of *Harris* v. *McCrae*,[3] the Supreme Court refused to set aside a federal statute banning federal payments for abortion unless the abortion was necessary to save the life of the mother. The Court denied that it was the responsibility of government to remove obstacles to securing an abortion which were ascribable to such causes as poverty - causes which were not directly attributable to government action. American constitutionalism promises the potentiality of securing certain freedoms. It promises that government will not interfere in the pursuit of those freedoms but it does not guarantee that government must help individuals realize those freedoms. As the Court said in the 1980 abortion case:[4]

> Although the liberty protected by the Due Process Clause affords protection against unwarranted government interference with freedom of choice in the context of certain personal decisions, it does not confer an entitlement to such funds as may be necessary to realize all the advantages of that freedom. To hold otherwise would mark a drastic change in our understanding of the Constitution.

Protecting First Amendment rights does not yet mean that government has an obligation to make these rights meaningful. Recognition of a constitutional right to a subsidy to broaden the meaningful exercise of free speech appears unlikely to be allowed by a Court that has declined to give support to an affirmative view of First Amendment freedom in far more limited situations.

The American print media are today insulated from any legal responsibility to provide fairness in the coverage of ideas or access for the presentation of ideas which otherwise might not be publicized. Government, on the other hand, at least in the case of the print media, seems unlikely to be able to fill the void by providing outlets for access not presently furnished by the private print media. The result of this press liberation from law has been called by some "an enviable freedom."[5] So it is. But when some have so much freedom that they are envied for it, one may usually suspect that others may lack it to a corresponding degree. The result of the relative immunity from law which the American press now enjoys raises a difficult question. Are the decisions of the press alone of the institutions of fundamental importance in our society to be immune from inquiry, accountability, and appeal? The answer in the long run is likely to be "no." The controversy over access to the press is too enduring a problem for it either to disappear or to be resolved forever by the result in a single case.

Increasingly, thoughtful and sensitive people in journalism have turned to attempting to build within journalism itself mechanisms for inquiry, accountability, and appeal. The formation of the National News Council, the existence of voluntary free press-fair trial codes in many states, the writings of journalism educators, all seem to suggest a concern that although fairness in the press may not yet be a requirement of press law it is an essential precept of journalism eithics. In short, if access to the media is not to be required by law, may it yet emerge as a matter of voluntary compliance through a press code enforced by consent rather than by law?

If access to the media is not to come by way of law, should it come by way of grace - in this case, the grace of the press? Peter Donaghue, journalist and scholar, has argued that "the lack of an access obligation on a constitutional level is a good reason to practice access on an operational level."[6] He suggests that the press adopt a voluntary code to provide public access and fairness. He asks the press to furnish of its own free will what it would fight if it were required by law. In this view, freedom is responsibility. The press, having won freedom in the battle for access, now must turn its attention toward the exercise of responsibility.

The procedures for access and fairness that Donaghue would have the press provide are challenging. They merit discussion as a means of focusing on the future of access to the press. In all, eight forms of access are proposed for voluntary adoption by the press. In the next section each precept is discussed and considered.

A VOLUNTARY PRESS CODE?

The first provision in Peter Donaghue's suggested voluntary press code for public access is that a newspaper will try to be a forum for a wide range of diverse opinions: "(1) An attempt will be made through news, editorial and advertising columns to provide an outlet for the expression of all segments of the public on a wide range of subjects from diverse points of view." Immediately, such a proposal raises questions of implementation. How can a more diverse range of opinion actually be achieved in our present print world of less than a score of syndicated columnists, homogenized editorials, and two wire services? Once we have added an op-ed page, improved the letters-to-the-editor column, and added a guest editorial column, where do we go from there? Before practical change can come in this area as in any other a theoretical understanding of what it is that we want must be arrived at. What is the function of the daily newspaper in the American city today?

Where a single daily newspaper provides the only news service in print in a community, its role is something like the utility company which brings the same community electricity. The public utility company is not free to refuse electric service to a person who wishes to be its customer. A daily newspaper is free to refuse to publish an advertisement which would provide information on a particular issue in a community. The question is whether this kind of power is permissible. If it is argued that such a cut-off of information is rare, it should be asked, how common is it for a newspaper involved in a labor dispute to carry news of the dispute in its pages during the life of the dispute?[7]

Whenever one asks, as Donaghue does, for the daily newspaper in a community to serve as an outlet for expression of "all segments of the public" one is taking a view of the press which looks at it at least in some respects as a common carrier. A common carrier view of press responsibility is sharply at odds with the plantation view of the press which is suggested in the Florida right of reply case. The press is the publisher's plantation and may be dealt with by the publisher as the planter governs his plantation.[8] The fundamental question endures: is the local newspaper to function as the voice of the community in a participatory sense or is the daily newspaper to be regarded as the property of the owner, to be dealt with entirely as he wishes? There are more answers available to this question than either the plantation theory or the common carrier theory suggest. Some newspapers have been arrested by a desire to present to their communities a sampling of the broad spectrum of issues on both local and national issues. It would be fair to characterize American journalism as either rigidly ideological *or* indifferent to ideas and entirely profit motivated. The advent of the ombudsman in the American newspaper as well as the burgeoning of op-ed pages illustrate that there is increasing sensitivity on the part of the press to the need for responding to the claim of public access.

The second precept in Donaghue's voluntary press code calls for press adherence to non-discriminatory access for advertising: "(2) Advertisements not in conflict with local, state, or federal laws will not be rejected because of their content. Space and mechanical restrictions may impose occasional limitations, but advertisements will not be discriminated against because of substance." The heart of this proposal is to encourage non-discriminatory access for advertising at least when it does not involve violation of law. The policy expressed is that while space and mechanical considerations may sometimes justify rejection of advertising, advertising should not be rejected because of its substantive or ideological content.

Non-discriminatory access for advertising is the minimal requirement of any meaningful access to the print media. Critics of access theory sometimes say that they find the proponents of access vague on the corrective remedies which they seek.[9] Yet the access literature from the beginning has emphasized the primacy of non-discriminatory access to advertising as the single most necessary advance in securing access to the media.[10]

Can a policy of non-discriminatory access to advertising be achieved in the daily press through voluntary means? I doubt it. The process of editorial discretion is being defended against any mode of legal inquiry with a fervor and an absolutism reminiscent of the claims of the Stuart kings of England. It is more doubtful than ever that publishers and editors would of their own volition limit their ability to decide what should fall "on the cutting room floor" even with respect to advertising. Furthermore, the suggested exceptions in the proposal for non-discriminatory access to advertising - space and illegality - may themselves frustrate the achievement of a goal of non-discriminatory access for advertising. Allowing the paper to make the unreviewable determination that if an ad violates the law, it need not be published, cuts a very large and perhaps fatally destructive hole in any effort to impose an ethical duty on the press to publish advertising. Similarly, the exception for space limitations contains an opportunity for abuse and evasion. If there is no threat of legal sanction, it seems unlikely that advertising columns would be much more open than they are today, particularly in the light of the new emphasis by some courts on editorial autonomy.[11] The proposal does not state whether the advertising would have to be paid or not. Presumably it would have to be paid.

A voluntary right of reply is the theme of the third precept in Donaghue's recommended voluntary press code: "(3) Persons or groups criticized will be given equal or adequate space in which to reply to the criticism." The press is unlikely to offer as a matter of grace that opportunity for reply which it fought so hard to oppose as a matter of law. The adverse editorial reaction across the country to Tornillo's claim for a right of reply to editorial attack and the avalanche of media *amicus* briefs filed against Tornillo's position in the Supreme Court reflect the passion in press opposition to a right of reply.

Many of the same objections launched against a legally imposed right of reply are readily available against a "voluntary" right of reply that is supposed to flow from conscience. If, as an editor, I know I must give my opponent an answer if I attack him, might I not choose to deprive him of the publicity altogether? If I do not attack him in the editorial, I avoid his answer. My attack gives him a voice. My silence leaves him speechless.[12] There is a kind of meanness to this strategy, but others argue that it merely demonstrates the chilling effect of a right of reply.

There is, of course, one difference between a voluntary right of reply and one imposed by law. Enforcement of a right of reply in the courts is seen as a kind of state surveillance of the press which, it is said, is simply inconsistent with press freedom. The merit of a voluntary right of reply is that compliance is a matter of choice for the press. Can we realistically expect that exercise of choice to provide any new opportunities for access? If press sensibilities are so fragile as to be chilled by a right of reply imposed by law, why should these sensibilities be any less tender if the grant of a right of reply is to be solely dependent on the even more fragile claims of conscience?

Further, it was argued against the establishment in law of a right of reply that space in the press is expensive, that the size of a paper is not infinitely expandable, and that newsprint is expensive. Space is what a publisher has to sell, but if that space is commandeered by conscience instead of law, it is still space that has been commandeered. If the foregoing problems are not obstacles to a right of reply to be enforced by conscience, it is hard to see why they should be obstacles to a right of reply to be enforced by law.

Newspapers are asked to refrain from insisting on having the last word in the fourth precept of Donaghue's voluntary press code: "(4) The editors in the same issue will not engage in debate with or challenge opinions of letter writers, or those replying to editorials, by appending editor's notes or keying remarks to accompanying rebutting articles or editorials." Once newspapers commit themselves to the principle of reply or response they should not still try to dominate the debate. Thus, a reply to an editorial should not be followed by a rebuttal editorial. Similarly, a letter to the editor should not be followed by an editorial note rebutting the thesis of the letter.

Those in the readership who disagree with a newspaper editorial are seldom afforded the opportunity of expressing their disagreement in the same issue of the paper in which the editorial appears. The best they may usually hope for is publication of a letter to the editor in a later issue. It seems elementary fairness would require newspapers to refrain from placing themselves in a superior position in this regard. The proposal Donaghue advances is fair and courteous, yet the chance of its acceptance as standard journalistic practice is slim. Balance and equality in the communications process and the present practice of editorial autonomy are not easily reconcilable objectives.

The fifth precept in this voluntary press code is that there should be no tampering with the letters to the editor column: "All letters to the editor may be edited for libel, brevity, and good taste, but such editing will not change their substance or context. While all letters to the editor cannot be published, the newspaper will make an effort to publish those reflecting a diversity of opinion. The newspaper will particularly invite comment contrary to the newspaper's editorial policy and opinions representing minority viewpoints and new ideas." Here the concern is that letters to the editor should not be edited to the point that their context and emphasis are altered. Furthermore, Donaghue suggests that newspapers publish "equitable guidelines for handling letters to the editor." If followed, this suggestion could allay the assumption that the letters to the editor column is used as a feature column. Publication of "equitable guidelines for handling" of letters to the editor at the head of the column would help it to be in fact what it purports to be: a public forum of representative community opinion on controversial public issues. Further, a specific line at the head of the column that contrary views are welcome may go far to remove suspicion that letters are selected to buttress the editorial page rather than to subject it to question.

An additional suggestion with respect to these proposals is in order. Would it not be helpful at least once a month for a daily newspaper to indicate the volume of letters received? What is the total number of letters received? Publication of the answers to these questions plus some indication of the subjects and points of view of the letters received would in itself be a helpful guide to reader action to community controversy and editorial opinion even if there is not sufficient space to print all the letters themselves.

The use of the letters to the editor column as a tool for increasing access to the media has sometimes been scorned on the ground that all letters submitted cannot be published owing to space limitations.[13] Space of course is a problem, but submission of a letter to the editor is at present a total non-event. Most letters are simply not published. If the foregoing suggestions were adopted, the reader would not be left as much in the dark about the extent to which a paper's letters to the editor column is a reliable or representative guide to the sentiments of at least that segment of the readership which writes letters to the editor.

The sixth precept in the voluntary press code is designed to increase and diversify the writers who write for a newspaper: "(6) An editorial board of non-newspaper people will be established, in an advisory capacity only, to encourage and screen articles and commentary for designated regularly scheduled space on the editorial or 'op-ed' page which will be open to writers not on the newspaper staff."

This is a remarkably perceptive proposal. Limiting access to the media to employees of a particular media outlet has now become the prevailing pattern both in print and electronic journalism. In the electronic media, the principal restraint on freedom of broadcasting emanates from broadcasting. The major networks insist on producing their own shows for nearly every minute of network television. As a result, independent producers have been frustrated. Non-network originated programming is virtually banished from prime time television.

Similarly, in newspapers and magazines the policy increasingly appears to be that all contributions must come from the in-house staff. The new barrier to the freelance journalist and the citizen-writer-critic are the media themselves. As bad as the situation is in the United States, it is even worse in England, where unionization of journalists has reached the point that unions seek to refuse all rights of publication to anyone not a member of the journalist's union.[14]

Any plea for hospitality to writers who come from the larger world outside the paper is welcome. In a time of tremendous cost consciousness and dwindling circulation, such a plea by the daily press to non-affiliated writers is unlikely to yield a receptive response. The shrinking of the market for a freelance journalist has an inevitable effect on the variety, contrariety, and vigor of what appears in the daily press. We may reasonably expect that the one-shot freelancer may more often hear the music of some far distant drummer than will the reporter on the payroll. Similarly, in electronic journalism, independent television producers and script writers find it increasingly difficult to secure production of their works on television.

Although the new trend in the media of concentrating production and distribution in the same hands stems from economic considerations, these developments often are defended on other grounds as well - the need for journalistic excellence or the importance of editorial autonomy. The broadcast news director and the newspaper editor say: if we publish the professional journalist who is in our employ, we assure excellence in journalism, a not inconsiderable argument. But limiting access to journalism to writers on the payroll can have less edifying consequences; it can lead to an incestuous and captive journalism.

A proposal that newspapers establish editorial advisory boards to counter in-house dominance of newspaper space does run counter to the principle of editorial autonomy. If openness in the media is to be achieved at all, however, some breach of the principle of untrammeled editorial discretion must follow. There have been some successful attempts to scale the wall of absolute editorial privilege even in this heyday of that doctrine. The creation in 1972 of the National News Council, after the example of the Press Council in Britain, is an example of the creation of a non-governmental reviewing board whose function is to review journalistic and editorial decision-making. Newspaper co-operation with the National News Council, both in specific cases and perhaps in the more basic area of giving the Council sufficient media exposure to make it important, has not been all that the Council would have liked,[15] but there has been considerable co-operation.

Creation of an editorial advisory board drawn from outside a particular network or station involves oversight. It involves a recognition, no matter how halting or incomplete, that the press, like every public institution, might benefit from the application of accountability. Development of private oversight mechanisms such as a proposed editorial advisory board or, on a larger scale, the National News Council, illustrate that institutions as important and central in our society as the daily press cannot escape examination with respect to their governance and operations, any more than the universities of this country, whether public or private, were able to escape a similar examination in the tumultuous days of the late sixties.

The suggestion that papers appoint editorial advisory boards to oversee the encouragement of writers beyond those outside the ranks of in-house is a valuable one. For one thing the proposal reveals that the problem of access to print involves more than just the access of the general public. The problem of access to the print media affects in the most fundamental way the opportunities of those who by their craft, training, skill, and credentials are writers. In a time of a limited but powerful number of media outlets, any claim for the exclusive limitation of expression only to those admitted to the staff of a newspaper or a broadcast station cannot go unexamined. It is a great mistake to regard the problem of access as a problem between us (the general public) and them (the media). A monopoly on access to the media silences one of the prime alternatives to complete in-house dominance of the mass media - the freelancer.

The seventh proposal in the voluntary press code is as follows: "While reserving for itself the right of final determination, the newspaper will co-operate with local, state, regional, and national press councils studying press policies and practices." This proposal appears to make the following appeal: if the press does not wish to see fairness and access administered by the courts, then it should establish some mechanism for accountability within journalism. When a council or institute is set up, Donaghue urges the press to abide by its decisions when complaints about press performance are upheld by such a council. This proposal is far more controversial than may appear. Journalists have no bar association and no society whose disciplinary procedures they may have to fear. To the extent that journalism submits to councils or organizations designed to review the performance of journalism, such submission is a relatively new phenomenon and press willingness to submit voluntarily to the edicts of press councils has been far from unanimous. Noteworthy in its refusal to co-operate has been the *New York Times*. In a much publicized action, the *Times* refused to co-operate with the National News Council when it was established.

For those for whom the principle of editorial autonomy is the ultimate value it is entirely consistent to decline, as the *Times* did, to join any private watchdog of the press such as the National News Council. To act in concert with other media necessarily calls for yielding some measure of editorial autonomy. For this reason the *Times* declined to join with other papers to pool resources to make a particular media foray into investigative journalism more formidable. In this matter, the *Times* acted consistently with its principles. One cannot reasonably insist on escaping control by law if one willingly submits to control by others. Of course we are involved here in differences in scale. Most broadcasters would rather yield to the NAB than the FCC, and many newspaper editors and journalists would rather yield to the National News Council than the orders of a state or federal court. Government, whether state or federal, is more greatly to be feared by the media than are kindred media organizations. But, on this point, one should protest the identification of the courts with government. Federal judges, for example, who serve in effect with life tenure, have a degree of independence and a record of sensitivity to First Amendment values that makes it unwise to lump them indiscriminately with "government."

Would a press code that secured wide adoption within the American press be truly "voluntary?" Broadcasting's experience with the National Association of Broadcasters and the NAB advertising code illustrates that it would not be. The fact that the NAB is a private rather than a public body does not make media co-operation with the Advertising Code of the NAB "voluntary."[16] For the media member of the NAB the price of disobeying the Code is expulsion, and the price of continued adherence is the submission of editorial autonomy to outside authority. To ask press councils to do what courts would not be permitted to do is to ask for the harmonizing of a theory of voluntary press responsibility with the new principle of absolute editorial autonomy. On the whole, American journalism does not at present appear willing to tolerate such an attempt at harmony.

The eighth proposal in the voluntary press code is as follows: "(8) The newspaper will maintain an ombudsman's office or bureau of fair play to handle with dispatch complaints levied against it concerning news, advertising or business practices." An internal complaint mechanism within a newspaper to deal with complaints from the public is valuable. Some newspapers already have ombudsmen. Perhaps the ombudsman proposal, as Donaghue describes it, is a complaint processing procedure, but it need not be limited to that. The chief of the office should himself be a person who is a distinguished journalist, and the office is particularly effective if the ombudsman is given his own column. In-house criticism and controversy about what should and should not be printed should be publicized occasionally. In short, the ombudsman needs a column to do an effective job; he needs a voice in the paper whose performance he is evaluating. The Donaghue ombudsman proposal should be further strengthened by providing that the ombudsman be treated somewhat differently from an ordinary newspaper employee. In order to assure some degree of independence, courage, and candor, the ombudsman should preferably have a contract for a specific term of years. Although the proposal that ombudsmen be under contract may seem self-evidently sound, it is not the general practice. When I spoke to a group of newspaper ombudsmen at a conference sponsored by the Washington Journalism Center of newspaper ombudsmen in the spring of 1980, I discovered - to my surprise - that no one in the room had a contract with his paper to serve as an ombudsman for a specific term. Nevertheless, when an ombudsman challenges in print the paper's editorial and advertising policy, he should not have to risk his job as the price of his forthrightness.

LAW OR ETHICS?

The difficulty with journalistic responsibility imposed as a voluntary matter is that in a crisis, solutions imposed by conscience often prove less serviceable than mandates directed by law. The apparently eternal conflict between the values of a fair trial and the values orginating in a free press is illustrative. The conflict between the First Amendment with its pledge of a free press and the Sixth Amendment with its pledge of a free and impartial trial is just as difficult as is the conflict in the access controversy. The access issue is not, like the free press-fair trial issue, a conflict between the First and the Sixth constitutional amendments, but is instead localized within the First Amendment. The heart of the access dilemma is that it poses a conflict between the free press rights of the media and the free expression rights of the public.

Is a "voluntary" approach to the access problem likely to work? In the free press-fair trial area a "voluntary" rather than a legal approach has been implemented in many jurisdictions. How has it worked? A vivid answer is found in the Supreme Court's 1976 decision in the *Nebraska Press Association* case.[17] The facts of the case are worth reciting in order to indicate the difficulties presented when conflicts between individual rights and media rights are pushed for solution alternately to ethics or conscience and then back again to law.

In the fall of 1975, six members of one family were murdered in their home in a tiny Nebraska town. A suspect was soon apprehended. Three days after the crime, counsel for the prosecution and counsel for the defendant joined in asking that the trial court issue an order restricting the matters that could be disclosed by the press. The order required, among other things, members of the press to adhere to the Nebraska Bar-Press Guidelines. One of the advertised virtues of bar-press guidelines is that they are voluntary standards which the news media and the bar both agree to regard as guidance for media coverage of criminal litigation.

Among the items the Nebraska Guidelines set forth as not

appropriate for reporting were confessions, opinions on the guilt or innocence of the accused, statements designed to influence the outcome of the litigation, the results of lie detector tests, comments on whether witnesses should be believed, and evidence that was presented to the court in the absence of the jury.[18] Several press and broadcast associations, individual journalists and publishers interested in the state court proceedings and the state district court modified the original restrictive order but the state district court's order still incorporated the Nebraska Bar-Press Guidelines.

Out of the foregoing facts arose the now famous Nebraska "gag order" case in the Supreme Court. When the sensational murder occurred which gave rise to that case, no confidence was shown by either counsel for the prosecution, the defense, or the court that an honor system approach to the Bar-Press Guidelines would work. Yet the basic function of such guidelines is to allay concern that coverage by the news media of criminal proceedings will prejudice the trial of the accused.[19]

What is equally interesting is that the press as a whole in effect refused to adhere to the "guidelines" by launching a major constitutional litigation against a restrictive order which in part consisted of bar-press guidelines which Nebraska lawyers and journalists had themselves voluntarily entered into. It is hard to resist the conclusion that once the bar-press guidelines were given teeth, organized journalism (perhaps understandably, given the scent of a big story) could hardly wait to knock the new teeth out.

The Nebraska Supreme Court in turn modified the restrictive order of the state District Court prohibiting the publication only with respect to three matters: (1) the nature of any confessions or admissions made by the defendant to the public; (2) any confessions or admissions made by the defendant to any third parties not including the media; (3) other facts "strongly implicative" of the accused.[20] The decision of the Nebraska Supreme Court in this regard was reversed by the Supreme Court. The restrictive order even as limited and modified by the Nebraska Supreme Court was held to have failed to meet the heavy presumption which First Amendment law placed on prior restraints on press publication.

Because the Nebraska Supreme Court did not rely in its decision on the Nebraska Bar-Press Guidelines, the United States Supreme Court did not have occasion to pass on the merits of a voluntary bar-press code. But is the implicit teaching of the case not that such voluntary codes do not present a viable solution? The press insists that it has a right to provide full coverage of criminal litigation and lawyers and judges insist that the accused should be shielded from pervasive media publicity which might so saturate a community that no subsequent trial no matter how punctilious procedurally could be regarded as fair to the accused. In the

Nebraska case, the lawyers were not willing to wait to see if the media followed the voluntary guidelines. After all, the national news media were not parties to the guidelines.

The Romans said that in war the laws were silent. The *Nebraska Press Association* case shows that, in the event of a confrontation between the media and those responsible for administering the system of criminal justice, ethical precepts, in the form of voluntary press codes, soon fall by the way and are rendered of little significance. In the *Nebraska Press Association* case, the Supreme Court took a long step toward outlawing "gag orders" directed against media coverage of criminal pre-trial proceedings. It should be noted, however, that the Court did not take the ultimate step in that endeavor; it did not simply outlaw "gag orders." What weaponry remains to safeguard the right of the accused to a fair and impartial trial in view of the new strength that as a matter of law has been given to unrestrained media coverage of criminal trials? The Court gave both explicit and implicit answers to this question. The hope was offered that relief would come through voluntary restraint on the part of the press. The press, it was said, received extraordinary protection from the First Amendment. As a result, Chief Justice Burger said the press should view itself as being subject to "something in the nature of a fiduciary duty to exercise the protected rights responsibly - a duty widely acknowledged but not always observed by editors and publishers. It is not asking too much to suggest that those who exercise First Amendment rights in newspapers or broadcasting enterprises direct some effort to protect the rights of an accused to a fair trial by unbiased jurors."[21]

A judicial appeal to the press to act as fiduciary for those whom it might otherwise injure has a doubtful chance of success. The unrestrained exercise by the press of its abundant freedom is easily capable of trampling the rights of those less powerful, whose freedom is less abundant. In the *Nebraska Press* case, the Court itself said that the trial judge was justified in concluding that there "would be intense and pervasive pre-trial publicity concerning the case." The Court agreed that it was reasonable for the trial judge to fear that "publicity might impair the defendant's right to a fair trial." In such circumstances, can the rights of one party be left solely to the hope that a judicial sermon rather than a judicial directive to act justly will be followed? With all respect, it is doubtful that the Court itself had much faith that its sermon to the press to act as fiduciaries would be heeded.

The Court in the *Nebraska Press* cases tried to suggest remedies to assure that the rights of the accused would not be left totally without recourse in situations where a media publicity barrage focused on a single criminal accused. The Court noted, very pointedly, that recommended guidelines by the American Bar Association had suggested that "trial courts in appropriate cases limit the extent to which the contending lawyers, police, and witnesses may talk to others." Here the Court implied that it might approve restrictive orders which "gagged" legal and law enforcement personnel so long as the press itself was not directly "gagged".[22] Furthermore, in a concurring opinion which asked for an end to "gag orders," Mr. Justice Brennan, jointed by Justices Stewart and Marshall, raised without deciding the question of whether preliminary hearings could be closed to the public consistent with the " 'Public Trial' Clause of the Sixth Amendment.[23]

In the *Nebraska Press Association* case, the Court says essentially to the press: do justly - or else. The "or else" here refers to two suggested solutions to direct restraints on publication in the form of "gag orders": (1) "gagging" the sources of journalistic information, particularly lawyers and police; (2) raising the threat of closing off preliminary hearings to the press altogether. Significantly, both options, to the anguish of journalists who had hoped the *Nebraska Press Association* case had ushered in a new day for press reporting of criminal litigation, were availed of by courts around the country in its aftermath.[24] In such circumstances, the media might well say, one more such victory and we are undone.

In the *Nebraska Press Association* case the appeal to moral conscience of the media is accompanied by the threat of future legal sanction if conscience fails to prevail, that is, "gag orders" against the non-media sources of crime stories, or preliminary hearings closed to the media and the public. The Court did not make any appeal for compliance with bar-press guidelines. Just as voluntary bar-press guidelines are not strong enough to relieve crisis situations in the free press-fair trial area, so it is with voluntary codes as a solution to the problem of access. Indeed, the merits of a voluntary solution are less hopeful of success in the access field because in the access area by definition something has *not* been printed. We are asked to hope for redress by means of conscience for a problem which is often unlikely to surface sufficiently for measurement.

Professor Donaghue's proposals are an excellent guide to access problems that currently exist in the daily press. It is unlikely, however, that a voluntary press code will be able to resolve the access controversy any more than voluntary bar-press guidelines were able to solve the collision between the media and the law in the Nebraska "gag order" case.

The idea that freedom of expression can be realized through reliance on the media is increasingly prevalent. In the *Richmond Newspapers* case[25] where the Court ruled that the right of the public and the press to attend criminal trials is guaranteed under the First and Fourteenth amendments, Chief Justice Burger remarked that people now acquire information about trials not from being present but through the print and electronic media: "In a sense, this validates the media claim of functioning as surrogates for the public. While media representatives enjoy the same right of access as the public, they often are provided special seating and priority of entry so that they may report what people in attendance have seen and heard."[26]

The problem of access to the media is not resolved by the press as the surrogate for the public theory. The press is unlikely to embrace voluntarily that which it resisted when it was imposed by law. The fundamental issue involved in the access controversy is still the same whether the appeal for access proceeds from the realm of ethics or from the realm of law: is freedom of expression realized by sharing that freedom or is it realized by lodging it with the media in the hope that their freedom is our freedom?

Notes

1. *Miami Herald Publishing Co. v. Tornillo*, 418 U.S. 241 at 256 (1974).
2. There has been considerable scholarly controversy on whether the freedom of the press clause and the freedom of speech clause in the First Amendment should each be accorded a separate constitutional definition. This debate essentially centers around whether, as George Orwell might have put it - assuming that we are all equal - is the press more equal than the rest of us? Or to put it another way, should the press be accorded a fuller measure of First Amendment protection than those who, not having press cards, must find shelter in the free speech clause? See Nimmer, introduction, *Is Freedom of the Press a Redundancy: What Does it Add to Freedom of Speech?*, 26 Hastings Law Journal 639 (1975); Lange, *The Speech and Press Clauses*, 23 U.C.L.A. Law Review 77 (1975); Nimmer, *Speech and Press: A Brief Reply*, 23 U.C.L.A. Law Review 120 (1975).
3. See *Harris v. McRae*, 100 S.Ct. 2701 (1980); see also *Maher v. Roe*, 432 U.S. 464 (1977). In Maher, the Supreme Court held that the states did not have an affirmative constitutional duty to subsidize abortions for mothers who cannot afford them.
4. *Harris v. McRae*, note 3, supra, at 2701.
5. See Lewis, "The American Press and the Law: An Enviable Freedom," *The Economist*, Apr. 2, 1977.
6. Donaghue, *Reconsideration of Mandatory Public Access to the Print Media*, 21 St. Louis Univ. L.J. 91 at 97 (1977). The eight precepts suggested by Professor Donaghue for a voluntary press code for fairness and access which are quoted subsequently in this chapter are set forth in the above-cited article.
7. The same pattern of reluctance to report media news is found in broadcasting. On Nov. 16, 1977, NBC-TV talk show host Tom Snyder criticized the failure of CBS and NBC to report employee cutbacks and executive reshufflings and firings. Snyder attributed the silence to paranoia about being fired and likened the atmosphere at NBC to that depicted in the movie, *Network*. See *Broadcasting*, "Snyder Wants a Mirror," Nov. 21, 1977, p. 39.

8. For examples of the "plantation view" of the press in judicial opinions, see the remarks of Judge Marovitz in *Chicago Joint Board* v. *Chicago Tribune Co.*, 307 F. Supp. 422 (N.D. Ill. 1969): "First and foremost, the press is treated with special Constitutional regard. No other private industry or organization has been afforded any protection similar to that granted to the press under the First Amendment. The only other industry that was ever treated specially in the Constitution was the liquor industry, but the Eighteenth Amendment was short-lived, being repealed within fourteen years by the Twenty-First Amendment. Consequently, any attempted regulation of the press' freedom stands in a different Constitutional light and must be viewed differently than regulations of other forms of private commerce and association."

Judge Burger stated the "plantation" view succinctly in the *Office of Communication of United Church of Christ* v. *FCC*, 359 F.2d 994 at 1003 (D.C. Cir. 1966): "A newspaper can be operated at the whim or caprice of its owners; a broadcast station cannot."

9. Daniel, *Right of Access to Mass Media-Government Obligation to Enforce First Amendment*, 48 Texas Law Review 783 at 787 (1970).

10. Barron, *Access: The Only Choice for the Media*, 48 Texas Law Review 766 at 774-7 (1970).

11. For a good example of the absolutist view of editorial autonomy, see *Herbert* v. *Lando*, 568 F.2d 974 (2d Cir. 1977) where the United States Court of Appeals held that a defendant television documentary producer did not have to comply with pre-trial discovery in a libel case brought by a plaintiff who was a public figure plaintiff. The claims of an "allegedly libeled plaintiff" were held to be of less importance than protecting "the vitality of the editorial process." This case was, of course, reversed by the Supreme Court. See *Herbert* v. *Lando*, 441 U.S. 153 (1979). See also Chap. 5, which discusses the *Lando* case as well as the Court's unwillingness to accept an absolutist view of editorial autonomy - at least when asserted by a libel defendant seeking to shield inquiry into his publication decisions on the basis of journalist's privilege.

12. See Lewin, "What's Happening to Free Speech?" *The New Republic*, July 27 and Aug. 3, 1974, p. 13.

13. Daniel, note 7, *supra*, at p. 785. See also Schmidt, *Freedom of the Press* v. *Public Access* 257 (1976).

14. See Beloff, *Freedom under Foot: The Battle over the Closed Shop in British Journalism*, pp. 15-16 (1976).

15. McKay, *National News Council as National Ombudsman*, 21 St. Louis Univ. L.J. 102 at 109 (1977).

16. Cf. *Writers Guild* v. *FCC*, 423 F. Supp. 1064 (C.D. Calif. 1976) where an alleged governmental suggestion to the NAB to set aside a certain segment of prime time on television as a "Family Viewing Hour" (the segment to be off limits to exploitation of sex and violence) was held to be impermissible *governmental* censorship. The case was vacated and remanded to the FCC by a panel of the United States Court of Appeal for the Ninth Circuit on the ground that the agency had primary jurisdiction to consider the issues in the case. See *Writers Guild* v. *ABC*, 609 F.2d 355 (9th Cir. 1979).

17. *Nebraska Press Association* v. *Stuart*, 427 U.S. 539 (1976).
18. The full text of the Nebraska Bar-Press Guidelines for Disclosure and Reporting of Information Relating to Imminent or Pending Criminal Litigation is set forth in Appendix A to the concurring opinion of Mr. Justice Brennan in the *Nebraska Press Association* case: See note 15, *supra*, at p. 613.
19. The first sentence of the Nebraska Bar-Press Guidelines is as follows: "These voluntary guidelines reflect standards which bar and news media representatives believe are a reasonable means of accommodating, on a voluntary basis, the correlative constitutional rights of free speech and free press with the right of an accused to a fair trial." See note 15, *supra*, at *id.*
20. *State ex rel. Nebraska Press Assn* v. *Stuart*, 194 Neb. 783, 236 N.W. 2d 794 (1975).
21. See note 15, *supra*, at p. 560.
22. See note 15, *supra*, at p. 564.
23. See note 15, *supra*, at 576, fn. 2. In *Gannett Company, Inc.* v. *Pasquale*, 443 U.S. 368 (1979), the Supreme Court, following up on the implications to that effect in *Nebraska Press Association*, held that the decision of a trial judge to close a supression hearing to the press in the interest of a fair trial did not offend either the First or Sixth Amendment rights enjoyed by the press or the public. *Gannett* was soon interpreted by trial judges and by the press to authorize closure of a criminal trial itself. After a continuing barrage of criticism of the *Gannett* case, the Court quietly yielded. In *Richmond Newspapers, Inc.* v. *Virginia*, 100 S. Ct. 2814 (1980), the Court held that there was a First Amendment right to be present at criminal trials which could be asserted by the press and the public. The extent to which *Richmond Newspapers* casts doubts on the power of trial judges to close even prelimiary or pre-trial suppression hearings is not yet clear.
24. See *Central South Carolina Chapter, Society of Journalists* v. *Martin*, 556 F.2d 106 (4th Cir. 1977) essentially upholding a "gag order" with respect to extrajudicial statements by non-media personnel such as lawyers, parties, witnesses, jurors, and court personnel. The press unsuccessfully sought review in the Supreme Court on the ground that the prohibition on communication between the press and trial participants violated the First Amendment.
25. *Richmond Newspapers, Inc.* v. *Virginia*, 100 S. Ct. 2814 (1980).
26. *Id.* at 2814.

4

Public Media and Editorial Autonomy: The Reflector and the Gay Alliance

In twentieth-century America the dominant mass media are not the individual voices of individual editors and printers, but are the property of large interlocking corporations. We search for some counterpoise to the enormity of such power. But what worthy rival for the modern mass media is there? Individuals and groups across the country who seek access to newsprint and airwaves for a particular idea or cause are like so many gnats to the media Goliath. The modern American mass media have only one real challenger and that is government. The difficulty with relying on government power as a rival to media power is that we suspect, and rightly, that for a free people, reliance on government power may present problems of its own.

The use of government to establish alternative media is still about us. The rise of public broadcasting is a dramatic illustration. Another illustration is the state university campus press. If ultimately most university education in America is to be public education, then are the newspapers at such institutions to be treated as private or public actors? The use of government to correct problems of distortion and monopoly has been rightly perceived as full of dangers. As one First Amendment scholar, Thomas I. Emerson, has described the matter, it is indeed a paradox:[1] "The paradox of looking to government for regulation of a system that, by definition, is immune from government control presents one of the most difficult problems of our age."

This section will focus on one example of public media - the state university student press. Here public funds and the lively play of ideas intersect. The readership served is a specific one. Most important, ideas battling to enter a forum do so, for once, under public auspices.

In the case of the state university student press, the abiding precept of our communications policy that private property rights define First Amendment freedoms is not applicable. What are the public's rights to the public press? This chapter will examine a particular controversy where the familiar claim of editorial freedom was matched by the less familiar claim that there is a right of public access to the public press.

In this area of our law, a right of access to the press has already been recognized. Where a newspaper or a magazine is operated by a state agency (for example, the campus newspaper at a state university), a number of court decisions have held that such papers cannot permit the publication of ads on one side of an issue and at the same time refuse to publish ads taking opposing viewpoints. Similarly, this body of decisional law declares that a policy of choosing to print all commercial ads but no political ads is also impermissible. To choose to print one category of material and to deny access to other categories was, in this view, to involve the state through its instrumentality, the campus newspaper of a state university, in an impermissible violation of equal protection of the laws. It was also discrimination by the state on ideological grounds and thus impermissible under the First Amendment.

Most of these cases come from the great debate and national travail over the Vietnam War in the late sixties and the early seventies. The present validity of these cases should, of course, be evaluated in light of *Miami Herald Publishing Co. v. Tornillo,*[2] where the Supreme Court invalidated a Florida statute conferring a right of reply to a newspaper attack on a political candiate. The future force of this part of the law should also be measured against the Burger Court's apparent determination to resist any concept that public property must be particularly hospitable to dissenting ideas at least as against the wishes of the primary custodians of that property.

A backward glance at the law conferring a right of access to the state press may be helpful. In *Radical Lawyers Caucus v. Pool,*[3] a federal court ruled in 1970 that the official journal of the Texas state bar association, the *Texas Bar Journal,* had to accept an ad designed to publicize a caucus of radical lawyers to be held during the annual convention of the Texas state bar. The court noted that the journal had published commercial ads as well as ads on political matters. These judicial observations were made in refutation of the argument of the *Texas Bar Journal* that the journal, as an organ of the Texas State Bar, was a state instrumentality and could not engage in political advertising. In view of the fact that the *Texas Bar Journal* had been hospitable to other points of view, denial of any obligation to publish the advertisement of the radical lawyers would be a violation of equal protection. The court particularly stressed that a state agency could not have a policy of accepting commercial advertising but not accepting political advertising.

A year earlier, in 1969, in *Zucker* v. *Panitz*,[4] a federal district court in New York held, as had the Texas federal court, that when a state facility lends itself to commercial advertising it cannot then refuse to accept political advertising. In *Zucker*, a high school newspaper in New Rochelle, New York, was involved.

In 1971, in *Lee* v. *Board of Regents*,[5] the federal court of appeals ruled in favor of a duty on the part of a state university newspaper in Whitewater, Wisconsin, to take ads the paper wished not to take. Three kinds of ads had been submitted by various people to the *Royal Purple*, the campus newspaper at Wisconsin State University. One ad sought to describe the purpose of a university employees' union. Another ad, signed by nine clergymen, declared the immorality of racial or religious discrimination. The third rejected ad concerned race relations and the Vietnam War. The federal trial court had granted summary judgment to the proponents of the various ads. The federal appeals court affirmed and framed the issue raised by the case as follows: "Whether the defendants, having opened the campus newspaper to commercial and certain other types of advertising, could constitutionally reject plaintiffs' advertisements because of their editorial character."

Has the ground underneath that small terrain where a right of access to the press had been recognized and implemented, even prior to *Tornillo*, been shaken by *Tornillo*? In short, has a right of access to the press of tax-supported public institutions survived *Tornillo*?

It may be helpful in examining the question to consider a major First Amendment case which arose at Mississippi State University. In the summer of 1973, the chairwoman of the Mississippi Gay Alliance presented a proposed ad to *The Reflector*, the student newspaper at MSU. The ad read as follows:

> Gay Center - open 6:00 to 9:00 Monday, Wednesday, and Friday nights.
> We offer - counselling, *legal aid* and a library of homosexual literature. [emphasis added]
> Write to - The Mississippi Gay Alliance, P.O. Box 1328, Mississippi State University, Ms. 39762.

Under Mississippi law, "unnatural intercourse" is a criminal offense. The Mississippi anti-sodomy law has been upheld as constitutional by the state courts. The tendered ad was a paid one. The editor of *The Reflector* rejected it. The leader of the MGA then tried unsuccessfully to get the same announcement published in the "briefs" section of the paper.

The MGA brought suit against the editor and others to compel publication of its paid advertisement. The MGA contended that it had been denied its First Amendment rights and asked that the defendants be required to print the rejected material. The federal appeals court refused to grant the relief sought by the MGA: "The district court refused to command publication. We affirm."⁶ In this case, Judge Coleman for the federal court of appeals held that the rejection of the ad by the student newspaper at Mississippi State did not constitute state action.

The cases where a right to access has been recognized are cases where "state action" was considered to be present. When state activity is present, the state agency involved, whether it be the bar journal in Texas or the state university newspaper in Wisconsin or the high school paper in New York, is required to meet constitutional standards which private actors, such as privately-owned newspapers, would not be required to meet. For the federal courts passing on the Mississippi Gay Alliance controversy, state action could not be established from the fact that the state aided in collecting the non-waivable student activities fee, a portion of which was assigned to the paper. Central to the conclusion that state action was not present was that university officials did not supervise or control what was to be published or not to be published by *The Reflector*. Suppose the president of the university had ordered the student editor not to publish the ad or else face losing any university help in transmitting any portion of student activity fees to the paper? By implication, at least, that kind of direct university interference in student editorial discretion constituted state action.

Would such direct university involvement in editorial decision-making constitute impermissible state action? The court suggests an answer: "University authorities could not have ordered the newspaper not to publish the Gay Alliance advertisement, had it chosen to do so . . ."⁷ This statement does not appear to be premised on the idea that such state intrusion would prefer one view to the exclusion of another and thus violate equal protection. This was the rationale of *Radical Lawyers Caucus, Zucker,* and *Lee v. Board of Regents.*

In the *MGA* case, a quite distinct view of the impermissibility of such hypothetical state involvement in the editorial process is taken. The court, quoting from *Tornillo*, suggests that an order from university authorities to a student editor not to publish would be invalid in light of the *Tornillo* stricture that the "choice of material to go into a newspaper" constitutes a protected exercise of editorial control and judgment.

The suggestion here appears to be that editorial autonomy itself whether exercised under public *or* private auspices is constitutionally excluded from judicial review. The implication is that the editorial function is protected by the First Amendment to an extent that requires its immunity from judicial review: editorial decision-making cannot be subject to government regulation. Government regulation in this context is considered to be review of a particular exercise of editorial functions in the courts. Thus, the court in *MGA* pointedly quoted what it called the Supreme Court's flat declaration in *Miami Herald Publishing Co. v. Tornillo*:[8] "It has yet to be demonstrated how *governmental* regulation of this crucial process can be exercised consistent with First Amendment guarantees of a free press as they have evolved to this time."

However, government regulation in *Tornillo* was posited against a private editor's exercise of editorial judgment. Does it make any sense to say that one government entity may never have any powers to call another entity within the government to account? Our whole constitutional system is animated by the idea of separation of powers. When units within the government sector collide we have come to expect courts to be the arbiters. Should the editorial function whenever it appears in the public sector be removed from judicial review? The court in *MGA* does not establish a doctrine of First Amendment-based preclusion of judicial review with respect to the exercise of editorial discretion in media run by public institutions, but it comes very close to doing so.

It is true that the court does say that there were "special reasons for holding that there was no abuse of discretion by the editor of *The Reflector*."[9] The special reasons appear to be based on the idea that a Mississippi statute makes sodomy a criminal offense. The court suggests that the advertisement, even though it might have only a peripheral connection to the activity specifically forbidden, was nonetheless illegal and therefore the editor was bound not to publish it. It is, of course, possible to argue that absent such "special reasons" abuse of discretion by a state university editor might be reviewed by the courts. However, the court's reading of *Tornillo* seems to resist such a conclusion.

In short, the novel idea which *MGA*, building on *Tornillo*, appears to be animated by is that editorial autonomy as a matter of First Amendment law is a principle so fundamental in our polity that it may never be reviewed by the courts.

If editorial autonomy, whether public or private, has become a new constitutional absolute, then it is irrelevant whether state action is or is not present in fact patterns in such cases as *Mississippi Gay Alliance*. In an access context, the hunt for state action is pursued in order to determine whether constitutional duty exists; in this theory the duty of state-supported institutions is to approach controversy on a non-ideological and non-preferential basis. If editors, regardless of whether they edit state-financed media or whether they edit private media, may never be directed to exercise their discretion fairly, then the search for state action in access cases is a wholly unnecessary quest. In such a view, editorial power, whether exercised by editors of public or private institutions, is sacrosanct in itself.

This judicial awe of editorial function in any context is found with respect to other public media. In public television, federal legislation tries to draw a line between journalistic independence and the reality that Congressional funding is a primary source of support for public television. In the case of public television, the stations which comprise public television are, at a minimum, bound by the fairness doctrine. The Corporation for Public Broadcasting, under the language of the Public Broadcasting Act of 1967, is directed to adhere to balance and objectivity in programming. However, in this context as in others the editorial function has been placed beyond the law. Even public broadcasting has been liberated from obligation to the public. A new decision has rendered the "balance and objectivity" standard of the Public Broadcasting Act legally unenforceable. In *Accuracy in Media, Inc. v. FCC*,[10] the federal court of appeals in an opinion by Judge Bazelon considered the provision of the Public Broadcasting Act which says that the Corporation for Public Broadcasting was to fulfill its responsibilities "with strict adherence to objectivity and balance in all programs or series of a controversial nature."[11] The "balance" and "objectivity" language was called "hortatory" by Judge Bazelon and it was ruled to be unenforceable by the FCC.[12]

The resolution of the *MGA* case was unfortunate in a number of respects. The case suggests that decisions concerning content by state-affiliated media can be left without recourse to law to the absolute discretion of anyone who can claim the title of editor. A casual editorial selection process - rather than hospitality to ideas - becomes the touchstone of First Amendment protection. In the *MGA* case, much is made of the fact that the editor operated independently of the state even though other earmarks of the paper's involvement with a state institution, MSU, are evident. These other earmarks derive from the fact that the university collects the student activities fee plus the fact that the students may not elect not to pay it. In short, the state is compelling students to support a newspaper whose views a student may not share. The cry of editorial freedom should be most carefully examined, particularly in media with a state connection. The fairness of the procedure whereby the editor is chosen and continues must also be examined in such cases.

In *Wooley v. Maynard*,[13] the Supreme Court held, per Chief Justice Burger, that the State of New Hampshire could not enforce criminal sanctions against a married couple, Jehovah's Witnesses, who covered up the motto on the state license place, "Live Free or Die." The couple covered up the motto because it was repugnant to their moral and religious beliefs. In this case, the Court observed:[14] "The First Amendment protects the right of individuals to hold a point of view different from the majority and to refuse to foster, in the way New Hampshire commands, an idea they find morally objectionable." A student who must support by his activities fee a newspaper endorsing views he opposes is being required by the state to foster those views. This in itself may not be objectionable. If alternative media are to develop, if some counterforce to the private commercial media is to arise, then obviously the editorial function must be given scope. If the campus newspaper is to publish editorials at all, they must take a point of view. The First Amendment impact on publicly supported media whose primary function is communication cannot be so rigid that all trace of viewpoint and conviction must be suppressed. On the other hand, the First Amendment impact on publicly sponsored media must have some procedure for entry for opposing viewpoints. Some part of the public media must be open. Public media must steer a course between being an editorial voice for a governing clique and being merely a common carrier for whatever content the community served wishes to have.

In the New Hampshire license plate case, the state argued that its interest in stimulating appreciation of "history, individualism and state pride" was sufficient to override the First Amendment objections of the couple.[15] The court's rejoinder to this argument was that such a state objective was not "ideologically neutral" because it sought "to communicate to others an official view."[16] In an *MGA*-type fact pattern the fortuity that an independently selected editor and state law were in harmony resulted in the communication of an official state view. To prevent the emergence of an official view, there must be some obligation on the public media to present opposing viewpoints. Otherwise, the state may too easily become impermissibly involved in sponsoring an ideology. One of the fundamental consequences of the First Amendment has been to minimize identification of the "established" view of things with state power and prestige. Inevitably, more media in an increasingly collectivist world will become intertwined with the state either administratively as in *MGA* or through the direct allocation of funds. But have we advanced the cause of encouraging expression for diversity of ideas if we let the editors of new and public media decide absolutely what goes in and what goes out?

Is editorial discretion, like divine judgment, not to be subject to earthly review? In the *Mississippi Gay Alliance* case, Judge Goldberg asks somewhat hypothetically: could a state newspaper called *Open Forum* refuse to "print a tendered statement on the ground that it expressed a political view contrary to that of the Governor, or on no stated ground at all"?[17] Judge Goldberg answers his own question: "Surely not."[18] Could the same paper refuse to publish a statement on the ground that the editor does not wish to print it? Here Judge Goldberg reaches a different conclusion. In reviewing the case law recognizing a right of access to state-sponsored publications, he points out that in the past where a right of access had been recognized (the duty to publish anti-

Vietnam War ads in the cases respectively of a public high school newspaper in New Rochelle, New York [*Zucker v. Panitz*], and a state university newspaper in Whitewater, Wisconsin [*Lee v. Board of Regents*]) "officials, not students, exercised ultimate responsibility for the censorship decision."[19]

In short, Judge Goldberg conceded that state officials rather than the editor had made the decisions to exclude the advertisements in controversy concerning the *Huguenot Herald* and the *Royal Purple* in Whitewater, Wisconsin. In the *Mississippi Gay Alliance* case, one factor that led the majority of the court to rule against the access claim was its view that the newspaper in controversy could not be viewed as a "state" publication. Since the state university through its officials had not been involved in the exclusion of the Gay Alliance from the advertising columns of *The Reflector,* the court concluded that the decision to ban the advertisement in question was not a situation where the "state" was acting impermissibly to choose sides in an ideological battle. It was instead an editorial decision and, therefore, under the First Amendment, immune from judicial review.

In dissent in the *Gay Alliance case,* Judge Goldberg quite properly argued that making a distinction between an "editorial" decision and an "official" decision with respect to what otherwise looks like a public instrumentality was an inadequate basis on which to make a determination as to whether state action existed or not. He pointed out that the funds that supported *The Reflector* were derived from a non-waivable student fee collected from MSU students by the university. The conclusion that followed from this that the funds supporting *The Reflector* came from a tax charged by the state to the students was reasonable.

What obligations are owed to the public by a public press? If the person given authority by the state to determine the composition of the paper's content is called "editor" rather than "principal" or "vice-chancellor," should that title be enough to exclude any obligation to the public or the readership? Although less true of the students of the seventies and eighties than the students of the sixties, student "editors" still are usually justly perceived as being less partial to establishment prejudices and rigidities than "vice-chancellors" and "principals." Fundamentally, a problem of fairness or access in the context of public media is really obscured by a focus which inquires whether the decision in controversy was made by a middle-aged "vice-chancellor" or by a young student "editor." The difficult and perplexing question in any public press is the question of the extent to which it is supposed to be innocent of ideology. The First Amendment is surely some guarantee of such innocence. If ideology can be manifested by the state through the broad delegation of authority to even a student editor, that circumspection with respect to the advocacy of a particular ideology which ought to be present wherever the state is involved is endangered. The Supreme Court denied review in the *MGA* case and so these problems remain unresolved.[20] Is it worth engaging in litigation all the way to the Supreme Court to determine whether or not a state university newspaper should publish an ad? Are such matters worth the lawyer's fees? Are they worth the printer's ink?

These battles *are* worth the pain, time, and expense that they occasion. The dissent filed in the *MGA* case by Judge Goldberg may ultimately point the direction of the law with respect to the role of the editorial function in the public media. He said that he would find a "narrowly circumscribed right of access which might extend to the MGA in this case."[21]

Judge Goldberg built his argument that a constitutional right of access to the state university campus press still endured, even after *Tornillo*, on the public forum concept popularized by the late Professor Harry Kalven of the University of Chicago. He describes the public forum concept as follows:[22] "When the state provides a communications forum generally open to the public, the state may not discriminatorily forbid the use of the forum by certain individuals because of the content of their proposed messages." Judge Goldberg believes this public forum doctrine, so described, can be applied to a "state newspaper." In his view, the state "cannot discriminate among potential speakers on the basis of the content of their message."[23] Judge Goldberg relied on Mr Justice Marshall's opinion in *Police Department of Chicago* v. *Mosley:*[24] "There is an 'equality of status in the field of ideas' and government must afford all points of view an equal opportunity to be heard." For Judge Goldberg, there was both a First Amendment and an equal protection foundation behind this non-discriminatory access principle: "Equality of access to public forums is compelled not only by speech and associational rights, but also by the full force of the equal protection clause."

Yet at the same time, he recognizes "a right to edit." He would permit "student editors of state newspapers unfettered discretion over what might be termed the "editorial product" of the newspaper."[25] Editorial product is defined by Judge Goldberg as including the "news and editorial columns of the paper." The advertising columns of a paper, on the other hand, are those parts of the newspaper which traditionally have been "open." Unlike the editorial columns, they were not involved in *Tornillo*. Judge Goldberg would require that "when the newspaper devotes space to unedited advertisements or announcements from individuals outside the newspaper staff, access to such space must be made available to other similarly situated individuals on a non-discriminatory basis."[26]

Judge Goldberg is not alone in suggesting that with respect to the state university campus press an unfettered "right to edit" and a principle of non-discriminatory access to the advertising columns can each be honored. Another student of the problem of the government as editor, who is equally sensitive to both the claim of editorial autonomy and the claim of public access to public media, is a former law clerk to Mr. Justice Douglas, Professor William Canby of the law faculty of Arizona State University. Professor Canby writes:[27]

> The advertising section of a school newspaper or a state university law review is also more effective when open and unrestricted, but the editorial, news and articles columns of these publications are not. As long as the alternative methods of expression are available, a right of access should be denied where the governmental enterprise cannot truly exist without the exercise of editorial discretion.

Canby's suggestion is that a principle of non-discriminatory access to advertising columns should be required with respect to state facilities whose primary function is communication. At the same time, Canby believes that protection of the editorial function with respect to such a public press is essential. Certainly a public press should have the right to editorialize and to make the editorial judgments essential to any communications media, but the exercise of editorial freedom in the public press must necessarily be subjected to a more intense level of public obligation than in the case of private media. Editorializing and editorial autonomy must be protected. However, public participation and public access to public media must also be secured. Editorial autonomy requires that the public press be able to take an editorial position. What must be watched carefully is that such an editorial position does not implicate the state in mandating that position as an exclusive position for the public press. Professor Canby apparently believes that the health of the editorial function, even when exercised under public auspices, requires that no access obligations should be recognized with respect to the news and editorial sections of the public newspaper, as opposed to the advertising columns of the public press.

Both Judge Goldberg and Professor Canby recognize that it is inconsistent for public media, which are by definition devoted to public service, to seal themselves off entirely from claims of public access. The question arises, however, whether it is necessary to insist that editorial and news columns of a state university campus newspaper must be closed to claims of public access and entry while the traditionally "open" section of the newspaper, the advertising columns, must be the sole host to claims of access to the public media. Is it not odd to talk of the news and editorial columns of public media as being "closed"? With respect to public media, should not such sections of the public press be, above all, "open"?

Insisting on rigid distinction between "closed" news and editorial columns and "open" advertising columns is, as a practical matter, clearly at odds with the phenomenon of the editorial advertisement. If the campus paper takes an editorial stance on a particular matter, the suggestion with respect to public media is that a claim to purchase an editorial advertisement by a group or individual opposed to the editorial should be honored. Suppose the same group or individual wants the paper to offer it a right of reply on the editorial page? How is the principle of editorial autonomy any more adversely affected than it would be if the right of reply were limited to the editorial advertisement? The editorial advertisement will, of course, involve the individual and group seeking it in paying the paper for the ad. A reply to the editorial if furnished by the paper by means of space in its news column or on its editorial page will be free. This distinction certainly affects the paper's treasury, but does it really affect the paper's editorial freedom? The private paper may say that if it must give voice to a view it does not believe, then its freedom is in some measure diminished. Although this is arguable, surely the editor of a public press is on far weaker ground if he should rely on such an argument. If a public press is so fanatic about its views as to exclude all criticism of itself, then such a press seems very susceptible to a charge that it is not adding to expression but rather propagandizing for an ideology.

In the private sector the claim may be urged that permitting a reply on the editorial page forces the editor or publisher to legitimize a position with respect to which the paper may in sincerity and out of deep conviction be opposed. In the case of public media, problems of viewpoint or editorial position cannot be seen just as expression of editorial autonomy to be treated the way such problems are treated in the case of private media. The state in our society creates media to add to expression and not to espouse a cause. Public toleration of such espousal as arises in public media is merely an inevitable and sensible recognition that instrumentalities which deal with ideas cannot pursue them intelligently in the absence of editing. Hence, editorial autonomy. But concern for the integrity of the editorial function in public media, which includes a respect for and encouragement of the taking of editorial positions, should not be pursued to the point where opposing viewpoints are, as a matter of First Amendment law, exiled from the news columns and the editorials of the public press.

The most persuasive justification in our society for permitting government to use public institutions and public funds to create new communications media is that such endeavors do not inhibit free expression but instead create new outlets for ideas. If this reasoning is accepted, then it is extremely important not to let the development of public media become a means for suggesting even implicitly that a viewpoint once taken by a public press will merit a response only by the grace of those managing the public press.

What better way to assure that the public media do not become vehicles for state ideology than to provide that in some circumstances a right of reply to an editorial taken by the public press is in order? There should be no absolute hierarchy with respect to opportunity for expression in public media. Expression cannot be keyed to the status of the author of the idea. The issue should not be whether an idea emanates from the editor of a public press or his staff or whether it emanates from a group or individual in the community served by that editor and staff. This should not be the exclusive touchstone guiding opportunity for expression in the editorial and news columns of public media. It will be tragic if the First Amendment is used to defeat public rights of expression to public media. The public cannot be excluded in all circumstances from claims of access and entry to the news and editorial columns of the public press.

First Amendment law must not become an abstraction whose protection covers trivial situations involving a few persons but grants less and less opportunity for expression in the communications media which affect the largest numbers in a community. Suppose, for example, that the MSU campus newspaper declared in an editorial that the Gay Alliance should not be accorded status as a recognized campus organization. As a First Amendment matter, in such circumstances, the Gay Alliance should have a right in the news and editorial columns to respond to the editorial advocating their exclusion.

The Supreme Court has said that the state cannot compel us to carry its motto on our auto license plates because that would compel us to endorse the state's philosophy. But if the state cannot compel us to place its philosophy on our license plates, it would be strange to allow the state at the same time to use our funds through a public press for the exclusive propagation of a particular philosophy. The claims of a due deference for editorial autonomy in the public press extend far, but not that far. Editorial autonomy is protected by allowing an editor to editorialize and to edit, but certainly in the case of public media, the right to editorialize should not be considered so fragile that it cannot withstand the just authentication of reply.

In the beginning of this chapter, this question was raised - how does the *Miami Herald* case affect those cases where a right of access had arleady been won? The existing case law recognizing a right of access to the public press should be viewed as unaffected by the *Miami Herald* decision because it cannot be said of public editors, as it may be of private ones, that they are the sole arbiter of what falls on the cutting room floor. Nevertheless, the *Gay Alliance* case does represent an assault on access to the press even in that one sector where it has been won - the publicly sponsored campus press. The case law makes clear that for state instrumentalities the mandates of the First Amendment with respect to freedom of expression are applicable. On a technical legal basis, it does not seem that the *Gay Alliance* case is in conflict with these older cases because the *Gay Alliance* case proceeds on the theory that there no state action was present. Such an interpretation, however, is disingenuous. The philosophy, as opposed to the law, of the *Gay Alliance* case is certainly at odds with the older cases. The *Gay Alliance* case proceeds on the theory that an editor - whether his editorial function is made possible by public funds or private funds - has a special status. In short, the theory seems to be that where an editor's claim of First Amendment right conflicts with a free expression right asserted by an individual, the editor's claim must necessarily prevail. The application of this doctrine, which uses the *Miami Herald* case for its support, reflects the pervasive impact of that decision. The *Gay Alliance* case also entails an enormous expansion of the *Miami Herald* doctrine because it applies that doctrine far beyond the context in which it originated - that involving a private newspaper rather than a public one.

A final word should be said about the *Gay Alliance* case as seen in the larger context of the effort to establish a right of access to the public campus press. The older access cases involving the public campus press involve matters like opposition to the Vietnam War. The *Gay Alliance* case involves an effort to secure equivalence of rights for those who have sexual preferences which do not meet the norm. The need for access to the media in a particular era is demonstrated, then, by the subject matters of the material in controversy. The material seeking media access is in truth a barometer of what is acceptable and what is not. Recognition of the access principle in a case like the *Gay Alliance* case, as was true in the older anti-Vietnam War cases, would usher into the opinion process issues which conformist editors proclaiming freedom of the press are otherwise quite willing to exclude.

Notes

1. Emerson, *Colonial Intentions and Current Realities of the First Amendment,* 125 U. of Pa. 737 at 756 (1977).
2. 418 U.S. 214 (1974).
3. 324 F. Supp. 268 (W.D. Tex. 1970).
4. 299 F. Supp. 102 (S.D.N.Y. 1969).
5. 306 F. Supp. 1097 (W.D. Wis. 1969); 441 F. 2d 1237 (7th Cir. 1971).
6. *Mississippi Gay Alliance v. Goudelock,* 536 F. 2d 1073 at 1074 (5th Cir. 1976).
7. *Id.* at 1075.
8. *Id.*
9. *Id.*
10. 521 F. 2d (D.C. Cir. 1975).
11. U.S.C. sect. 396(g) (1)(A). Judge Bazelon observed in the *Aim* case,

note 10, *supra*, that sect. 398 of the Public Broadcasting Act states that no "agency . . . of the United States" should have authority to supervise or control the Corporation for Public Broadcasting. Judge Bazelon reasoned that the FCC is an "agency" of the United States, *ergo*, sect. 396 cannot be read as giving jurisdiction to the FCC to enforce sect. 396. Would the statutes not be more reasonably read as meaning merely that sect. 398 is *pro tanto* qualified by the plain meaning sense of sect. 396 which is that the FCC should enforce the "balance and objectivity" requirement of sect. 396?

12. 47 U.S.C. sect. 396 (g) (1)(A) (1970) sets forth the "balance and objectivity" of the Public Broadcasting Act of 1967. This provision was interpreted in *Accuracy in Media, Inc.* v. *FCC*, 521 F.2d 288 (D.C. Cir. 1975).

13. 430 U.S. 705.

14. *Id.* at 1436.

15. *Id.*

16. *Id.*

17. Note 6, *supra*, at 1082.

18. *Id.*

19. *Id.* at 1084.

20. *Mississippi Gay Alliance* v. *Goudelock, cert. denied*, 430 U.S. 982 (1977).

21. *Id.* at 1076.

22. *Id.* at 1080.

23. *Id.*

24. 408 U.S. 92, 95-6 (1972).

25. Note 6, *supra*, at 1087.

26. *Id.*

27. Canby, *The First Amendment and the State as Editor: Implications for Public Broadcasting*, 52 Tex. L. Rev. 1123 at 1133-4 (1974). Professor Canby is now a federal appellate judge.

5

The Rise and Fall of a Doctrine of Editorial Privilege: Reflections on Herbert v. Lando*

In that ever-growing area of law that is concerned with conflicts between the competing claims for liberty asserted by the media on the one hand and individuals on the other, a particularly interesting case has arisen. The case - a prototype, perhaps, of this type of conflict - is *Herbert v. Lando*.[1] The television showcase of investigative journalism, "60 Minutes," had undertaken an inquiry into charges by Colonel Anthony Herbert that war crimes had been committed by American military personnel in Vietnam.[2] Barry Lando, producer of "60 Minutes," made a serious inquiry into Colonel Herbert's allegations that American military authorities in Vietnam had declined to investigate numerous atrocities committed by American military in Vietnam.[3] In a program called "The Selling of Colonel Herbert," which was aired on February 4, 1973, Lando expressed serious doubts about some of Herbert's major assertions.[4]

The full extent of his research for the "60 Minutes" program was set forth by Barry Lando in an article in the *Atlantic Monthly* entitled "The Herbert Affair."[5] Herbert then brought a suit for more than $44 million in damages against Lando.[6] The discovery in the case was extensive and defendant Lando extended the fullest co-operation to plaintiff Herbert.[7] Lando refused, however, to answer some questions concerning his beliefs, intentions, and conclusions in connection with his preparation of the program, on the ground that the questions probed an area which was protected by a First Amendment-based editorial privilege.[8] Lando asserted that the editorial function itself was being endangered by the kinds of questions that Herbert was propounding.[9]

---

* This article was published in 47 Geo. Wash. L. Rev. 1002 (1980). Reprinted with the permission of the George Washington Law Review, 1979.

On a motion to compel discovery, a federal district court held that Lando should be compelled to answer even those questions.[10] The court, per Judge Haight, denied Lando's assertion that the First Amendment entitled him to refuse to answer the questions propounded on the ground that they invalidly impinged on editorial freedom.[11] Furthermore, the court noted that the appropriate balance between protection of one's reputational integrity and the right of the news media freely to disseminate information had been struck in *New York Times* v. *Sullivan*[12] in the form of the now famous "actual malice" doctrine.[13] The doctrine of actual malice requires that if the libel plaintiff is a public figure or a public official (it was conceded that Colonel Herbert was a public figure), then he may recover damages from the defendant only if he can prove by clear and convincing proof that what the defendants had said about him was published in reckless disregard of the truth or falsity of what was said.[14]

How can one prove recklessness without showing the state of mind of the defendant? If the defendant is determined to defame the plaintiff whatever the facts, for example, how will the plaintiff be able to ferret this out if the plaintiff is not permitted to ask questions about the defendant's state of mind? In short, it may be impossible to satisfy the rigorous requirements of the actual malice test if the plaintiff is not able to inquire into anything that might show "reckless disregard" on the part of the defendant.

If a new and imprecise doctrine of editorial privilege is tacked on to the existing rigors of the *New York Times* v. *Sullivan* standard of liability, the fragile equilibrium between reputational integrity and editorial freedom which had previously been struck by the Supreme Court in the *New York Times* case will be seriously disturbed. For these reasons, Judge Haight denied the defendants' plea for the establishment of an editorial privilege exception to discovery requests.[15] Chief Judge Kaufman, however, speaking for the majority of a three-judge panel for the United States Court of Appeals for the Second Circuit, disagreed.[16] Judge Kaufman ruled that the First Amendment required recognition of an editorial privilege doctrine in these circumstances.[17] The Supreme Court reversed the decision of the Second Circuit in *Herbert* v. *Lando*.[18]

Before we directly examine the Supreme Court opinion in *Lando*, however, a careful examination of the sources of the Second Circuit's decision to recognize an editorial process privilege is in order if the full implications of the Supreme Court's contrary decision in *Lando* are to be understood. The relationship of the editorial privilege recognized by Judge Kaufman in *Lando* to the emphasis on untrammeled editorial discretion in the Supreme Court's unanimous decision in *Miami Herald Publishing Co.* v. *Tornillo*[19] must be stressed.

The doctrine of *Miami Herald Publishing* v. *Tornillo*, rejecting a right of access to the press on the ground that such a right is at variance with the protection necessary for unfettered editorial freedom,[20] is the essential source of the Second Circuit decision in *Lando*. The rejection of a right of access in the name of editorial freedom was, by analogy, a principal source for the attempt to create an editorial privilege in the new public law of libel. As perhaps a matter of recompense, it is entirely right that a doctrine of editorial privilege should attempt to take root in the specific context of a *New York Times*-type libel case. The need for recognition of First Amendment rights of individuals as well as the First Amendment rights of the media, developed to some extent by way of a reaction to the disequilibrium which resulted from the *New York Times* v. *Sullivan* case.[21] Judge Kaufman, in his opinion in the *Lando* case, relied directly on the *Tornillo* decision.[22] After all, *Tornillo*'s defense of the editorial function was a ringing one: "The choice of material to go into a newspaper and the decisions made as to limitations on the size and content of the paper, and treatment of public issues and public officials - whether fair or unfair - constitute the exercise of editorial control and judgment."[23]

On its fact, the *Tornillo* decision blocked the development of a new legal control of the press - a right of access and reply. The somewhat extravagant language[24] of that decision, however, has proved quite serviceable in producing new arguments to attack even long-standing legal controls on the press, such as the law of libel itself, including that new branch of the law of libel inaugurated by the advent of *New York Times* v. *Sullivan,* the public law of libel.

Chief Justice Burger stated for the Court in *Tornillo* that "press responsibility is not mandated by the Constitution."[25] In this post-Watergate world, these are seductive words and it is not surprising that they should have been seen by some as a call to arms. After all, if press responsibility cannot be enforced at law by a right of reply, it is not unreasonable to ask why press responsibility should be enforced by laws to vindicate reputation. In a sense, the issues in *Lando* present this kind of argument in a more moderate form. In short, the argument of the defense in *Lando*, accepted by the Second Circuit, did not ask directly for an end to the law of libel. Rather, it sought indirectly to knock out some of the remaining teeth in that law, teeth which have survived the imposition of the actual malice test.

Judge Kaufman's opinion in *Lando* took a broad view of the right of the press to disseminate news. He defined it to include not merely the decision to publish or not to publish, but the whole process of pre-publication decision-making.[26] Judge Kaufman relied directly on *Miami Herald Publishing Co.* v. *Tornillo*[27] and *Columbia Broadcasting System, Inc.* v. *Democratic National Committee*[28] for the idea that the claims of editorial freedom should take precedence even over the carefully developed accommodation between the law of libel and First Amendment values that the

Supreme Court had already struck in *New York Times* v. *Sullivan*. In *Lando*, Judge Kaufman made his preference for the new editorial freedom cases - *Tornillo* and *CBS* - over the requirements of the *New York Times* doctrine unmistakably clear:

> The unambiguous wisdom of *Tornillo* and *CBS* is that we must encourage, and protect against encroachment, full and candid discussion within the newsroom itself. In the light of these constitutional imperatives, the issue presented by this case is whether, and to what extent, inquiry into the editorial process, conducted during discovery in the *New York Times* v. *Sullivan* type libel action, impermissibly burdens the work of reporters and broadcasters.[29]

To this new emphasis on editorial freedom, Judge Kaufman brought an expanded conception of the editorial function. Kaufman believed that if a reporter or editor must function under the awareness that his "thoughts might have to be justified in a court of law,"[30] he would be discouraged from the "creative . . . probing" and hypothecation that are "the sine qua non of responsible journalism."[31] In *Lando*, Judge Kaufman concluded that Barry Lando did not have to answer questions that he believed would impermissibly pierce the exercise of his editorial judgment.[32] In a sense, this doctrine comes near to reviving the doctrine of absolute privilege in public libel cases advocated by Mr. Justice Black in *New York Times* v. *Sullivan*[33] and implicitly rejected by the majority of the Supreme Court in the opinion of Mr. Justice Brennan.[34]

Judge Kaufman relied further on *Branzburg* v. *Hayes*[35] to reach his conclusion that Lando should be permitted to assert a defence of editorial privilege against answering the questions about his state of mind.[36] Objectively, it would seem that the *Branzburg* decision would be seen as a precedent against Lando rather than for him. In *Branzburg*, the plurality opinion, per Mr. Justice White, declined to exempt journalists from any duty to appear and testify before a grand jury. The Court noted that this was a duty that bound all citizens, including the President of the United States.[37] Under this reading, the following postulate, derived from *Branzburg*, should be applied to the *Lando* controversy. Just as a journalist has a duty along with other citizens to respond to the grand jury's inquiry, assuming it is conducted under otherwise permissible general constitutional norms, so a media defendant in a libel case has the same obligation to make discovery in a libel case which other libel defendants are required to make. Objectively, therefore, *Branzburg* was a precedent for Herbert and not for Lando. Judge Kaufman did not see it that way. He focused his attention[38] not on the plurality opinion of the Court in *Branzburg*, but on the concurring opinion of Mr. Justice Powell, which suggested that in some circumstances, as when the requested information had only a remote and tenuous relationship to the subject of investigation, a qualified First Amendment privilege would be recognized on behalf of a journalist in a grand jury proceeding.[39]

In the aftermath of *Branzburg*, the case law in the lower courts, particularly in civil litigation, has increasingly come to recognize the existence of a qualified First Amendment-based journalist's privilege.[40] The courts in some of these later libel cases have, in fact, appeared ready to offer to journalist defendants a measure of First Amendment protection that non-journalists cannot claim.[41] Although some of these later developments were inconsistent with the egalitarian First Amendment theory posited by the plurality in *Branzburg*, they were consistent with the establishment of a new doctrine of editorial privilege that might be used by media defendants in libel cases.

If the foregoing analysis of the manner in which Judge Kaufman used *Branzburg* in *Lando* is correct, it is another illustration that the new doctrine of editorial privilege is essentially an aspect of a novel movement for a special constitutional status for the media.[42] In this view, the First Amendment is not a mandate that freedom of the press shall not be abridged, but that the press shall be free from law. The post-*Branzburg* cases on which Judge Kaufman relied recognize only a qualified First Amendment-based privilege. Even if his decision had not been reversed, it would have left unresolved many questions that would have perplexed the application of an editorial process privilege. For example, did Judge Kaufman, on the *Lando* facts, mandate the creation of an absolute editorial process privilege? Would the media defendant ultimately have been permitted to decide for himself the extent to which the discovery sought by the plaintiff impermissibly trespasses on editorial freedom?

The answers to these questions are not clear. On the one hand, Judge Kaufman said: "We cannot permit inquiry into Lando's thoughts, opinions, and conclusions to consume the very values which the *New York Times* landmark decision sought to safeguard."[43] He then stated that if a legislature were to insist on inquiring into the thought processes of a journalist "such an intrusion would not be condoned."[44] But the remand he issued gave more discretion to the trial court than these comments suggest. The trial court was not instructed to preclude discovery with respect to the matters sought by Herbert, but merely to evaluate "the interrogatories in the light of the principles articulated in this opinion."[45]

Judge Kaufman said the principles of the *New York Times* doctrine require the extension of protection to a journalist's pre-publication editorial decision-making. Yet, the *New York Times* Court advisedly refused to create an absolute privilege in libel litigation when the plaintiff was a public plaintiff.[46] The *New York Times* actual malice test attempts to give weight to the competing values of untrammeled publication and reputational integrity. The rejection of editorial freedom as the ultimate constitutional value in libel actions against the media was specifically discussed by Mr. Justice Powell in his opinion for the Court in *Gertz v. Robert Welch, Inc.*:

> The need to avoid self-censorship by the news media is, however, not the only societal value at issue. If it were, this Court would have embraced long ago the view that publishers and broadcasters enjoy an unconditional and indefeasible immunity from liability for defamation ... Such a rule would, indeed, obviate the fear that the prospect of civil liability for injurious falsehood might dissuade a timorous press from the effective exercise of First Amendment freedoms. Yet absolute protection for the communications media requires a total sacrifice of the competing value served by the law of defamation.[47]

The Second Circuit decision in *Lando* received, appropriately, a considerable degree of attention. Illustrative of this attention is a provocative article in which Professor Randall Bezanson of the University of Iowa Law School seeks to make the results of the *New York Times* case and the *Tornillo* case cohere.[48] Professor Bezanson wrote before the Supreme Court announced its decision in *Lando*, but his comments on that case are particularly relevant because the Supreme Court basically shared his distaste for the extension of a concept of editorial privilege to *New York Times*-type libel cases.

Professor Bezanson stated that "editorial freedom does not demand editorial non-accountability."[49] He rightly rejected the idea that there should be "editorial freedom from law."[50] It is implicit from his position that he fears that an absolute editorial privilege for the rights of media defamers in practice may result in an absolute trespass on the reputational rights of individuals. As a result, he justly protests a theory of the First Amendment which, as applied to libel cases, would leave the media "free of liability for the calculated or reckless misuse of its freedom."[51] On the other hand, as against individual rights for access to the press, he is quite willing to allow editorial freedom to be "a central principle."[52] He is fearful that "drafting the press into the service of the marketplace of ideas would erode and ultimately destroy its capacity to serve as a check on the system of government in which we participate."[53] He believes that government intervention in the form of judicial recognition of the right of access is dangerous because the "marketplace is too vulnerable to control by government or those with economic or political power who might subvert it or, more likely, suffocate it in the interest of bland balance."[54]

What I find paradoxical in this point of view is that the contemporary function of the law of libel as a tool for accountability of the media is willingly accepted, despite the apparent injury such accountability does to complete editorial freedom. Yet governmental intervention with respect to increasing the flow of ideas is rejected as impermissible. Large libel judgments rendered by courts (which, after all, are instrumentalities of the state) in some cases may pose far more of a threat to editorial freedom than the provision of modest remedies of access and reply.

In his dissent from the Second Circuit majority in *Lando*, Judge Meskill wisely cautioned against giving the precepts of editorial autonomy or editorial privilege a status of First Amendment inviolability.[55] In Judge Meskill's view, the long history in the common-law world of the libel law (a history that has flourished in the United States both before and after the adoption of the First Amendment) should in itself be enough to silence any extravagant claims for editorial freedom or editorial privilege as an absolute constitutional dogma to which all competing constitutional values must necessarily be subordinated. Judge Meskill explained the matter as follows: "The mere existence of a libel cause of action chills the exercise of editorial judgment. That is the whole idea. It is exactly this kind of chill that *New York Times* v. *Sullivan* condones."[56]

In my view, *Miami Herald Publishing Co.* v. *Tornillo* and *New York Times* v. *Sullivan* are profoundly inconsistent.[57] I do not agree with the result reached by Judge Kaufman[58] and Judge Oakes[59] in *Herbert* v. *Lando*. Yet in a sense they chose the more recent of two competing judicial principles. In so doing, the Second Circuit fairly applied conventional legal and judicial techniques. The difficulty with the *Tornillo* doctrine and its implicit suggestion of absolute editorial privilege and freedom is that in fact it has no stopping place. Technically the *Tornillo* decision can be seen as the invalidation of an order to tell a newspaper what to say, that is, to require it to publish a reply to an editorial attack which it does not wish to print. In this sense, the result in *Tornillo* falls in line with the heavy presumption that is supposed to accompany any direct restraint on publication.[60] On the other hand, the law of libel falls more on the subsequent punishment side of the line. Theoretically, the alleged defamer has said what he wanted to say and now may be required to pay damages for it. Yet, as a practical matter, the intended message has gotten out.[61]

How consequential are these distinctions? An order requiring that something be printed is quite different from an order not to print something.[62] An order not to print something, a "gag order," for example, falls in the classic tradition of unwelcome prior restraint which is justifiably suspect. An order that does not prevent the speaker from saying anything at all, but merely requires him to let another speak hardly falls into the category of cases involving judicial orders silencing the speaker. In a sense, the current debate about the *Lando* case betrays the present state of confusion in First Amendment theory. This confusion, in my view, is revealed even on the face of the decision of the majority of the Supreme Court in *Tornillo* in which the first third of the opinion objectively states the arguments for access, and the balance of the opinion proceeds to ignore them. In short, the Court, like the rest of us, is concerned about trends of monopoly and concentration of ownership and centralization of editorial decision-making in ever fewer hands.[63] And the Court, like the rest of us, is perplexed about how to resolve the problems produced by these phenomena.

Although I have said that *Miami Herald Publishing Co. v. Tornillo* and *New York Times v. Sullivan* are in principle in conflict, in a sense there is one common ground in their fact patterns. In each case, a private plaintiff is suing a private media defendant. First Amendment interests are far more difficult to reconcile in the context of private battles about ideas than in cases involving conflicts between the state and an individual in which the state attempts to silence a particular point of view. The whole tradition of our First Amendment law makes the latter category of cases far easier to resolve than cases in which First Amendment rights collide in the context of battles by one private actor against another.

The recent effort to attribute a distinct meaning to the press clause[64] of the First Amendment is, at bottom, an effort to avoid an egalitarian approach for access to ideas when the censor is a private entity rather than the state. Mr. Justice Stewart's view of the special meaning of the press clause, set forth in his now celebrated lecture at Yale Law School,[65] is entirely consistent with the absolute editorial privilege interpretation of *Tornillo*. The idea that the press clause confers unique protection on the press in a way that the free speech clause does not protect the rest of us is an effort to enlist the constitutional text, and, it is hoped, history, in the cause of subordinating individual claims for expression to media-enforced efforts toward silence.[66]

The dilemma of the *Tornillo* case is that it presents a problem for First Amendment interpretation that involves not a state desire to censor, but a media desire to censor. In the past, we have relied on the First Amendment to assure much-needed protection for the press against government-designed efforts to silence it. It is an unaccustomed and unwelcome task for First Amendment interpretation to have to deal with media silence policies. Indeed, if we look at the *New York Times* case backwards through the lens of *Nebraska Press Association v. Stuart*,[67] it may be argued that the refusal of the *Miami Herald* to publish Pat Tornillo's reply to the *Herald*'s editorial attack on him was in effect a media gag order directed against an individual. What is the proper First Amendment equation to solve such problems? I submit we have not yet found it.

In short, I fully share Professor Bezanson's view that the absolute editorial privilege doctrine of the Second Circuit in *Lando* contained a potential for placing the media beyond the law, certainly beyond the reach of the law of libel.[68] On the other hand, I cannot agree that the Second Circuit's result in *Lando* is wrong,[69] but that the Supreme Court's result in *Tornillo* is right.[70] In my view, the result reached by Judge Kaufman in *Lando* is the necessary consequence of the doctrine of the *Tornillo* case.

In *Herbert v. Lando*,[71] the Supreme Court, per Mr. Justice White, determined that no editorial privilege should be created that would prevent discovery of matters that might show actual malice on the part of a media libel defendant in an action brought by a public plaintiff.[72] Basically, the Court did not believe that the accommodation reached in *New York Times v. Sullivan* between the interest in reputation of public figures, and the interest, to use the *New York Times* phrase, of the "citizen critic of government"[73] in uninhibited discussion of public persons and public events should be revised.[74]

Just as Mr. Justice White had done in *Branzburg* for a plurality of the Court, so in *Lando* he asserted for a majority of the Court that the creation of new evidentiary privileges in litigation are disfavored; that "even evidentiary privileges rooted in the Constitution must give way in proper circumstances."[75] In addition, the Court was troubled by the imprecision of an editorial privilege. Justice White declared that neither the court below nor counsel for Lando had adequately been able to explain "when the editorial process begins and when it ends."[76] It should be remembered that in *Branzburg*, Mr. Justice White had been similarly troubled by another kind of imprecision: the question of who, in fact, could be identified as a journalist.

Insofar as the argument that editorial privilege would have an "intolerable chilling effect"[77] on the editorial function, Mr. Justice White responded that *some* inhibition of press publication was directly contemplated by the *New York Times v. Sullivan* rule:

> But if the claimed inhibition flows from the fear of damages liability for publishing knowing or reckless falsehoods, those effects are precisely what *New York Times* and other cases have held to be consistent with the First Amendment. Spreading false information in and of itself carries no First Amendment credentials.[78]

In a sense, what Mr. Justice White is saying in *Lando* is that the cry of the press for the creation of a doctrine of editorial privilege in libel litigation proves too much. Even if Lando had won the case, the creation of a constitutionally-based editorial privilege would still not have been able to quiet the basic unease of the press in the area of libel law: "Only complete immunity from liability for defamation would effect this result, and the court has regularly found this to be an untenable construction of the First Amendment."[79]

The decision in *Herbert v. Lando* suggests that the Court perceived the whole effort to tack an editorial process privilege onto the workings of the actual malice rule as an attack on the accommodation between libel law and freedom of the press that had been struck in *New York Times*. In short, the *Lando* litigation was conceived of as basically an implicit media request for an overhaul of the doctrine of *New York Times*. Although the *New York Times* doctrine has given the press a measure of freedom from libel, the movement for recognition of a new editorial process privilege reflects a journalistic disenchantment with the *New York Times* doctrine, a disenchantment that the majority of the Court refuses to encourage. Oddly enough, the Court may also be unhappy with the *New York Times* rule but for different reasons. Indeed, if there is any disenchantment with the *New York Times* doctrine on the part of the Supreme Court as manifested in Mr. Justice White's opinion in *Lando*, it is that the *New York Times* rule strikes the balance too much against the individual interest in reputation and too much in favor of press dissemination of what may turn out to be false information.[80] Indeed, one may wonder to what extent there is some nostalgia in the long discussion in Mr. Justice White's opinion about the definition of malice in the law of libel in its pre- *New York Times* v. *Sullivan* form.[81] State-of-mind evidence, he insists, preceded the *New York Times* rule and indeed in his view has survived it.[82] Establishing the legitimacy of state-of-mind evidence in libel litigation appears to be an essential purpose of the Court's decision in *Lando*.

On balance, what are some of the significant conclusions that can be drawn from the decision of the court in *Lando*? The first is that the Supreme Court will continue to employ the actual malice test created by *New York Times* v. *Sullivan* in cases in which public plaintiffs sue media defendants for libel. Perhaps this should be regarded as something of a media victory because there is no suggestion in *Lando* that the very significant protection accorded the press by the actual malice test vis-à-vis public plaintiffs under the rules set forth by the Court in *New York Times* and *Gertz*[83] should be reassessed in favor of the libel plaintiff.

The second conclusion that can be drawn from the *Lando* case is that inquiry into state-of-mind evidence may be undertaken pursuant to the actual malice test in the public law of libel and that such inquiry was always assumed to be permissible. To be sure, considerable commentary in the press in the aftermath of the *Lando* case has suggested that now, for the first time, courts may inquire into the state of mind of journalists.[84]

The Court in the *Lando* decision was at pains to show that the actual malice test as administered by the Court in *New York Times* and its progeny always assumed an inquiry into matters of editorial judgment. Thus, according to Justice White in *Lando*, the separate opinion of Chief Justice Warren in *Curtis Publishing Co.* v. *Butts*,[85] which applied the *New York Times* standard to public figures,[86] relied on

> conversations among the editors and author concerning the research and development of the article ... decisions and reasons

relating to who should be interviewed and what should be investigated ... conclusions as to the importance and veracity of sources and information presented in the article ... and conclusions about the impact that publishing the article would have on the subject ...[87]

To be sure, a majority of the *Butts* court did not explicitly rely on evidence of editorial judgment. Nevertheless, Mr. Justice White's analysis of *Butts* appears to be a reasonable assessment of the Court's analysis of the record in that case: "It is quite unlikely that the [*Butts*] Court would have arrived at the result it did had it believed that inquiry into the editorial processes was constitutionally forbidden."[88]

Mr. Justice Stewart, in his dissent in *Lando*, contended otherwise and asserted that "inquiry into the broad "editorial process" is simply not relevant in a libel suit brought by a public figure against a publisher."[89] It is possible, of course, to argue that the *New York Times* rule should be so approached. The Stewart analysis in *Lando* of the *New York Times* rule, however, is a better description of what the law would have been if the Court had affirmed the Second Circuit's decision in *Lando*. As a statement of the post-*New York Times* v. *Sullivan* law, Mr. Justice White's *Lando* analysis, relying at least by way of analogy on *Butts*, is more persuasive. How else can one explain the language in *St. Amant* v. *Thompson*,[90] which characterizes the proof that would establish reckless disregard for truth as evidence that discloses that the defendant "in fact entertained serious doubts as to the truth of his publication"?[91]

Moreover, as Mr. Justice White pointed out in *Lando*, the Court in *Gertz*, in defining the actual malice standard, had spoken of the defendant's "subjective awareness of probable falsity."[92] How, one may ask, can one show serious doubts about the truth or subjective awareness of probable falsity without showing the state of mind of the libel defendant? *St. Amant*, *Butts*, and *Gertz* all appear to suggest that the availability of state-of-mind evidence on discovery by a libel plaintiff operating under the requirements of the *New York Times*-*Gertz* rules has been of long standing. In addition, media lawyers must be very uncomfortable with the argument of their journalist clients that inquiry into the state of mind was never part of the essential workings of the *New York Times* v. *Sullivan* actual malice test. An overview of post-*New York Times* v. *Sullivan* libel litigation indicates that counsel for media defendants have made extensive discovery of state of mind in order to show there was no actual malice, that is, reckless disregard.[93] Of course, it is one thing if counsel for the media defendant wishes to make available state-of-mind evidence. Arguably, what the First Amendment forbids is that the state, including its courts, should require such inquiry. On the other hand, one must wonder whether thoughtful media lawyers are really altogether saddened by the results of the *Lando* case. If Justice Stewart's view that only objective evidence is available in *New York Times* v. *Sullivan*-type cases had prevailed, then the opportunity of media counsel to show by subjective evidence that in fact there was no actual malice or no intent to publish in reckless disregard of the truth or falsity of what was said might well have been precluded. In short, it seems apparent that the workings of the *New York Times* actual malice test always assumed the availability of inquiry into state of mind on the part of the media defendant. If that is true, then all that the *Lando* decision had done is to clarify the law on this point. The decision keeps open, by pre-trial discovery, a line of inquiry that may aid the media defendant as well as injure him.

The third conclusion to draw from the *Lando* decision is an apparent distaste on the part of the Court for the creation of new judicially created First Amendment-based privileges in matters affecting media liability. The question for the future is whether *Lando* suggests that when the Supreme Court actually passes on specific lower court holdings recognizing qualified First Amendment-based journalist privilege in civil litigation, the Court will reverse the lower court rulings that have moved in this direction and declare that there is no justification for the creation of a First Amendment-based qualified journalist's privilege.[94] Judge Kaufman of the Second Circuit has been as receptive to the creation of First Amendment-based privileges in the area of media liability as the majority of the Supreme Court has been unreceptive. Thus, in *Edwards v. National Audubon Society, Inc.*[95] the United States Court of Appeals for the Second Circuit, per Judge Kaufman, recognized a doctrine of neutral reportage, which permits a journalist to claim the benefit of the *New York Times* doctrine when he disseminates an accurate account of an informant's charges even though the journalist has serious doubts about the truth of the information.[96] Assuming that the neutral reportage doctrine is itself a revision of the original accommodation between individual reputation and free discussion struck in *New York Times v. Sullivan*, it would appear that the *Lando* decision will gravely undermine the future of the neutral reportage doctrine and of other newly developed First Amendment-based privileges.[97]

The fourth conclusion to be drawn from *Herbert v. Lando* is that the editorial function, even though it is entitled to First Amendment protection, is not to be approached as an absolute value to which all other values must be subordinated. The cases giving subordinating protection to the editorial function against competing free speech values - *Miami Herald Publishing Co. v. Tornillo*[98] and *Columbia Broadcasting System, Inc. v. Democratic National Committee*[99] - were given a far narrower scope by the Supreme Court than they had received in the opinion of Judge Kaufman and Judge Oakes below. Speaking for the Court in *Lando*, Mr. Justice White was sharply impatient with the attempt to inflate the protection afforded the editorial function in the context of a right of access to encompass the domain of libel: "Holdings that neither a State nor the Federal Government may dictate what must or must not be printed neither expressly nor impliedly suggest that the editorial process is immune from any inquiry whatsoever."[100] He rejected the entire effort to transplant an editorial privilege concept in the new terrain of the public law of libel: "It is incredible to believe that the Court in *Columbia Broadcasting System* or in *Tornillo* silently effected a substantial contraction of the rights preserved to defamation plaintiffs in *New York Times, Butts,* and like cases."[101] He emphasized that *Tornillo* and *Gertz*" were announced on the same day."[102] In short, he suggests that the freedom from legal accountability that journalists had won in *Tornillo,* that is, an immunity from the duty to provide those attacked in print with a right of reply, was to be balanced out by a new reliance on the law of libel to provide some measure of accountability for individuals injured by press attacks. Indeed, in *Gertz,* Mr. Justice White spoke out in dissent against alterations in state libel law that were suddenly deemed constitutionally ordained by the Court in *Gertz*: "I fail to see how the quality or quantity of public debate will be promoted by further emasculation of state libel laws for the benefit of the news media. If anything, this trend may provoke a new and radical imbalance on the communications process."[103]

Reflecting on these observations of Mr. Justice White in his dissent in *Gertz* and in his opinion for the Court in *Lando,* one may conclude that he believes, as perhaps a majority of his colleagues do also, that equality in legal contests between individuals and the large media corporations in the communication process can be attained by continued adherence to the accommodation between the individual interest in reputation and the press interest in free discussion reached in *New York Times.*

There is a fifth conclusion that can be drawn from the *Lando* decision. One of the issues left unsettled by the *Gertz* case was whether the focus of the *New York Times* rule was to be limited to media defendants. If the *New York Times* doctrine, as reinterpreted by *Gertz,* was to be applied only to media defendants, and if the editorial privilege doctrine was tacked on to the actual malice standard of liability, then the *New York Times* rule would really have been transformed.[104] In a public law of libel case, the media defendant would have been in a far better position than the nonmedia defendant because the media defendant alone would be able to assert some resistance to pre-trial discovery on the basis of an editorial process privilege.

At least implicitly, the result in *Lando* suggests that the status of a media defendant, even in a public law of libel case, does not call for any change in the workings of the *New York Times* standard of liability. To this extent, the Court in *Lando* rejects Mr. Justice Stewart's view that the press clause grants specific and unique protection to the press. By rejecting an editorial process privilege, *Lando* treats all libel defendants, whether media or non-media, as the same. In so doing, it restores the *New*

York Times v. Sullivan rule to its true beginnings. For it should be remembered that the emphasis in New York Times on stimulating free and vigorous debate was not directed to the press alone, or even to the press specifically, but to "citizen critics of government" which, happily, include the press and the rest of us as well.

Mr. Justice Brennan's dissent in part in Lando provides a fascinating retrospect on the doctrine of New York Times by the justice who wrote that enormously influential decision. Two essential themes run through the Brennan dissent. The first reflects an appropriate anxiety about the recurrent but unresolved issue of who is the ultimate addressee of First Amendment protection. The second theme reflects an unmistakable loyalty to the basic premises of the New York Times doctrine. Mr. Justice Brennan tried to reconcile the new emphasis on a special meaning for the press clause and the related claim for special First Amendment protection for the institutional press with older and more populist perspectives provided by such First Amendment decisions as Red Lion Broadcasting Co. v. FCC[105] with its emphasis on a public right of access to socio-political and other ideas. He recalled that affording a privilege to "the citizen critic of government"[106] had been a focal point of the decision in New York Times. On the other hand, he recognized that, in Gertz, the Court had spoken specifically of "press and broadcast media."[107] Similarly, though the Court in First National Bank v. Bellotti,[108] the corporate speech case, refused to accord media corporations a preferred First Amendment status, he mentioned, with apparent approval, the carrot that was thrown to the press clause theory in the Court's opinion in the Bellotti case: "The press cases emphasize the special and constitutionally recognized role of that institution in informing and educating the public, offering criticism, and providing a forum for discussion and debate."[109]

Mr. Justice Brennan shied away, however, from ruling that the evolution of the New York Times privilege from a qualified privilege designed to protect the critics of government should now be reinterpreted as a privilege directed to the media alone. Although he thought that the editorial process should have some protection, he was insistent that editorial privilege should be recognized not for the press *qua* press, but on a theory that the press was agent or surrogate for the public.

Unlike Mr. Justice Stewart, Mr. Justice Brennan was unwilling to assert that an agency theory required an absolute editorial privilege. He contended that the rules set forth in New York Times v. Sullivan were "generous standards."[110] Only a modest revision of the New York Times doctrine was appropriate or necessary in his view: "The First Amendment requires predecisional communication among editors to be protected by an editorial privilege, but ... this privilege must yield if a public-figure plaintiff is able to demonstrate to the prima facie satisfaction of a trial judge that the libel in question constitutes defamatory falsehood."[111]

Mr. Justice Brennan said that the Second Circuit decision had divided the editorial process into two components.[112] The first component, as both Judge Oakes, in his concurring opinion, and Judge Kaufman, for the majority, recognized, consisted of the thought process of individual editors.[113] The second part of the editorial process included what Judge Kaufman called "free interchange of ideas within the newsroom"[114] and what Judge Oakes called "the relationship among editors."[115]

Mr. Justice Brennan rejected the conclusion of the court of appeals that permitting discovery into the thought processes of journalists, the first component of the editorial process, would fatally chill the editorial process. Discovery, in his view, could not chill a journalist's thought processes: "Since a journalist cannot work without such internal thought processes, the only way this aspect of the editorial process can be chilled is by a journalist ceasing to work altogether."[116] With respect, however, to the second aspect of the editorial process, the pre-publication editorial conference, he thought that inquiry into this kind of information "might well dampen full and candid discussion among editors of proposed publications."[117]

From a press point of view, Mr. Justice Brennan's opinion may be particularly unsatisfactory because, in his view, pure state-of-mind evidence should not be privileged at all. He would recognize a privilege, in some circumstances, only for editorial discussion of a publication, a category of information that is, in a sense, "objective evidence." Even this privilege, however, could be pierced. If the public figure plaintiff can make a prima facie case to show that the alleged libel did in fact constitute a "defamatory falsehood," the privilege falls.[118] In such circumstances, pre-trial discovery about what was said at the pre-publication editorial conference would be permissible.[119]

Mr. Justice Brennan's willingness to erect a modest editorial privilege on the edifice of the *New York Times* doctrine, however, is hardly enthusiastic or wholehearted:

> I fully concede that my reasoning is essentially paradoxical. For the sake of more accurate information, an editorial privilege would shield from disclosure the possible inaccuracies of the press; in the name of a more responsible press, the privilege would make more difficult of application the legal restraints by which the press is bound.[120]

These comments reflect some unhappiness that recognition of even a qualified editorial privilege reduces the present legal constraints under which the press operates. This expression of concern is not surprising, because Mr. Justice Brennan's dissent in part in *Lando* manifests a basic allegiance to the purposes behind *New York Times* v. *Sullivan*. One of those purposes was to provide "a substantive standard defining that speech unprotected by the First Amendment."[121] Therefore, the editorial process of the media defendants in *Lando* could not be shielded merely so as to block judicial determination of whether media defendants have in fact engaged in unprotected speech.[122]

The tension between reliance on the press clause for creation of an editorial privilege specifically benefiting the press and the old individualistic focus in the *New York Times* v. *Sullivan* case itself on the "citizen critic of government" is left unresolved by Mr. Justice Brennan. Indeed, his dissent in part in *Lando* shows he has a foot in both worlds - one foot in the old access-oriented, populist, and individualistic perspective of the *New York Times* case, and another in the media-oriented post-Watergate movement for recognition of a special status for the press. The press, he says, is not entitled to an absolute editorial privilege, but it may be entitled to a qualified privilege to protect part of the editorial process. The pre-publication conference should be protected, at least until the point the plaintiff can show, without reliance on pre-publication editorial discussion, that a defamatory falsehood in fact occurred.[123]

If the first theme of the Brennan opinion is absorbed with the unresolved conflict between a populist and a media-oriented interpretation of the First Amendment, the second theme is concerned with loyalty to the essential accommodation between individual reputation and uninhibited discussion struck in *New York Times*. At the same time as Mr. Justice Brennan seeks to preserve the essence of the precepts of the *New York Times* doctrine, he strives mightily to provide a justification for a slight alteration of the original formulation of the *New York Times* rule by recognizing, at least partially, a qualified editorial privilege. It is intriguing, however, that he does not consider the recognition inconsistent with the use of discovery to probe for state-of-mind evidence into the "thought processes" of journalists. Indeed, he insists that state-of-mind evidence was within the original contemplation of the *New York Times* v. *Sullivan* actual malice test.[124] His fidelity to the basic precepts of *New York Times* is such that he agrees with Mr. Justice White that the actual malice test always contemplated the ability to inquire into state-of-mind evidence:

> Subsequent decisions have made clear that actual malice turns on a journalist's 'subjective awareness of probable falsity.' *Gertz* v. *Robert Welch, Inc.* . . . It would be anomalous to turn substantive liability on a journalist's subjective attitude and at the same time to shield from disclosure the most direct evidence of that attitude.[125]

Even the modified qualified editorial privilege that Mr. Justice Brennan would recognize offers the media defendants in *Lando* very little protection from the matters that media counsel sought to shield from discovery in *Lando.* Mr. Justice Brennan described the matters which Lando refused to make discovery about as follows:

> The Court [of Appeals] grouped the discovery inquiries objected to by respondents into five categories:
> 1. Lando's conclusions during his research and investigations regarding people or leads to be pursued, or not to be pursued, in connection with the "60 Minutes" segment and the *Atlantic Monthly* article;
> 2. Lando's conclusion about facts imparted by interviewees and his state of mind with respect to the veracity of persons interviewed;
> 3. The basis for conclusions where Lando testified that he did reach a conclusion concerning the veracity of persons, information or events;
> 4. Conversations between Lando and Wallace about matter to be included or excluded from the broadcast publication; and
> 5. Lando's intentions as manifested by his decision to include or exclude certain material.[126]

Of these five categories, Mr. Justice Brennan says four cannot be covered by an editorial privilege because they involve mental processes.[127] He believes that only the fourth category - conversations between Lando and Wallace about matters to be included or excluded from broadcast publication - can be protected "by a proper editorial privilege."[128]

His opinion reflects the error in portraying the result in *Lando* as merely a manifestation of the Burger Court's alleged hostility in the media. Mr. Justice Brennan, bulwark of the Warren Court, was the author of the *New York Times* decision but his dissent, which is a dissent only in part, manifests a basic unwillingness not only to change the essential workings of *New York Times* v. *Sullivan,* but also to accept the argument of the media defendant in *Lando* that the First Amendment affords the media some kind of absolute categorical protection for matters impinging on the editorial process.

Mr. Justice Marshall's dissent in *Lando* reflects a unique viewpoint on the present Court. He is the only justice who is frankly willing to confront the possibility of conflict between the new editorial autonomy cases - *Tornillo* and *CBS* - and the doctrine of *New York Times* v. *Sullivan.* For him, faithfulness to the constitutional considerations that underlay the *New York Times* decision are more important than technical adherence to the "actual malice" test. In short, he is prepared to recognize some procedural shortcomings with the *New York Times* rule:

> Yet this [*New York Times* v. *Sullivan*] standard of liability cannot of

itself accomplish the ends for which it was conceived. Insulating the press from ultimate liability is unlikely to avert selfcensorship so long as any plaintiff with a deep pocket and a facially sufficient complaint is afforded unconstrained discovery of the editorial process. If the substantive balance of interest struck in *Sullivan* is to remain viable, it must be reassessed in light of the procedural realities under which libel actions are conducted.[129]

Mr. Justice Marshall argued that the First Amendment concerns that prompted the *New York Times* Court to limit the occasions for liability for libel should now also cause the Court to limit discovery.[130] A fundamental question is immediately provoked by the very breadth of this suggestion: does Mr. Justice Marshall wish to qualify the scope of discovery in all libel cases? In all libel cases in which there was a media defendant? Or only in libel cases in which there is a media defendant and the public status of the plaintiff has occasioned the invocation of the *New York Times* rules? Presumably, it is the last category - *New York Times* v. *Sullivan*-type libel cases alone - in which he would create an editorial process privilege for use in pre-trial discovery. His opinion is hardly clear on this point.[131]

Because Mr. Justice Marshall, unlike the majority of the Court, saw a need to reassess the *New York Times* doctrine, it is hardly surprising to find that, in his view, the *Tornillo* case and the *CBS* case greatly affected an appropriate resolution of the issues presented in *Lando*:

> I do not mean to suggest, as did the District Court here, that *Tornillo* and *Columbia Broadcasting* have 'nothing to do' with this case ... To the contrary, the values of editorial autonomy given recognition in those decisions should inform district courts as they monitor the discovery phase of defamation cases.[132]

What is surprising about his *Lando* dissent is that his willingness to recognize a privilege for the editorial process in pre-trial discovery in *New York Times* v. *Sullivan*-type libel cases is far more limited than the contours of the privilege delineated by Judges Kaufman and Oakes in the Second Circuit decision in *Lando*.

Like Mr. Justice Brennan, Mr. Justice Marshall concluded that state-of-mind evidence should not be privileged in the name of editorial autonomy:

> So long as *Sullivan* makes state of mind dispositive, some inquiry as to the manner in which editorial decisions are made is inevitable. And it is simply implausible to suppose that asking a reporter why certain material was or was not included in the given publication will be more likely to stifle incisive journalism than compelling disclosure of other objective evidence regarding that decision.[133]

Mr. Justice Marshall believed, however, that the creation of editorial privilege for the "pre-publication dialogue" was appropriate.[134] Here he parted company with Brennan, who believed that according a privilege for pre-publication dialogue only to plaintiffs who were able to make a prima facie showing of falsity would provide insufficient protection to safeguard a "climate of free interchange among journalists."[135] As a result, Mr. Justice Marshall concluded that discovery should be foreclosed in defamation cases "as to the substance of editorial conversation."[136] Such a conclusion constitutes a significant amendment to the present workings of the *New York Times* doctrine. His position, however, is much less of a revision of *New York Times* v. *Sullivan* than the media had argued for in *Lando* or the Second Circuit had afforded.

Mr. Justice Marshall was quite conscious that his willingness to extend an absolute privilege against pre-publication dialogue in defamation cases[137] constituted a revision of the *New York Times* doctrine,[138] but he asserted that protections of First Amendment interests have been extended beyond *New York Times* before, citing cases in which the Supreme Court has denied review to lower federal court cases that gave a qualified First Amendment privilege some degree of recognition in libel cases.[139] On the other hand, in an apparent effort to square the result he would like to reach in *Lando* with the Supreme Court's holding in the *Branzburg*[140] case, he conceded that "different considerations would, of course, obtain if a privilege for editorial communications were sought in conjunction with criminal proceedings."[141]

Mr. Justice Marshall's dissent presents a complete contrast with Mr. Justice White's majority opinion in *Lando*, which holds, relying on the *Branzburg* precept, that the First Amendment should not be regarded as receptive terrain for the sowing of evidentiary privileges. Mr. Justice Marshall, of course, contended that the lower courts have in fact been recognizing a qualified First Amendment-based journalist privilege in libel cases.[142] Of significance for the future is that he specifically called the Court's attention to these developments. The majority of the Court nonetheless chose to agree with Mr. Justice White: "Evidentiary privileges in litigation are not favored, and even those rooted in the Constitution must give way in proper circumstances."[143] In short, a question that the Marshall dissent raises is whether the future of First Amendment-based privileges which the lower courts have recognized in libel contexts in areas not involving the fact pattern of *Lando* is secure.

In a well-known Idaho case, *Caldero* v. *Tribune Publishing Co.*,[144] the Idaho Supreme Court refused to recognize the claim of a First Amendment-based journalist privilege in a libel case, and the Supreme Court denied review.[145] Mr. Justice Frankfurter's memorable lecture to the bar on the point that denial of *certiorari* has no substantive significance still reflects the last word on that subject.[146] Nevertheless, Mr. Justice Marshall's dissent in *Lando*, coupled with the majority's manifest distaste for proliferation of First Amendment-based evidentiary privileges will certainly fuel speculation that if *certiorari* had been granted in *Caldero*, the Court would have affirmed the state court decision rejecting a First Amendment-based privilege.

A word is in order about Mr. Justice Powell's concurrence.[147] He stated that the "explicit constitutional protection of First Amendment rights in a case of this kind, as articulated by *New York Times* v. *Sullivan* . . . should not be expanded to create an evidentiary privilege."[148] Powell uses the *Lando* fact pattern to treat the issues presented as basically a problem in the workings of pre-trial discovery in federal civil practice. The extent to which "a discovery demand arguably impinges on First Amendment rights"[149] is simply one more matter that should be factored into a district court's decision when an objection is made to a request for discovery by a party. Exactly how these First Amendment considerations should be factored in is a matter which Mr. Justice Powell says - perhaps to the exasperation of federal court judges - is "hardly an exact science."[150]

As one surveys all the opinions in the *Lando* case, it is clear that Mr. Justice White, Chief Justice Burger, and Justices Blackmun, Rehnquist, and Stevens are steadfast in their view that *New York Times* v. *Sullivan* and its actual malice test should not be amended or revised to create a doctrine of editorial privilege with respect to pre-trial discovery in *New York Times*-type libel cases. It is clear that Mr. Justice Powell is also of that opinion. Furthermore, despite his dissent in part, Mr. Justice Brennan, like the majority of his brethren, is also basically unwilling to make more than a slight amendment to the *New York Times* actual malice test. Only Mr. Justice Marshall, as we have seen, is frankly willing to take on the challenge of overhauling the *New York Times* doctrine. Even he would provide less of an overhaul than perhaps many of those who have been entranced by the new theory of the special meaning of the press clause and a special status for editorial privilege would like. Even Justice Marshall, as we have seen, would not provide an editorial privilege for state-of-mind evidence.

What of Mr. Justice Stewart? What is the reaction of the author of the special meaning press clause theory[151] to the problems of the *Lando* case? In my view, his position is curious, for he contends that under "the constitutional rule of *New York Times* v. *Sullivan* . . . inquiry into the broad "editorial process" is simply not relevant in a libel suit brought by a public figure against a publisher."[152] In his view, *New York Times* v. *Sullivan* simply never assumed the availability of inquiry into state-of-mind evidence in pre-trial discovery. Phrases such as "intent" and "improper motive"[153] should have no role in the life of the *New York Times* doctrine. If they have had a role, it is simply an unfortunate consequence of the fact that the Court took a phrase which had an established meaning in the private law of libel - actual malice - and gave it a new meaning in the *New York Times* variety of libel cases. This, Mr. Justice Stewart says, has caused "judges and lawyers" to be "led astray by the phrase "actual malice" in the *New York Times* opinion."[154]

Mr. Justice Stewart's dissent is terse, but one sentence in his opinion summarizes his position: "What was *not* published has nothing to do with the case."[155] Although his dissent is not clear on the point, I gather from his remarks that he is suggesting that in the *Lando*-type fact pattern neither pre-publication dialogue nor state-of-mind evidence should be available on discovery. Both lines of inquiry are designed to probe what was not published rather than what was. An interesting consequence of Mr. Justice Stewart's analysis is that his reasoning lines him up with seven other justices for the position that the *New York Times* case needs no revision, though to be sure his view of the *New York Times* case is quite different from that of his brethren. Thus, if I am right in my assessment that the *Lando* case was basically a much-heralded effort to prompt the Supreme Court into changing the workings of the actual malice test of *New York Times* v. *Sullivan* to give even greater protection in libel cases to the media defendants than the *New York Times-Gertz* rules already provide, I think we can conclude that the request was massively repudiated in *Lando* because only Mr. Justice Marshall endorsed this position, and even he did not do so fully.

The Second Circuit decision in *Lando* may be seen as an example of pushing the principle of editorial privilege too far. As Mr. Justice Cardozo characterized another field of law, so we may characterize a recent post-Watergate First Amendment interpretation: "When I view the subject as a whole, I find logic to have been more remorseless here, more blind to final causes than it has been in other fields. Very likely it has been too remorseless."[156] Perhaps, with the Supreme Court decision in *Lando,* an era of "remorseless logic" in First Amendment interpretation is over.

Cardozo said that there were fields in the "domain of law where fundamental conceptions have been developed to their uttermost conclusions by the organon of logic."[157] The emergent post-*Tornillo* doctrines of editorial privilege and a special-status-for-the-press interpretation of the press clause of the First Amendment are consummate examples of this phenomenon. The Second Circuit decision in *Lando* proceeded out of an effort to apply the protection accorded the editorial process in *CBS* and *Tornillo* to libel cases governed by the *New York Times* doctrine. To the extent the two lines of cases were in conflict, Judges Kaufman and Oakes chose the later line of cases - *CBS* and *Tornillo*. On the other hand, to the extent that there was tension between *New York Times* v. *Sullivan* and the workings of its actual malice test and the *Tornillo* case and its doctrine of unfettered editorial autonomy, the Supreme Court limited the scope of *Tornillo* to be faithful to its original understanding of the *New York Times* case. The Supreme Court chose advisedly and particularly to curtail the transformation of the editorial autonomy doctrine of the *Tornillo* case into a general First Amendment doctrine of absolute editorial privilege.

It is important to remember, as Mr. Justice Brennan pointed out for the Court in a post-*New York Times* case, *Time, Inc. v. Hill*,[158] that the guarantees of the First Amendment "are not for the benefit of the press so much as for the benefit of all of us."[159] The First Amendment grants great protection to the press but it does not protect the press alone. In this regard, the First Amendment's lack of exclusivity is its strongest claim to our common allegiance. In reminding us of these precepts, the decision of the Supreme Court in *Herbert v. Lando* restores the individual "citizen critic" to a central place in First Amendment protection.

Notes

1. 73 F.R.D. 387 (S.D.N.Y.), rev'd, 568 F. 2d 974 (2d Cir. 1977), rev'd, 441 U.S. 153 (1979).
2. 568 F.2d at 980-2.
3. *Id.* at 981-2.
4. *Id.* at 982.
5. *Id.*
6. *Id.*
7. The extent of Lando's co-operation may be gauged by the 26 deposition sessions in which he participated. *Id.*
8. *Id.* at 982-3.
9. *Id.* at 983.
10. 73 F.R.D. at 396.
11. *Id.* at 395.
12. 376 U.S. 254 (1964).
13. 73 F.R.D. at 404.
14. See Restatement (Second) of Torts 580A, Comment d (1977).
15. 73 F.R.D. at 396.
16. 568 F.2d at 984.
17. *Id.*
18. 441 U.S. 153 (1979).
19. 418 U.S. 241 (1974).
20. *Id.* at 258.
21. *See* Barron, *Access to the Press: A New First Amendment Right*, 80 Harv. L. Rev. 1641, 1657 (1967): "It is paradoxical that although the libel laws have been emasculated for the benefit of defendant newspapers where the plaintiff is a 'public official,' the Court shows no corresponding concern as to whether debate will in fact be assured. The irony of *Times* and its progeny lies in the unexamined assumption that reducing

newspaper exposure to libel litigation will remove restraints on expression and lead to an 'informal society.' But in fact the decision creates a new imbalance in the communications process."
22. 568 F.2d at 978.
23. *Miami Herald Publishing Co. v. Tornillo*, 418 U.S. 241, 258 (1974).
24. See note 23 *supra* and accompanying text.
25. 418 U.S. 256.
26. 568 F.2d at 977.
27. 418 U.S. 241 (1974).
28. 412 U.S. 94 (1973).
29. 568 F.2d at 979.
30. *Id.* at 980.
31. *Id.*
32. See *id.* at 984.
33. 376 U.S. 254, 293-7 (1964) (Black, J., concurring).
34. *Id.* at 283.
35. 408 U.S. 665 (1972).
36. 568 F.2d at 977-8.
37. *Branzburg v. Hayes*, 408 U.S. 665, 689 n.25 (1972).
38. 568 F.2d at 977.
39. 408 U.S. at 710 (Powell, J., concurring).
40. See *Baker v. F & F Investment*, 470 F.2d 778, 783 (2d Cir. 1972), *cert. denied*, 411 U.S. 966 (1973). See also *Silkwood v. Kerr-McGee Corp.*, 563 F.2d 433, 437 (10th Cir. 1977); *Gilbert v. Allied Chem. Corp.*, 411 F. Supp. 505, 510-11 (E.D. Va. 1976); *Democratic Nat'l Comm. v. McCord*, 356 F. Supp. 1394, 1398 (D.D.C. 1973). Interestingly, lower courts have begun to recognize a qualified First Amendment journalist's privilege, using to some extent criteria set forth in Mr. Justice Stewart's *Branzburg* dissent, in criminal cases also. See *State v. St. Peter*, 132 Vt. 266, 315 A.2d 254, 256 (1974); *Brown v. Commonwealth*, 214 Va. 755, 757, 204 S.E.2d 429, 431, *cert. denied*, 419 U.S. 966 (1974). But cf. *New York Times Co. v. Jascalevich*, 439 U.S. 1304, 1305 (1978) (Marshall, J., in chambers) (Court refused to issue a stay of state court order which required journalists to produce certain documents in the course of a criminal trial).
41. See *Cervantes v. Time, Inc.*, 464 F.2d 986, 995 (8th Cir. 1972), *cert. denied*, 409 U.S. 1125 (1973). See also *Carey v. Hume*, 492 F.2d 631, 636 (D.C. Cir.), *cert. dismissed*, 417 U.S. 938 (1974) (although the journalist's claim of a qualified First Amendment privilege was not honored on the facts, it was recognized as a matter of doctrine). But cf. *Caldero v. Tribune Publishing Co.*, 98 Idaho 288, 294, 562 P.2d 791, 797, cert. denied, 434 U.S. 930 (1977) (court steadfastly refused in the context of a libel case to give any recognition whatever to the assertion of a First Amendment-based qualified journalist's privilege by a media defendant).
42. For Justice Stewart's elaboration of a special meaning for the press clause and his claim, based on the press clause, for a special First Amendment status for the press, see Stewart, *Or of the Press*, 26 Hastings L.J. 631 (1975) (reprint of the influential lecture on the subject that Justice Stewart delivered at Yale Law School).

43. 568 F.2d at 984.
44. Id.
45. Id.
46. See notes 33-4 *supra* and accompanying text.
47. Gertz v. Robert Welch, Inc., 418 U.S. 323, 341 (1974).
48. See Bezanson, Herbert v. Lando, Editorial Judgment, and Freedom of the Press: An Essay, 1978 U. Ill. L.R. 605.
49. Id. at 630.
50. Id.
51. Id. at 631.
52. Id. at 618.
53. Id. at 619-20.
54. Id. at 620.
55. 568 F.2d at 997-8 (Meskill, J., dissenting).
56. Id. at 997 (Meskill, J., dissenting).
57. I recognize that it is more often suggested that *Red Lion Broadcasting Co. v. FCC*, 395 U.S. 367 (1969) and *Miami Herald Publishing Co. v. Tornillo*, 418 U.S. 241 (1974) are inconsistent. See Van Alstyne, *The Mobius Strip of the First Amendment: Perspectives on Red Lion*, 29 S. Car. L. Rev. 539, 547-8 (1978). But cf. Geller, *Does Red Lion Square with Tornillo?*, 29 U. Miami L. Rev. 477 (1975) (argues that the two cases can be reconciled).

I confess that a decade ago I suggested that *New York Times* and *Red Lion* were inconsistent. But there I was concerned with the fact that the Court in *New York Times* extolled debate as a First Amendment value but took no effort to achieve it. See Barron, *Access: The Only Choice for the Media?*, 48 Tex. L. Rev. 766, 768-74 (1970).

The inconsistency I speak of here between *Tornillo* and *New York Times* concerns a different point. *New York Times* afforded libel defendants sued for libel by public plaintiffs only a qualified privilege against libel, that is, the actual malice test. *New York Times*, in other words, assumed some infringement on editorial autonomy if the libel defendant was a journalist. On the other hand, *Tornillo* predicates a media defendant's immunity from legally imposed right-of-reply legislation on a doctrine of editorial autonomy that on its face appears absolute in scope.

Some commentators have pointed out that editorial autonomy need not have been made absolute. Professor Benno Schmidt observed that *Tornillo* represented a clash between the competing First Amendment values of editorial autonomy and the need for diversity of expression. See B. Schmidt, Freedom of the Press v. Public Access 237 (1976). Schmidt has suggested that the resolution of such a conflict might have been undertaken in a manner that could have given recognition to each of these values. Under such an approach, depending on the facts and the relative strength of the competing values in relation to each other, sometimes the value of editorial autonomy would emerge as the dominant value and at other times the First Amendment value in encouraging diversity of expression would be given the subordinating preference. The mode of analysis which might have been employed had editorial autonomy not been given an absolute preference in *Tornillo* is described by Professor Schmidt as follows:

The aim of analysis would be to determine which 'publishers' should be protected from access so that the values of autonomy can be best preserved. And, conversely, analysis would have to determine which other 'publishers' should be made accessible to serve the goal of diversity. Rights of access would have to be allocated to particular publishing units in such a way that the aim of diversity would be served to the maximum, but jeopardy to the values of autonomy would be kept to a minimum.

Id. at 36.

58. See 568 F.2d at 984.
59. See id. at 984 (Oakes, J., concurring).
60. See *Nebraska Press Ass'n v. Stuart*, 427 U.S. 539, 568-70 (1976) (on the basis of the heavy presumption against prior restraints, the Court created new and perhaps insurmountable barriers to the issuance of judicial "gag orders" directed against the press to protect a defendant's right to fair trial).
61. Chief Justice Burger noted this very distinction in his opinion for the Court in *Nebraska Press*:

Prior restraints on speech and publication are the most serious and the least tolerable infringement on First Amendment Rights. A criminal penalty or a judgment in a defamation case is subject to the whole panoply of protections afforded by deferring the impact of the judgment until all avenues of appellate review have been exhausted. Only after judgment has become final, correct or otherwise, does the law's sanction become fully operative.

A prior restraint, by contrast and by definition, has an immediate and irreversible sanction. If it can be said that a threat of criminal or civil sanctions after publication "chills" speech, prior restraint "freezes" it at least for the time.

Id. at 559.

62. It is interesting to note that the *Tornillo* doctrine equates an order to a publisher to print with an order not to print. But an order to a speaker, an advertiser, to spend substantial sums of money for corrective advertising is valid even though the advertiser was just as unwilling as the publisher to engage affirmatively in the expression in controversy. See *Warner-Lambert Co. v. FTC*, 562 F.2d 749, 756-64 (D.C. Cir. 1977) (FTC order requiring an advertiser, Warner-Lambert, to correct in its future advertisements because deceptive statements had been made in prior advertisements upheld). The First Amendment legitimacy of compulsory speech is at least on its facts apparently distinguishable from compulsory publication, a result which is at least implicitly a victory for a theory of the First Amendment that accords a special status to the press. See note 41 *supra*.

63. The First Amendment danger presented by such developments was only recently voiced by the Court in *FCC v. National Citizens Comm. for Broadcasting*, 436 U.S. 775 (1978), in which the FCC prospective ban on newspaper-broadcast combinations in the same city was upheld.

Particularly in the context of broadcasting, the Court, per Mr. Justice Marshall, declared: "We see nothing in the First Amendment to prevent the Commission from allocating licenses so as to promote the 'public interest' in diversification of the mass communications media." *Id.* at 799. See Chap. 9.

    64. See generally Lange, *The Speech and Press Clauses*, 23 U.C.L.A. L. Rev. 77 (1975); Nimmer, *Introduction: Is Freedom of the Press a Redundancy: What Does It Add to Freedom of Speech?*, 26 Hastings L.J. 639 (1975); Stewart, *supra*, note 42.

    65. See generally Stewart, *supra* note 42.

    66. Judge Oakes quoted the distinction Justice Stewart drew between the greater protection the press clause gives the press than the free speech clause presumably offers others as a ground for recognizing an editorial process privilege in libel cases. 568 F.2d at 988 (Oakes, J., concurring) (quoting Stewart, *supra* note 42, at 633-4).

    67. 427 U.S. 539 (1976).
    68. See Bezanson, *supra* note 48, at 630.
    69. See *id.*
    70. See *id.* at 610.
    71. 441 U.S. 153 (1979).

    72. The Court refused to hold for the first time that when a member of the press is alleged to have circulated damaging falsehoods and is sued for injury to the plaintiff's reputation, the plaintiff is barred from inquiring into the editorial process of those responsible for the publication, even though the inquiry would produce evidence material to the proof of a critical element of his cause of action. *Id.* at 169-75.

    73. *New York Times Co. v. Sullivan*, 376 U.S. 254, 282 (1964).
    74. 441 U.S. at 167-71.
    75. *Id.* at 175.
    76. *Id.* at 170.
    77. *Id.* at 171.
    78. *Id.*
    79. *Id.* at 176.
    80. *Id.* at 169-70.
    81. *Id.* at 163-4.
    82. *Id.* at 165.
    83. *Gertz v. Robert Welch, Inc.*, 418 U.S. 323 (1974).
    84. See, e.g., N.Y. Times, Apr. 19, 1979, at 1, col. 2.
    85. 388 U.S. 130 (1967).

    86. The *New York Times* doctrine proved to be fecund and moved quickly from its elected public official setting to embrace non-elected public officials. See *Rosenblatt v. Baer*, 383 U.S. 75, 85-6 (1966). The *Butts* case much expanded the scope of the doctrine by extending the *New York Times* rule to "public figures." 388 U.S. at 164 (Warren, C.J., concurring in result).

    87. 441 U.S. at 160 n. 6.
    88. *Id.*
    89. *Id.* at 199.

90. 390 U.S. 727 (1968).
91. See *id.* at 731, quoted in *Herbert v. Lando*, 441 U.S. 153, 156 (1979).
92. *Gertz v. Robert Welch, Inc.*, 418 U.S. 323, 334 n.6 (1974), quoted in *Herbert v. Lando*, 441 U.S. 153, 156 (1979).
93. Mr. Justice White in *Lando* cited more than three dozen libel cases in which matters that would be embraced under an editorial process privilege were deemed to have been relevant and admissible when offered by both libel plaintiffs and media defendants. 441 U.S. at 165 n.15.
94. See notes 40-1 *supra*.
95. 556 F.2d 113 (2d Cir.), *cert. denied*, 434 U.S. 1002 (1977).
96. The philosophy of the neutral reportage doctrine as set forth by Judge Kaufman is that when a reliable informant makes "serious charges against the public figure, the First Amendment protects the accurate and disinterested reporting of those charges, regardless of the reporter's private views regarding their validity." 556 F.2d at 120.
97. See notes 40-1 *supra*.
98. 418 U.S. 241 (1974); see note 23 *supra* and accompanying text.
99. 412 U.S. 94 (1973). In *CBS*, the Court, per Chief Justice Burger, relying on the fairness doctrine, rejected a claim for a First Amendment right of access to broadcasting and made the following influential defense of the editorial function in both broadcast and print media:

> For better or worse, editing is what editors are for; and editing is selection and choice of material. That editors - newspaper and broadcast - can and do abuse this power is beyond doubt, but that is no reason to deny the discretion Congress provided. Calculated risks of abuse are taken in order to preserve higher values.

Id. at 124-5. This egalitarian approach to the print and broadcast media contrasts oddly in retrospect with Mr. Justice Stevens' observation in *FCC v. Pacifica Foundation*, 438 U.S. 726 (1978); "And of all forms of communication, it is broadcasting that has received the most limited First Amendment protection." *Id.* at 748.
100. 441 U.S. at 168.
101. *Id.*
102. *Id.*
103. *Gertz v. Robert Welch, Inc.*, 418 U.S. 323, 399-400 (White, J., dissenting).
104. A kindred question has arisen in the context of the *Gertz* case. *Gertz* held that strict liability and presumed and punitive damages (in the absence of actual malice) are inconsistent with the First Amendment protection afforded media libel defendants. *Id.* at 349. May the rules curtailing strict liability and presumed and punitive damages be invoked by a non-media defamation defendant? In *Jacron Sales Co. v. Sindorf*, 276 Md. 580, 592-5, 350 A.2d 688, 695-6 (1976), the Maryland Court of Appeals answered in the affirmative. Contra *Calero v. Del Chem. Corp.*, 68 Wis. 2d 487, 500, 228 N.W.2d 737, 747-8 (1975).
105. 395 U.S. 367 (1969).

106. See *New York Times Co.* v. *Sullivan,* 376 U.S. 254, 282 (1964), cited in *Herbert* v. *Lando,* 441 U.S. 153, 189 n.8 (1979) (Brennan, J., dissenting in part). The "citizen-critic" aspect of the *New York Times* doctrine is the product of Alexander Meiklejohn's view that the purpose of First Amendment protection is to equip the individual citizen for the task of democratic decision-making. See generally, A. Meiklejohn, Free Speech and Its Relation to Self-Government (1948). In the recent post-Watergate phase of First Amendment theory in which the press is seen as the guardian angel of individual rights, this view has been criticized as obsolete: "The Meiklejohn thesis vision of active, continual involvement by citizens fails to describe not only the reality but also the shared ideal of American politics..." Blasi, *The Checking Value in First Amendment Theory,* Am. Bar Foundation Research J. 523, 562 (1977). For Blasi, the press rather than the individual citizen is better equipped to provide a counterforce to government. In playing such a role, the press instrumentally fulfills the "checking value" which in Blasi's view should be the contemporary key to First Amendment protection. The Supreme Court's *Lando* decision, by rejecting a doctrine of editorial privilege, refused to take an entirely media-oriented view of the First Amendment. By maintaining fidelity to the fact that the focus of *New York Times* was on the citizen critic and not merely the media critic, *Lando* will help restore First Amendment theory to its more individualistic and egalitarian *New York Times* origins and thereby move its focus away from its post-Watergate phase, the apotheosis of which is reflected by the *Tornillo* decision's now somewhat diminished suggestion of absolute editorial autonomy.

107. 441 U.S. at 188-9 (1979) (Brennan, J., dissenting in part) (quoting *Gertz* v. *Robert Welch, Inc.,* 418 U.S. 323, 343 (1974)).

108. 435 U.S. 765, 781-2 (1978) (holding that free speech rights could be asserted by business corporations and rejecting the thesis based on the press clause that media corporations have a special and preferred claim to First Amendment protection).

109. 441 U.S. at 189 (1979) (Brennan, J., dissenting in part) (quoting *First Nat'l Bank* v. *Bellotti,* 436 U.S. 765, 781 (1978)).

110. 441 U.S. at 192 (Brennan, J., dissenting in part).

111. *Id.* at 181 (Brennan, J., dissenting in part).

112. *Id.* at 192 (Brennan, J., dissenting in part).

113. Judge Oakes characterized this aspect of the editorial process as "the mental processes of the press regarding 'choice of material'," 568 F. at 995 (Oakes, J., concurring). Judge Kaufman stated that the editorial process included an editor's "thoughts, opinions, and conclusions." 568 F.2d at 984.

114. 568 F.2d at 980, quoted in *Herbert* v. *Lando,* 441 U.S. 153, 193 (1979) (Brennan, J., dissenting in part).

115. 568 F.2d at 993 (Oakes, J., concurring), quoted in *Herbert* v. *Lando,* 441 U.S. 153, 193 (1979) (Brennan, J., dissenting in part).

116. 441 U.S. at 192 (Brennan, J., dissenting in part).

117. *Id.* at 194 (Brennan, J., dissenting in part).

118. *Id.* at 181 (Brennan, J., dissenting in part).

119. *Id.*

120. *Id.* at 196 (Brennan, J., dissenting in part).
121. *Id.* at 191 (Brennan, J., dissenting in part).
122. *Id.*
123. *Id.* at 181 (Brennan, J., dissenting in part).
124. *Id.* at 192-3 (Brennan, J., dissenting in part).
125. *Id.*; see notes 84-93 *supra* and accompanying text.
126. 441 U.S. 181-2 (Brennan, J., dissenting in part).
127. *Id.* at 198 (Brennan, J., dissenting in part).
128. *Id.*
129. *Id.* at 204 (Marshall, J., dissenting in part).
130. *Id.* at 206 (Marshall, J., dissenting). See generally *Schlagenhauf* v. *Holder,* 379 U.S. 104 (1964); *Hickman* v. *Taylor,* 329 U.S. 495 (1947).
131. A similar question is provoked by Mr. Justice White's recitation of a great many pre-*New York Times* libel cases in which matters that might have a claim to protection under an editorial process privilege were deemed relevant and admissible. See 441 U.S. at 165 n.15; note 93 *supra.* Perhaps the implication was that editorial process privilege, once recognized, could not logically be limited merely to the *New York Times* variety of cases.

Certainly on the lower court level the *New York Times* rule has already occasioned changes in the normal way courts approach some of the more routine problems of civil procedure. Thus, in *New York Times Co.* v. *Connor,* 365 F.2d 567 (5th 1966), Commissioner "Bull" Connor of Birmingham, Alabama, brought a libel action against the *New York Times* because of his objection to an article by *Times* reporter Harrison Salisbury on racial conditions in Alabama, *id.* at 568. The case raised the question whether the circulation of 395 copies of the *Times* a day in Alabama was sufficient to constitute the requisite "minimal contacts" that would justify as a matter of due process, submitting the *Times* to service in Alabama under the state "long-arm" statute. See generally *International Shoe Co.* v. *Washington,* 326 U.S. 310 (1945). Certainly, an out-of-state business that serves over 300 customers would normally be considered to satisfy the "minimal contacts" rule. The Fifth Circuit in *Connor* ruled otherwise: "First Amendment considerations surrounding the law of libel require a greater showing of contact to satisfy the due process clause than is necessary in asserting jurisdiction over other types of tortious activity." 365 F.2d at 572.

132. 441 U.S. at 208 (1979) (Marshall, J., dissenting).
133. *Id.* at 207 (Marshall, J., dissenting).
134. *Id.* at 209-10 (Marshall, J., dissenting).
135. *Id.* at 209 (Marshall, J., dissenting).
136. *Id.*
137. *Id.* at 209 n.6 (Marshall, J., dissenting); see note 131 *supra* and accompanying text.
138. 441 U.S. at 209 n.6 (Marshall, J., dissenting).
139. *Id.* (citing *Cervantes* v. *Time, Inc.,* 464 F.2d 986 (8th Cir. 1972), *cert. denied,* 409 U.S. 1125 (1973); see *Washington Post Co.* v. *Keogh,* 365 F.2d 965, 972-3 (D.C. Cir. 1966), *cert. denied* 385 U.S. 1011 (1967).
140. *Branzburg* v. *Hayes,* 408 U.S. 665, 708-9 (1974).

141. 441 U.S. at 209 n.6 (Marshall, J., dissenting).
142. Id. See also notes 40-1, 138 supra and accompanying text.
143. 441 U.S. at 175.
144. 98 Idaho 288, 562 P.2d 791, cert. denied, 434 U.S. 930 (1977).
145. 98 Idaho at 291, 562 P.2d at 794.
146. See *Maryland* v. *Baltimore Radio Show*, 338 U.S. 912 (1950), in which the Court stated:

> Inasmuch, therefore, as all that a denial of a petition for a writ of certiorari means is that fewer than four members of the Court thought it should be granted, this Court has rigorously insisted that such a denial carries with it no implication whatever regarding the Court's views on the merits of a case which it has declined to review. The Court has said this again and again; again and again the admonition has to be repeated.

Id. at 919.

147. In *Lando,* as in Branzburg, Mr. Justice Powell joined in the Court's no-privilege conclusion, but filed a special concurrence. In both cases, his opinion appears to promise more than it delivers. See *Branzburg* v. *Hayes,* 408 U.S. 665, 709-10 (1974) (Powell, J. concurring). The Stewart dissent in *Branzburg, id.* at 743 (Stewart, J., dissenting), with its threefold test for the application of a qualified First Amendment-based journalist's privilege, has proved to be far more influential in keeping a constitutionally-based privilege than has the Powell concurrence. See generally J. Barron & T. Dienes, *Handbook of Free Speech and Free Press* 443-58 (1979).

148. 441 U.S. at 178 (Powell, J., concurring).
149. Id. at 179 (Powell, J., concurring).
150. Id. at 180 (Powell, J., concurring).
151. See note 42 *supra* and accompanying text.
152. 441 U.S. at 199 (Stewart, J., dissenting).
153. Id. at 201 (Stewart, J., dissenting).
154. Id. at 200 (Stewart, J., dissenting).
155. Id.
156. See *Selected Writings of Benjamin Nathan Cardozo* 294 (M. Hall, ed. 1947).
157. Id. I am indebted to my colleague Professor David Robinson, Jr, for these references in Cardozo's writings concerning the tendency of fundamental principles in law to be expanded to the outermost limits of their logic.
158. 385 U.S. 374 (1967).
159. Id. at 398.

6

Whose First?*

Does the First Amendment, or more specifically the Press Clause of the First Amendment, belong to the press alone or is its protection more broadly aimed and more widely shared? If we ask this question, we are in a better position to understand recent press law developments. Critics of the Burger Court have contended that in both the print and the broadcast media the Supreme Court has been waging a vendetta against the press by promulgating a series of decisions which is steadily eroding First Amendment rights. This charge is overstated. Often in these much-criticized opinions what is involved is not a judicial desire to punish the press but rather a judicial effort to reconcile competing but weighty claims of media freedom versus individual freedom. The state of libel and libel-related actions from the *Gertz*[1] case in 1973 to the *Lando*[2] case in 1979 are illustrative.

What we have been witnessing is a post-Watergate press, encouraged by its important and honorable role in that national trauma, seeking new legal advantages. It is not unusual that powerful groups in society should seek to become more powerful. The fact that its efforts to secure ever new immunities from law have been unsuccessful should not blind us to the fact that our press remains, and happily so, freer than any press in the world. In 1978, the Court held that the writ of the Fourth Amendment runs to newspaper premises as well as to other premises so long as the command of the Fourth Amendment with respect to the probable cause requirement is met. After that decision - *Zurcher* v. *Stanford Daily*[3] - there was much talk in the media that the press would be victimized by midnight police raids into newsrooms across the country. That phenomenon did not occur. It did not occur because in our country a free press is more than a part of our law - it is part of our culture and tradition.

---

* This chapter is based on an address which was delivered at the First Amendment Congress in Philadelphia on Jan. 16 and 17, 1980. A number of press groups sponsored the First Amendment Congress in order to deepen the popular understanding of the First Amendment. Four speakers addressed the Congress: Dan Rather, George Gallup, jr, Mayor Ernest Morial of New Orleans, and myself. The speech was reprinted in *Vital Speeches* in Mar. 1980.

The anxiety expressed by the press about the disinclination of the courts to allow it to expand its privileges is in stark contrast to press insensitivity to the beam in its own eye. Since the second World War, the number of American dailies in the hands of independent ownerships has declined from 1376 to 715. In the meantime, the number of daily newspapers owned by groups or chains has risen from 368 to 1047. At the present time, 165 chains dominate more than 60 per cent of the nation's 1762 daily newspapers and account for more than 71 per cent of the national daily newspaper circulation.[4] Four newspaper chains - Newhouse, Knight-Ridder (itself an example of a merger), Chicago's Tribune Company, and Gannet Company - account for no less than 25 per cent of the total daily newspaper circulation in the United States. Furthermore, out of 1548 cities with a daily newspaper, two or more papers are published in only 187 cities.[5]

These figures are truly examples of a world which nobody ever made or sought. In short, it is doubtful that many perceive concentration of the media to be a particularly desirable phenomenon. Nevertheless, it is a reality which we have to confront. The pattern of chain domination of the daily press when coupled with network domination of broadcast television suggests that our dominant media are in too few hands. It is from the perspective of increasing concentration of ownership that we should examine the question "whose First Amendment?"

Mine is a populist view, if you will, of the First Amendment. I believe the First Amendment confers rights on everyone. The guarantee of freedom of speech is no less significant than is the guarantee of freedom of the press. Freedom of the press should not be aggrandized at the expense of freedom of speech. Furthermore, the guarantee of "freedom of the press" is not a particular conferral of specific rights on the print media alone. After all, the language of the First Amendment guarantees freedom of the press, not press immunity from law. It does not say that Congress may not abridge the press itself.

The Supreme Court has recognized this distinction since it has consistently held, against vigorous press opposition, that the press is bound, like other business enterprises, by the labor laws and the antitrust laws. The claims of absolute protection for the press and the claims for a unique status for the press are exactly that - absolutist claims. Whenever the claim for one group in society is absolute, the necessary consequence of such a claim can only be at the expense of the freedom of others. Increasingly, the Supreme Court has been unwilling to recognize claims that would diminish individual liberties and individual autonomy. A recent example is the case of *Herbert* v. *Lando*,[6] where the Court properly rejected a claim of editorial privilege in a public law of libel case on the ground that such a claim would eat too deeply into the already limited protection that is accorded the claims of reputation.

Not all recent press law decisions of the Burger Court strike the proper balance between individual and media rights. The *Gannett*[7] case, where the court was closed to the press, in a pre-trial suppression hearing was unwise and ill considered, particularly when viewed from the perspective of "whose First Amendment?" It was particularly ill considered in its insistence that the right to an open courtroom was a right that could be asserted by the defendant alone.

Since the First Amendment belongs to the public at large, the view that the press may cover a courtroom only at the wish of the defendant is too myopic a perception of the functions served by an open courtroom. Happily, the Supreme Court has now made clear that in its view the policy of our Constitution favors an open criminal trial.[8]

In short, the question "whose First Amendment?" in this context as in others is answered by saying that the First Amendment belongs to the public at large. The media comprise a part of that public but their First Amendment rights are not exclusive any more than a defendant's Sixth Amendment rights should have been deemed the exclusive consideration involved in *Gannett*.

We must be very careful to understand the significance of Mr. Justice Brennan's October 1979 speech at the Newhouse Law Center of Rutgers University.[9] In that speech, he objected to the fact that the "vehemence of the press reaction" to recent Supreme Court decisions has been "out of all proportion to the injury suffered." The appropriate place for law in the affairs of the press is very clear to Mr. Justice Brennan. He says that there are two distinct models for the role of the press in our society. One he calls the "speech" model. Under this model, the press is accorded absolute protection under the First Amendment. However, there is another model with respect to the role of the press which Brennan spoke of which he called the "structural" model. This model does not involve directly the publication of news but instead involves "myriad tasks necessary" to the gathering and dissemination of news. In this area, press claims for absolute protection should be less encompassing. In Brennan's view, the structural model does not "fit comfortably with the absolutist rhetoric associated" with the "speech model of the press."

I do not know whether Mr. Justice Brennan would agree. But in my view, his structural model of the press is capable of helpful expansion.[10] A decision like the *Red Lion*[11] case, which upheld the fairness doctrine - that is, the statutorily imposed duty on broadcasters to provide a balanced presentation of controversial issues of public importance - is a further example of the structural model of freedom of the press. Under the fairness doctrine, a broadcaster is admonished that he may not as a continuous policy air only those views on public affairs to which he is partial, and no others. The broadcaster is urged to present opposing views as well. This policy of balanced presentation encouraging non-media voices to express themselves is properly deemed an implementation of freedom of speech and press and not a violation of it.

Another example of the structural mode of the freedom of the press would be the recent case of *Federal Communications Commission v. National Citizens Committee for Broadcasting*.[12] In that case, the Supreme Court upheld a prospective ban on a common ownership of a newspaper and a VHF television station in the same community. Newspapers bitterly protested that this prospective ban on cross-ownership was a restriction on their First Amendment rights. In that case, Mr. Justice Marshall said for the Court: "Requiring those who wish to obtain a broadcast license to demonstrate that such would serve the "public interest" does not restrict the speech for those who are denied licenses; rather, it preserves the interest of the 'public as a whole . . . in free speech'."

The language just quoted is extremely important. Justice Marshall speaks of free speech rights of the people as a whole. It would be the greatest caricature of the First Amendment to say that at the end of the twentieth century it is meant only to protect the freedom of those who have an ownership interest in the great corporations that control our print and broadcast media. In these matters it is important not to be misunderstood. The suggestion is not that these great corporations should be government controlled. As powerful as they are, their power is nevertheless more atomized and, therefore, less menacing than if all their power were gathered together and placed in the hands of the government as is the case in totalitarian regimes.

On the other hand, it would be the greatest irony if those justly and sincerely concerned with the freedom of the press were not sufficiently mindful of the position the ordinary citizen finds himself in today. The individual finds himself placed between the two behemoths of contemporary life - giant government and giant media. It has been the genius of the American experiment that we have managed in our pragmatic way to allow, insofar as our polity has deemed just, a free scope to business, and at the same time to be ever mindful of the rights and claims of individuals to privacy, reputation, and expression. These latter values are somewhat embattled as a result of the recent claims of giant media. The solution is not government control or ownership of the media, but solutions will have to be found that give additional protection to individuals in the furtherance of the values mentioned above.

By century's end, perhaps our courts will be more sympathetic to the need to recognize rights of reply than they have been up to now. Already we can see a new sensitivity on the part of our courts to the claims of reputation. In *Wolston v. Readers Digest Ass'n, Inc.*,[13] as in *Time,*

Inc. v. Firestone,14 the Supreme Court has defined the scope of who is a public figure. It has done this to broaden the availability of the general law of libel to citizens who believe themselves to have been defamed by media. In *Herbert v. Lando,* the Court refused to allow a claim of editorial privilege to completely shield the aggressive exercise of investigative journalism from its consequences with respect to those individuals who might find themselves victimized by it. In short, as in so many human problems, what is necessary is the development of a sensitivity and a disposition to secure an accommodation between competing claims for liberty and expression. So far the press has been valiant and eloquent in defense of its own rights to liberty and expression. It has been somewhat less eloquent and less valiant in its valuation of the rights to expression, privacy, and reputation of those whom it serves.

Notes

1. *Gertz v. Robert Welch, Inc.,* 418 U.S. 323 (1974).
2. *Herbert v. Lando,* 441 U.S. 153 (1979).
3. *Zurcher v. The Stanford Daily,* 436 U.S. 547 (1978).
4. See the 1978 *Editor and Publisher Yearbook.*
5. See Sobel and Emery, *U.S. Dailies' Competition in Relation to Circulation Size: A Newspaper Data Update,* Journalism Quarterly (Spring 1978), which indicated that only 39 cities had competing dailies in 1976. (The figures reported above are recorded in Gillmor and Barron, *Mass Communication Law* (West Publishing Co., 3d ed. 1980), p. 690.)
6. See note 2, *supra.*
7. *Gannett Co., Inc. v. De Pasquale,* 443 U.S. 368 (1979).
8. In *Richmond Newspapers, Inc. v. Virginia,* 100 S. Ct. 2814 (1980), the Court, in an opinion authored by Chief Justice Burger, and joined by Justices White and Stevens, said the common law tradition of open criminal trials was guaranteed by the First and Fourteenth amendments. Those amendments protected the right of the public and the press to attend criminal trials. Mr. Justice Brennan, joined by Mr. Justice Marshall, declared in a separate opinion that the First and Fourteenth amendments secured the public a right of access to trials. Agreement on the part of the judge and the parties was not sufficient to constitutionally close a trial to the public. *Gannett* had allowed the closure to the press and public, in some circumstances, in a pre-trial suppression hearing. Some lower court judges had therefore reasoned that the criminal trial itself could be closed to the press and the public. Except for the most extraordinary circumstances, the *Richmond Newspapers* case has now foreclosed this line of reasoning.
9. Address by Mr. Justice Brennan, Dedication of Samuel I. Newhouse Law Center, Rutgers University, Newark, New Jersey, Oct. 17, 1979.

10. When I made this point before the First Amendment Congress, Floyd Abrams, the able and distinguished lawyer for CBS in *Herbert* v. *Lando*, note 2, *supra*, see Chap. 5, rose from the audience to state that he believed that the "structural" model of the press could not be expanded to justify procedural mechanisms to assure debate, such as the fairness doctrine. It was a fair point.

On Jan. 21, 1980, I wrote Justice Brennan to get his reaction to whether under his "structural" model freedom of the press, a decision like the *Red Lion* case validating the fairness doctrine could be seen as an example of the "structural" model of freedom of the press.

On Feb. 19, 1980, Justice Brennan responded to my inquiry as to whether he would share my view on the "structural" model as follows:

> I agree that the 'structural' mode of the First Amendment has application to the questions you discuss. The model mediates between the First Amendment and the structure of communications necessary for a democracy to survive, and in that sense provides a conceptual foundation for the existence of constitutional interests that are not personal. In your address, however, you argue that these constitutional interests should in some situations prevail over the personal First Amendment rights of the media.
>
> As I understand your address, therefore, you use the 'structural' model of the First Amendment as a premise for your argument. While I certainly agree with this premise, I'm afraid that I must reserve judgment at this time about your conclusion. I would prefer to resolve such conflicts in the context of a concrete case.

On Feb. 26, 1980, I replied to Mr. Justice Brennan's letter:

> I realize, of course, that it is not possible to pass judgment on whether emergent rights should be recognized outside the context of a particular case. However, I would like to say that what I think is particularly vital and fundamental in your work on the First Amendment is its sense, reflected in your letter, that the question of 'the structure of communications necessary for a democracy to survive' and the task of First Amendment interpretation have the closest possible relationship. In my view, the latter necessarily must influence the former.

11. *Red Lion Broadcasting Co.* v. *Federal Communications Commission*, 395 U.S. 367 (1969).

12. 436 U.S. 775 (1978).

13. 443 U.S. 157 (1979).

14. 424 U.S. 448 (1976).

7

Access for Advertising in the Print Media and the Commercial Speech Boom

INTRODUCTION

The Florida right of reply case dealt a heavy blow to the movement seeking to establish rights of access and reply in the newspaper press. However, that situation did not involve claims of entry into the private press with respect to the advertising columns of the private press. Even those who have generally taken a very limited or narrow view of the proper claims of a right of access have not claimed that the Florida right of reply case controls the question of the First Amendment status of claims for access to the advertising columns of the daily newspaper press.[1] The cause of a First Amendment status for a right of nondiscriminatory access to the advertising columns of the private newspaper press has recently received new support. The theme of this chapter is that the legal foundations of the movement can be recharged by the new protection the Supreme Court has begun to give commercial speech in general, and advertising in particular.

WHAT IS COMMERCIAL SPEECH?

What is meant by the phrase "commercial speech"? From its beginnings, the commercial speech doctrine has primarily been concerned with the propriety under the First Amendment of government regulation of commercial product advertising. The doctrine is perhaps best explained by examining the circumstances of its birth, a birth which involved, appropriately enough, a commercial product advertisement.

In a 1942 Supreme Court case, *Valentine* v. *Chrestensen*,[2] the owner of a Navy submarine sought to exhibit it in New York City at a state pier in the East River. The exhibitor prepared and printed a handbill advertising the boat and soliciting the public for a fee to come and have a look at it. When the exhibitor tried to distribute the handbill in the city streets, he was advised by the police commissioner that such distribution violated a city ordinance prohibiting the distribution on city streets of commercial advertising. He was also told at the same time that he was free to distribute handbills containing information concerning matters of public protest. Chrestensen proved sufficiently inventive to find something to protest. He took the blank side of his handbill and used it to protest the action of the City Dock Department, which had denied him wharfage facilities at a city pier for the exhibition of his submarine. On the other side of the handbill, he retained the original commercial advertisement of the submarine, which he altered only by deleting any reference to an admission fee.

In the view of the police commissioner, the submarine exhibitor could distribute a handbill containing the protest about the city's denial to him of wharfage facilities but he could not combine it with commercial advertising. The submarine exhibitor tried to distribute the double-faced handbill anyway but the police restrained him from doing so. He then went to court to prevent the police commissioner from interfering with the distribution of the handbill.

From these rather humble facts a major First Amendment doctrine was spun. Freedom to disseminate information and opinion in city streets was recognized, as was the authority of cities and states to regulate such dissemination as long as the regulation was "not unduly burdensome." The Court went on to suggest that the power of government to regulate advertising was particularly extensive.[3] "We are equally clear that the Constitution imposes no such restraint on government as respects purely commercial advertising."

This doctrine established a hierarchy for the protection of expression. Under this doctrine, matters of political or social controversy had merit and greater claim to First Amendment protection than did speech of a commercial character. Making a distinction between commercial and non-commercial speech, however, poses a particularly difficult issue for First Amendment law - the problem of motive. In the *Chrestensen* case, the court said that it was very clear that "the affixing of the protest against official conduct to the advertising circular was with the intent, and for the purpose of evading the prohibition of the ordinance."[4] Obviously, there is potential for abuse in a motive approach to the distinction between commercial and non-commercial speech. If the speech in question is unappealing to the reviewing authority, there may be a temptation to call the speech in question commercial speech and thereby subject it to a greater measure of regulation by the state.

From an access point of view, how has the commercial speech doctrine worked? The report is mixed. Suppose a public facility, such as a publicly owned bus company, makes its car card space open only to commercial advertisements and rejects political advertisements? Under the older approach to commercial speech, the distinction between purely commercial speech and political speech would come to the rescue of a ban on political advertisements. The state would not be permitted to discriminate in favor of commercial speech and against political speech, that is, to accept commercial advertisements and to refuse political advertisements. After all, the whole purpose of the distinction between commercial and political or "public" speech was to protect speech which dealt with ideas.

In recent years, the Burger Court, unlike the Warren Court, has shown itself increasingly disposed to sympathize with the claims of property, whether that property is public or private. As a result, the commercial speech doctrine has worked against the access concept. If all paid advertisements are treated simplistically as "commercial speech" without regard to whether their content and purpose is commercial rather than political, then the traditional commercial speech doctrine could be used easily as a vehicle to justify even the total exclusion of, say, editorial or political advertisements from a public facility. The reason for this is that advertising, as commercial speech, is much more vulnerable to restrictive governmental legislation than legislation affecting so-called protected speech.

An example of how the commercial speech doctrine buttressed a decision that there was no right of access to political advertising in one public facility is the well-known case of *Lehman* v. *City of Shaker Heights*.[5] The facts of the case follow.

POLITICAL ADVERTISING IN SHAKER HEIGHTS

Harry Lehman was running for the Ohio legislature. He thought it would be nice to advertise his candidacy by purchasing car card space on the rapid transit system owned by the City of Shaker Heights, Ohio. The city had delegated management of the advertising for car cards on the rapid transit cars to a private advertising agency, Metromedia, Inc. Metromedia rejected Harry's ad. The content of the ad in controversy was as follows:

> Harry J. Lehman is old-fashioned!
> About honesty, integrity, and good government.
> State Representative. District 56.
> (X) Harry J. Lehman.

Metromedia rejected the ad on the ground that the contract between the city and the agency forbade political advertising. Harry Lehman thought his First Amendment rights had been violated and brought suit. When the Shaker Heights case reached the Supreme Court, the Court held, 5-4, that car card space on a city transit system was not a First Amendment forum. A principal factor in Mr. Justice Blackmun's plurality decision for the Court appeared to be that the state had a wider latitude to regulate communication in public facilities whose primary purpose was not communication, particularly when those facilities have not in the past been associated with communication. For the four justices who participated in the plurality opinion for the Court in Shaker Heights, the facts failed to reveal the existence of a public forum.

The city transit system in Shaker Heights was held to have acted constitutionally in banning political ads on its buses despite the fact that the transit system accepted commercial ads. Mr. Justice Douglas furnished the essential fifth vote which made the result possible. In a separate concurring opinion, Justice Douglas joined the plurality opinion for the Court only with respect to the result reached. Surprisingly, for Douglas, protection for the vagrant gaze of the transit rider against Harry Lehman's innocuous political ad was the pivotal issue in the case. In this view, the rights of the captive audience should prevail against the intrusion of unsought messages from political candidates. Furthermore, Douglas appeared to assume that political candidates have no First Amendment right to have non-discriminatory access to advertising on a content-neutral basis to a state-sponsored facility. It is noteworthy that in a later case the Court rejected a contention that a total ban on nudity in films in the community was justified because nudity on an outdoor movie screen could be seen by passers-by who would be offended by it. The Court remarked quite sensibly that the passer-by could merely avert his gaze.[6]

There were a number of factors which contributed to the ultimate result in the Shaker Heights case. Crucial to the Court's plurality decision, however, appears to be the idea that a municipal transit authority's car card space was not a public forum and, therefore, no First Amendment rights attached. There is also an implication in the plurality decision for the Court that since the state was regulating advertising, albeit political advertising, there was no basis for a claim of First Amendment protection since even political advertising is a species of commercial speech, a lesser and constitutionally unprotected breed of speech. There is specific reliance in the *Shaker Heights* decision on a 1932 case which is apparently cited for the proposition that display advertising, like advertising in general, does not rise to First Amendment stature.[7]

The four dissenters, led by Mr. Justice Brennan, rejected the notion that no public forum was involved in the *Shaker Heights* case. The dissenters relied on what may be called a First Amendment-equal protection principle prohibiting invidious discrimination by the state against expression of ideas on the basis of content. Application of such a principle required the publication of Harry Lehman's ad: "The City created a forum for the dissemination of information and expression of ideas when it accepted and displayed commercial and public service advertisements on its rapid transit vehicles. Having opened a forum for communication, the City is barred by the First and Fourteenth Amendments from discriminating among forum users solely on the basis of message content."[8]

The dissent appears to reject a distinction between commercial speech and political or ideological speech for purposes of First Amendment protection: a public forum was present and no selective discrimination against expression because of content, whether commercial or noncommercial, was permissible. Mr. Justice Brennan declared that the difficulty with protecting ideological speech and yet according the state wide regulatory scope over commercial speech was clear: the process of distinguishing ideological speech from commercial speech is essentially a subjective one. Harry Lehman's ad was a perfect example of the difficulty in making such a content evaluation. The copy Lehman submitted to the transit system for publication was certainly an advertisement, but as a political ad it was also ideological speech. The aversion of the four dissenters in the Shaker Heights case to the old commercial/non-commercial speech distinction is made clear. In retrospect, this aversion, even though it was expressed by the dissent, was the true harbinger of a transformation in First Amendment doctrine.

Finally, there is a specific passage in Mr. Justice Brennan's dissent which addresses the plurality opinion's reliance upon the 1932 case referred to earlier, holding that display advertising did not raise a First Amendment issue. The dissenters responded that the contention that such advertising could not be regulated "consistent with the First Amendment had never been authoritatively decided." In the years since the *Shaker Heights* decision, the First Amendment status of "commercial speech" *has* been authoritatively decided.

THE NEW COMMERCIAL SPEECH BOOM

Does an access claim for a right to publish advertising in a communication medium operated by the state enjoy a higher legal status now than it did at the time of the *Shaker Heights* case? Judge Goldberg, the dissenting judge in the *Mississippi Gay Alliance* case, answered this question in the affirmative.[9] The reason? The Supreme Court's historic turnaround on the commercial speech doctrine.

In the 1976 *Virginia Pharmacy* decision, Mr. Justice Blackmun wrote an opinion for the Court which appeared to erase any distinction between commercial and political speech insofar as the point of the distinction was to suggest that commercial speech character of itself removed it from full First Amendment protection.[10] The dissenters had argued in the *Shaker Heights* case that for First Amendment purposes there could be no distinction between commercial and political speech. Blackmun had not agreed with the dissenters in the *Shaker Heights* case, but in the *Virginia Pharmacy* case he adopted this point of view for the Court. In *Virginia Pharmacy,* the Supreme Court invalidated as inconsistent with the First Amendment a state statute which prohibited advertising the price of prescription drugs. In a landmark opinion, the Court said that even purely commercial speech is not removed from First Amendment protection. The Court ruled that whatever may be the bounds of time, place, and manner restrictions on commercial speech, they are exceeded by a statute which singles out speech of a particular content and seeks to prevent its dissemination. Our forgetful judges! In the *Shaker Heights* case, only two years before, one of the issues had been whether the state could single out a particular class of speech, political advertising, and seek to prevent its dissemination entirely.

From an access point of view, the significant feature of the *Virginia Pharmacy* case is that it takes a far more inclusive view of the identity of the ultimate addressees of First Amendment protection than do cases like the *Shaker Heights* case or the Florida right of reply case. In the latter two situations, the First Amendment interests of the consumers of information, the rapid transit riders in the *Shaker Heights* case, and the voters and readers of the Miami *Herald* in the Florida right of reply case, were necessarily subordinated to other values. What are these values? To a large extent, these newly dominant values appear to be editorial autonomy and editorial discretion. If decision-making can be viewed as editorial in nature, should such decision-making automatically be considered inviolate? Before we answer this question it might be worthwhile to apply such an approach to a specific problem. It is possible to view the decision of the rapid transit authority in *Shaker Heights* to ban political advertising from its car card space as an exercise of editorial judgment. Is the decision of the authority, therefore, to be unreviewable because "editing is what editors are for"? If the definition of what is included by the phrase "editorial judgment" is made too encompassing, then other First Amendment interests are likely to atrophy. Using editorial autonomy as a standard for judgment in resolving First Amendment problems is too narrow a focus for analyzing problems which so often involve a clash between competing rights. If judicial protection of editorial autonomy is too ruthless, then the only First Amendment interest which may survive may be that of the nominal editor, and this would be true in the case of either public or private media.

Virginia Pharmacy looks at First Amendment problems from another vantage point than that of the editor. The case takes a far richer and broader view. The decision reasons that the First Amendment cannot permit a class of advertising to be banned entirely because the consumer and the society have a strong and protected interest in the flow of information.

Has *Virginia Pharmacy* revitalized the case for a right of access to publicly-sponsored media for political advertising? It is certainly now possible to argue that political advertising should be protected against total banishment from the advertising space of a city bus company or rapid transit system. Political advertising is a form of advertising, and advertising is now protected by the First Amendment. Even more fundamentally, there is a citizen interest in such advertising. Political advertising is part of the lifeblood of politics in a democracy. In a truly inclusive theory of First Amendment protection, government should have an obligation to expose the largest relevant audience to the political candidates and choices which will determine that audience's future.

If the core area of First Amendment protection is to protect the process of self-government by permitting the criticism of government, it is a strange result which allows the state to choose commercial speech over political speech, to "prefer" commercial speech and to banish political speech.

The difference that the new status that has been won for commercial speech can make for the movement for public access to the public media can be seen quickly if the facts of the *Shaker Heights* rapid transit case are kept in mind. In that case, the political ads were treated as just another form of advertising. They, therefore, could be regulated as commercial speech: "The car card space, although incidental to the provision of public transportation, is a part of the commercial venture."[11] As commercial speech such ads could be regulated to the point of denying them all access to car card space.

But if the doctrine of *Virginia Pharmacy* that "the notion of unprotected commercial speech [has] all but passed from the scene" is combined with the principle of equality of access to public forums a different result follows. The legal status of access claims such as Harry Lehman's request that his political advertisement be displayed in the rapid transit car cards in Shaker Heights and of the Mississippi Gay Alliance's request that its advertisement be published in *The Reflector* at Mississippi State University has been greatly strengthened by the new commercial speech cases.

It is perhaps inherent in the perverse character of legal ideas that even those ideas which are supposed to have been properly buried have a way of fleeing from their coffins. Such is the case, perhaps, with the right of non-discriminatory access for advertising to state-sponsored media. The rise of a new constitutional status for commercial speech may have the unintended consequence of providing a new basis for establishing a right of access to advertising.

THE CONSUMER INTEREST IN COMMUNICATION

In the light of more recent Supreme Court developments, the case for the establishment of a right of access to advertising has become stronger. An additional indicator, if any was needed, that a new constitutional status for commercial speech is a continuing theme of the Burger Court is the Court's landmark case permitting lawyers to advertise. In late June 1977, toward the end of term, the Court held that a disciplinary rule of the Arizona state bar restricting advertising by lawyers violated the First Amendment insofar as the rule prohibited truthful and non-misleading advertisements by lawyers concerning the availability and the terms of routine legal services. The case, *Bates* v. *State of Arizona*,[12] should prove to be one of the most significant First Amendment decisions of the seventies. The Court relied heavily on its decision a year earlier in *Virginia Pharmacy* where a state law was invalidated which made a pharmacist who advertised the prices of prescription drugs guilty of unprofessional conduct. Like the prescription drug advertising case in Virginia, the lawyer advertising case had a listener-reader-consumer focus which differed sharply from the focus on the editor or the journalist which had marked cases such as the Florida right of reply case.

In the lawyer advertising case, the Court gave a new and different answer to that hardy perennial among constitutional questions: whose interests is the First Amendment designed to protect? In a fascinating passage on this issue, Mr. Justice Blackmun made the following observations:[13] "Advertising, though entirely commercial, may often carry information of import to significant issues of the day... And commercial speech serves to inform the public of the availability, nature, and prices of products and services, and thus performs an indispensable role in the allocation of resources in a free enterprise system . . . In short, such speech serves individual and societal interests in assuring informed and reliable decision-making . . ."

In cases like the *Shaker Heights* rapid transit case and the Florida right of reply case, the interests of the recipient of the communication rather than the communicator were the source of the First Amendment claim advocated by the losing party. In the *Shaker Heights* case, it had been urged that the political candidate, Harry Lehman, should not be excluded from being permitted to advertise in the car card space of a public transit system. There was a First Amendment interest in facilitating the task of a political candidate in reaching the electorate, whose support was essential for election. The simple thesis of state legislature candidate Harry Lehman was that there was a First Amendment interest, an interest particularly compelling in the case of a publicly owned forum, in political advertising. It was hardly shocking to suggest that the First Amendment, the constitutional provision designed to protect political freedom, should be interpreted to deny to a public facility the power to exclude only that advertising which related to the exercises of political freedom and political advertising. Yet this simple and unremarkable thesis was in fact rejected.

In the Florida right of reply case, Tobias Simon and I, as counsel for Pat Tornillo, the labor leader and political candidate seeking space to reply to an editorial attack, emphasized in both the Supreme Court of Florida and the United States Supreme Court that the Florida right of reply statute was found in the Florida Election code. This was the section of the Florida statutes designed to achieve fair and open election campaigns. The Florida right of reply law was not intended to accomplish the large task of imposing a right of access on the Florida press. Instead, it set for itself the far more modest task of assuring that when a newspaper attacks a political candidate during the course of a political campaign the candidate should be afforded a right of reply by the newspaper.[14] The objective of the statute was to insure that the voters had sufficient information to make a judgment on the candidate. Under the scheme of the statute, the voter would reflect on the editorial attack and on the reply to it. Then the voter would make his assessment of whether he wished to vote for the candidate or against him as the paper had urged. In this sense, the Florida right of reply law, even though it was drafted in 1913, reflected what the late Edmund Cahn called the consumer perspective.

Yet in both the Florida right of reply case and the *Shaker Heights* case the recipient interest, or non-press aspect of the First Amendment protection, was subordinated. In the *Shaker Heights* case there was even an implication that public institutions had no particular First Amendment obligations. This implication was certainly out of line with a good deal in the way of previous lower court case law and previous Supreme Court case law as well. In the Florida case, the candidate's interest in expression, and the implicit public benefit in terms of providing new and fuller information to the Miami citizenry, were all subordinated to a conception of First Amendment protection which made its focal point the immunity from judicial oversight of the exercise of the editorial function. The doctrine of *Miami Herald* v. *Tornillo*[15] focuses First Amendment protection on the communicator. The rights of the communicator are deemed so weighty as to subordinate all other claims.

Why are the First Amendment interests of the voter and the reader, the transit rider, all necessarily subordinate to the editor and the publisher? Is the merit of the First Amendment claim of a right to information by its recipient to be exclusively reckoned by the judicial perception of the *need* for that information? Under such a theory, the access claims of advertising for pharmaceuticals or bread will always prevail over advertising that deals with politics and social conflict. In a short and brutish view of social need, we need bread and pharmaceuticals more then we need advertisements concerning controversies and politics. Surely such an attitude to First Amendment claims is to make constitutional dogma of philistinism. It would be a paradox if the constitutional guarantee ostensibly designed to protect the marketplace of ideas should, in the end, protect only the marketplace.

It is all too true, as Mr. Justice Blackmun said for the Court in the lawyer advertising case, that the "consumer's concern for the free flow of commercial speech often may be far keener than his concern for urgent political dialogue."[16] The comparative indifference of many to ideas that do not appear to have an immediate material impact on them can hardly be the basis for the construction of First Amendment theory. If majoritarian preference alone were the guide for our approach to problems of freedom of expression, we would do as most democratic countries still do, and we would leave such matters to the good, it is to be hoped, but in any case absolute, judgment of the legislature.

There is now new attention directed by the Supreme Court toward speech concerned with matters more vivid and tangible than those found in the marketplace of ideas. This new attention, to some extent at least, has its origin in the concern of the Court for property. The Florida right of reply case makes it clear that free expression rights are determined by property rights: he who does not own the *Miami Herald* may not as of right be published there. In the commercial speech cases, the injury that the state by statute may do to various forms of commercial property by restricting the opportunity to advertise such property has now been greatly limited. Because the Court has ostensibly abandoned economic regulation under the Fourteenth Amendment in the name of the due process clause, the novelty is that this latest judicial effort to strike at state economic regulation (state statutes restricting advertising) is done in the name of the First Amendment.

The link between the Florida right of reply case and new commercial advertising cases is that each is motivated at least in part by a deep concern to protect property. In the *Shaker Heights* case what was involved was not property but political ideas. It is still surprising that a claim for access to advertising in a public facility should not be viewed as suffused with First Amendment obligation when the advertising involved concerned the essence of political controversy, that is, who should be elected. It is an odd fate that the language of the First Amendment, designed as it was to protect and secure political freedom, should be read to accord greater rights of acquisition to commercial information than to political dialogue. Are the rights of acquisition to political information worthy of less protection because the Court *knows* that to the public political information is a bore and a distraction?

There is a new concern for the recipient of commercial information and for the advertiser desiring to convey that information. Why is there no equivalent First Amendment concern for the political candidate, like Harry Lehman, who wants to tell the voters in his constituency about his candidacy? Why is there no equivalent concern about the public's need for information about a political candidate, like Pat Tornillo, who wants to tell the voters in his constituency that the editorial about him in the state's largest paper is untrue? One reason, of course, is found in the fact patterns of the new commercial speech cases that have reached the Supreme Court. Thus far, the cases have not presented a clash between a claim for expression by someone outside the formal communications process and the custodian of the communications process itself, the editor and the publisher. In the new commercial speech cases, journalism and the group excluded from expression have been on the same side. The excluder has not been the press but the state.

The precursor of the Supreme Court's new approach to commercial speech was a 1975 decision, *Bigelow* v. *Virginia*,[17] where a Virginia weekly newspaper editor published an advertisement stating that placements for low-cost abortions could be made in New York, where they were legal. At the time of the ad, Virginia had in force a state law prohibiting the publication of information encouraging abortion and the editor was convicted under the statute. The Court reversed the editor's conviction and declared that advertising was not devoid of First Amendment protection. The Court emphasized that the "advertisement conveyed information of potential interest and value to a diverse audience - not only to readers possibly in need of the services offered, but also to those with a general curiosity about or genuine interest in the subject matter . . ."[18] Significantly, the Court stressed that the First Amendment interests of the editor *"coincided with the constitutional interests of the general public."* [Emphasis added.]

In both the lawyer advertising case and the *Virginia Pharmacy* case, it was the state that presented the access barrier. The open question is whether the case for First Amendment protection for a right to advertise is weakened when it is the editor rather than the state who is the censor.

The present Court has an attachment to the *Tornillo* doctrine. As far as the Court is concerned, the question of First Amendment protection for a right to advertise in the private press is only theoretically open. Its attachment to the *Tornillo* doctrine has been frequently proclaimed in recent cases, but the inequality in the communications process nevertheless persists. Interestingly enough, even Mr. Justice Rehnquist, the champion of the *Tornillo* doctrine and the absolute property rights of the media, has begun to question whether the "marketplace of ideas" is still an acceptable model for First Amendment theory. Even that champion of laissez-faire, Mr. Justice Rehnquist, recently complained about applying the "marketplace of ideas" metaphor in contexts where it does not make sense: "There is no reason for believing that the marketplace of ideas is free from market imperfections any more than there is to believe that the invisible hand will always lead to optimum economic decisions in the commercial market."[19]

The point is that as a matter of First Amendment theory, compelling expression in some cases has been permitted by the present Court. On the basis of these developments, a Court more sensitive to imbalances in the communications process than this one may yet construct a First Amendment theory rich enough to provide public rights to the print media. Must the interests of the consumer and the recipient necessarily become subordinated when the editor wishes to prohibit a certain class of advertising?

It is worthy of note that before the advent of the new status for commercial speech in a context where the interests of journalism and the state conflicted, the state prevailed. In a 1973 Supreme Court case involving the *Pittsburgh Press*[20] it was held that that city's human relations commission could validly require Pittsburgh daily newspapers to abolish sex-designated advertising columns. The decision was rationalized by the court on the lesser protection accorded commercial speech. Would the *Pittsburgh Press* case be decided another way if the case were litigated today? Is it still good law?

These questions are not easily answered. It is difficult to assess the continuing significance of the *Pittsburgh Press* case. The Supreme Court's justification in that case for validating an intrusion into a newspaper's management of its own space was two-pronged. First, the justification was based on the fact that a want ad involved the proposing of a commercial transaction and that such a proposition was at the heart of what was meant by the term commercial speech. Under the older approach to commercial speech which reigned at the time of the decision of *Pittsburgh Press*, an advertisement proposing a commercial transaction was clearly subject to a greater measure of state regulation than other kinds of expression. Second, the justification of the regulation of the want ad columns of *Pittsburgh Press* was upheld on the ground that something more was involved than merely weighing a state interest in the regulation of newspaper space against a First Amendment claim that the regulation was impermissible. In *Pittsburgh Press*, the Court reasoned, the state interest outweighed the First Amendment interest because the advertising involved was itself illegal in that it involved prohibited discrimination in employment. Interestingly enough, Chief Justice Burger, who later wrote the *Tornillo* decision, dissented in *Pittsburgh Press*. For him, the majority in *Pittsburgh Press* had impermissibly intruded on editorial discretion. He protested that this intrusion constituted a worrisome "enlargement of the 'commercial speech' doctrine."

The difficulty in trying to identify the authoritative status of the

Pittsburgh Press case today is that the new commercial speech cases which have followed it have not dealt, as *Pittsburgh Press* did, with a clash between a claim of editorial discretion and a state contention of an overriding state interest which would be served by subordinating such a claim. As we have seen, much was made of the fact in *Pittsburgh Press* that the advertising itself involved an underlying legal violation of law, employment discrimination. Can state intrusion on editorial discretion be justified with respect to advertising whenever the state intrusion coincides with state regulation of underlying conduct which the state has made illegal but which the newspaper advertising at issue allegedly furthers? If the answer to this question is in the affirmative, the protection for editorial discretion spoken of in *Tornillo* may easily be undone by the emphasis on an underlying violation of law in *Pittsburgh Press*. Conversely, it is possible to conclude that *Pittsburgh Press* and *Tornillo* are not in conflict. Viewing the two cases together, it may be argued that the two cases stand for the proposition that the advertising columns of a daily newspaper, unlike its news and editorial columns, are subject, consistent with the First Amendment, to a greater measure of state-imposed obligation.

An area of newspaper advertising which has recently become a source of controversy involves advertising for x-rated movies. Usually such ads do not themselves violate obscenity laws. Again, most often such ads advertise films which themselves do not violate obscenity laws. Should a daily newspaper be allowed to ban ads for x-rated movies altogether? Such a question presents a fundamental clash between the Court's new emphasis on prohibiting bans on entire classes of advertising and its equally new emphasis on the claims of editorial autonomy. Does the new constitutional status that has been won for commercial advertising still hold when the claim for a right of access for advertising is made against the press itself rather than the state in a situation where the press rather than the state is the censor? It is to these questions that we next proceed.

THE MEDIA AS ADVERTISING CENSOR

In the summer of 1977, the *Los Angeles Times* announced it would no longer take ads for x-rated movies. As of July 1, 1977, the *New York Times* announced a similar policy although it said it would list the names and times of such movies but not otherwise carry advertising or illustrations for such movies. The movie exhibitors affected in New York have not chosen to list their shows and times, but are boycotting the *New York Times* in protest. *Los Angeles Times* staff writer Kent MacDougall, in a study of this issue, stated that eight California dailies as well as a few elsewhere have joined "about 35 dailies known to have banned x-rated movies for years."[21] MacDougall reported that the x-rated movie producers, distributors, and exhibitors affected by the new *Los Angeles Times* advertising ban have filed a $45 million damage suit against the *Times* on the basis of censorship.

With the new status of commercial advertising, the porno movie houses certainly have a basis to argue that they have a First Amendment right to non-discretionary access to advertising in the daily press. This is particularly true if the Florida right of reply case is interpreted to apply only to the news and editorial columns of the paper. How much scope should be granted in this context for the claims of absolute right of editorial autonomy? Are the claims of editorial autonomy of equal weight when made with respect to a paper's advertising columns as when such claims are made on behalf of the paper's editorial and news columns?

In the battle between the x-rated movie houses and the metropolitan dailies, the state action problem once again intrudes to the center of the problem. A state university press, such as a campus newspaper, may have a duty to provide non-discriminatory access to its advertising. Presumably, this duty has arguably attained a new stature in light of the Court's increasing emphasis on the importance of advertising to consumers as a basis for intelligent decision-making. Do private newspapers have any duty to comply with a right of non-discriminatory access to advertising? When the *Los Angeles Times* bans a class of advertising, can such a policy be considered "censorship"? Certainly it is censorship in a real or practical sense, but it is not now censorship in a legal sense. For the present at least, courts, on constitutional grounds, refused to view the situation where a private newspaper bans an entire class of expression from its advertising pages as censorship. The question for the future is quite clear: is a private newspaper, no matter how powerful or how arbitrary, forever immune from accountability for censorship because of its "private" status? The movie ad access problem provokes the issue which communications controversies so frequently raise: should the rights to freedom of expression be completely defined in terms of the interests of the communicators and against the interests of the recipients of the communication?

The ingredients of a First Amendment argument for a right of access to the advertising columns of the privately owned press would include the following components. Neither the facts nor the opinion in the *Tornillo* case went beyond the news and editorial columns of a newspaper. On the other hand, the *Tornillo* decision was in part predicated on the idea that a newspaper is private property and can be dealt with by its owner as he chooses. Yet *Pittsburgh Press* should be recalled for its holding that the captions on the "help wanted" advertising columns of a newspaper must be titled as state law directs rather than as editorial discretion desires. The *Tornillo* decision could be used to provide still another argument against a right of access to advertising. It may be argued that the primary rationale of *Tornillo* is that the editorial function, as a process, is insulated by the First Amendment against demands for compulsory publication because without such protection the editorial function could not survive. But compulsory publication with respect to commercial advertising does not present the same dangers to the news and editorial columns that would be presented by a recognition of a compulsory right of access or response to the news and editorial columns of a newspaper. In the new commercial speech cases, the Supreme Court emphasized that commercial speech is hardier speech than political or ideological speech. Furthermore, in the new commercial speech cases, the Supreme Court has stressed that the First Amendment interests of those who are communicated with as well as the First Amendment interests of the communicator are worthy of nurture and protection.

The quarrel between the porno movie houses and two metropolitan dailies in New York and Los Angeles involves censorship, and a particularly interesting form of censorship at that. Most of the movie advertisements which are now banned concern subject matter which on the whole does not violate a constitutional application of state and federal obscenity law. Metropolitan newspapers have circulations and prestige that endow them with what is in economic terms a life-and-death power to empty or fill a theatre. Denying such theatres access to these papers is a powerful sanction. Can the theatres be held to a standard of censorship more intense and more demanding than that imposed by the state? May private individuals be permitted to utilize a censorship standard that would be denied to the state? The immediate answer to this question is affirmative. The act of editing involves, by necessity, a censorship aspect. Surely the blue pencil can strike out the blue line. But if the blue pencil is used to preserve the family newspaper, why is that objectionable? Perhaps it is because the "family newspaper" may be the only real or effective advertising medium open to the excluded business house. The issue then becomes, should monopoly or semi-monopoly corporate power in the form of a mass circulation newspaper (which at least in its circulation area is without rivals) be allowed to exercise a censorship role which is denied to the state?

A CASE FOR PRINT MEDIA COUNTER-ADVERTISEMENTS?

The Supreme Court now says that commercial speech merits First Amendment protection. At the same time, the Court says that commercial speech, because of its greater hardihood, may command state-imposed opportunities for correction and compulsory publication which could not be imposed on political speech:[22] "[T]he greater objectivity and hardiness of commercial speech, may make it less necessary to tolerate inaccurate statements for fear of silencing the speaker. Compare *New York Times* v. *Sullivan,* supra, with *Dun & Bradstreet, Inc.* v. *Grove,* supra. *They may also make it appropriate to require that a commercial message appear in such a form, or include such additional information, warnings and disclaimers, as are necessary to prevent its being deceptive.* Compare *Miami Herald Publishing Co.* v. *Tornillo,* . . . with *Banzhaf* v. *FCC."*

What is the meaning of this passage? It may have a startling message: some mandatory corrective remedies for abuses in print media advertising may be constitutionally permissible. Will a public right of entry to the press which was thrown out through the First Amendment's front door, at least with respect to a right of reply to a private newspaper's editorials, reassert itself in the advertising columns of that same private newspaper? The answers to these questions are unclear. What is clear is that new constitutional "protections" inevitably stimulate a movement toward the creation of new obligations. So it is with the new protection the Supreme Court has accorded commercial advertising.

In the passage quoted above, the Court makes specific reference to the fact that in the broadcast media, there are already some legal rights of response to commercial advertising. Furthermore, the Court is trying to make sure that corrective remedies which have already been established to counter abuses in commercial advertising are not destroyed by according a fuller measure of First Amendment protection to advertising. In addition, at least with respect to commercial advertising, this cautionary language can also be used to anticipate the argument that the *Tornillo* principle requires subordinating claims of access to advertising to claims of editorial discretion and autonomy.

New legal remedies may now be possible as a result of the new status of commercial speech. One such corrective that may be arguably implicit is a right of entry for counter-commercials. If commercial advertising cannot be banned in the interests of informing the consumer, then why should requiring the publication of material responding to that advertising in order to inform the consumer not also be in order? The philosophy of the new commercial speech cases is motivated at least in part by a policy of bringing information to the consumer. In light of this policy, a movement either for some mandatory response to commercial advertising in the print media to match the reply time already available to some commercials in broadcasting under the fairness doctrine would be a logical development. Similarly, recognition of a right of non-discriminatory access to the print media would also be authorized under this approach. In the lawyer advertising case, it was emphasized that more in the way of regulation was still possible with respect to commercial speech than was possible with forms of speech which had less recently won First Amendment protection:[23] "Indeed, the public and private benefits from commercial speech derive from confidence in its accuracy and reliability.

Thus, the leeway for untruthful or misleading expression that has been allowed in other contexts has little force in the commercial arena."

If a commercial advertisement makes a false statement about the quality of the legal services offered, perhaps the local bar association, or a group of lawyers who are competitors of the advertiser, may be able to compel an unwilling publisher to sell space for rebuttal in order to challenge the false claim. The First Amendment protects truthful lawyer advertisements against legislation restricting their publication. It is still possible that the state will provide for a remedy against print media lawyer advertisements which might involve false or misleading claims about the *quality* of legal services being advertised. Could a state legislature enact a law affording a right of response to false lawyer advertisements? Suppose an informed practitioner and/or a bar association sought to avail itself of such a statute? Are compulsory counter-commercials in the print media implicitly legitimized by the First Amendment status recently accorded to lawyer advertising? The court's commentary, insofar as it answers these questions, is laconic but tantalizing:[24] "We do not foreclose the possibility that some limited supplementation, by way of warning disclaimer or the like, might be required of even an advertisement of the kind ruled upon today so as to assure that the consumer is not misled."

The suggestion has been made that corrective relief may be particularly important with respect to misleading expression that is directed to an audience lacking the requisite sophistication. As authority for this proposition, the Supreme Court relied on a lower federal court of appeals decision which accorded a significant measure of latitude to the Federal Trade Commission to deal with deceit by advertisers.[25] The reference is to a passage which states:[26] "Ever since the enactment of the Federal Trade Commission Act, the courts have sustained orders which sought to limit the use of language which, although seemingly innocuous to the expert was likely to deceive the unlearned and the gullible. To cope with the great variety of deceit they have devised varied means of combatting them. They have ordered *additions* or omissions of words, phrases, or disclosures, positive or negative, as the circumstances of the situation demanded. And the courts, without deviation, on review, have sustained them."

The broad language of this passage suggests that in regulating advertising the Federal Trade Commission has the power both to prohibit and to compel speech. The court of appeals in this decision was not addressing itself to the large question of whether legislation requiring media to provide time or space for counter-commercials was permissible under the First Amendment. It should be noted, however, that the court had no doubt that the advertiser could be compelled to correct his advertisement through additional speech.

In the same segment of the *Bates* case where the Court discussed the greater susceptibility of advertising to legislative forms of compulsory correction to assure accurate and reliable information, the Court relied on a passage in the *Virginia Pharmacy* case quoted earlier in this chapter, where the court stressed that legislative efforts to furnish correctives to inaccurate advertisements are less vulnerable to First Amendment objection than are legislative efforts in the First Amendment heartland, a newspaper's news and editorial columns.

At this juncture, I should add my own disclaimer. The new commercial speech cases in the Supreme Court have certainly not explicitly pointed to the availability of mandatory rights of reply to print media ads. Clearly, the language about the greater hardihood of commercial speech is designed to insure that the state will still be able to require the inclusion in advertisements of warnings and disclaimers and the excision of false or misleading statements. It is nonetheless significant to note that after the Supreme Court has accorded commercial speech a new and higher First Amendment status, the court still insists on the right of the state to compel the exclusion and inclusion of content with regard to such "newly" protected speech. If protected speech can be the subject, consistent with the First Amendment, of state directives with respect to content, then at least in the case of advertising it seems difficult to conclude that all mandatory publication legislation is unconstitutional. As a result of the new commercial speech cases new strength has been furnished for a statutory basis for various kinds of compulsory reply or access statutes, at least as long as such legislation is directed to the advertising columns of newspapers.

THE LISTERINE CASE

If any proof were required that government was still going to be able to regulate advertising even after the emergence of a greater measure of First Amendment protection for commercial speech, the now celebrated Listerine case provides it. The Listerine case involved a complaint brought by the Federal Trade Commission (FTC) against Warner-Lambert's claim for its product, Listerine antiseptic mouthwash, that it was "beneficial for colds, cold symptoms and sore throats." After a long hearing, the FTC concluded that Warner-Lambert had misrepresented the usefulness of Listerine against the common cold.

The FTC demanded two things from Warner-Lambert by way of sanction. One sanction prohibited speech, and the other compelled it. First, Warner-Lambert was required to cease and desist from advertising that Listerine prevents, cures, or alleviates the common cold. The second sanction was more controversial. This one compelled speech. The FTC ordered Listerine to make the following disclosure in future advertising: "Contrary to prior advertising, Listerine will not help prevent colds or sore throats or lessen their severity." The part of the FTC order which compelled the foregoing disclosure was no vague admonition. The FTC joined this order with a requirement that the duty to make the disclosure about the inefficacy of its product is to lapse only when Warner-Lambert had spent on Listerine advertising "a sum equal to the average annual Listerine advertising budget for the period of April 1962 to March 1972, approximately ten million dollars." The FTC demanded that the consumers of America should obtain ten million dollars worth of free rebuttal time provided by the advertiser.

On review, the federal court of appeals affirmed the validity of both parts of the FTC order but deleted from the "required disclosure" the phrase "contrary to prior advertising."[27] The court of appeals held that Congress had given the Federal Trade Commission authority to order corrective advertising in appropriate cases. Corrective advertising, the court declared, did not violate the First Amendment. The restrictions on the advertiser's freedom of expression was no greater than was necessary to meet the government needs - informing the consumer by curing past deception.

The advertising industry argued that "since the Supreme Court has recently extended the First Amendment protection to commercial advertising, mandatory corrective advertising is unconstitutional."[28] Judge Wright, rejecting the argument, replied that the Supreme Court had specifically stated in *Virginia Pharmacy* that there was no First Amendment barrier to the prohibition or regulation of misleading advertising. Relying on a passage in *Virginia Pharmacy* discussed above, which appeared specifically to authorize the relief at issue, Judge Wright noted that the Supreme Court had perceived differences in commercial speech from other forms of speech which made it " 'appropriate to require that a commercial message appear in such a form, or include such additional information, warnings and disclaimers, as are necessary to prevent its being deceptive'."[29] A chief difference between commercial speech and other forms of speech which the Supreme Court had emphasized was its greater "hardihood," its capacity to endure a higher degree of government regulation. As Judge Wright put it, "the Supreme Court clearly foresaw the very question before us, and its statement is dispositive. . . ."[30]

The Supreme Court may well have agreed. In the spring of 1978, the Supreme Court declined to review the Listerine case.[31] A mandatory corrective remedy, in the newly protected commercial speech field, had successfully survived a full-scale First Amendment attack.

Because of the novel First Amendment issues raised by the FTC order in the Listerine case, counsel for Warner-Lambert petitioned for a rehearing of the case by the full court. Warner-Lambert specifically referred to "the conflict between approval in this case of mandated speech and the

First Amendment principles enunciated in other decisions, including a recent decision by this Court."[32] Warner-Lambert further points out that the FTC affirmative disclosure order involved represents the "first litigated case in which the Federal Trade Commission had ordered a company to disseminate 'corrective advertising'." The developments Warner-Lambert is talking about refer to the Supreme Court's new commercial speech decisions. Warner-Lambert also says the case is the first to litigate an FTC affirmative disclosure order. This highlights the mandatory speech aspect of the December 1975 FTC order. It was issued *after* a manadatory statute in the political speech area was declared to be a violation of the First Amendment by the Supreme Court in 1974. The Listerine case is a post-*Tornillo* development.

In the petition for rehearing, Warner-Lambert, the advertiser, complained: "Not only would the Commission prohibit Warner-Lambert from urging the position which it holds in good faith about its product; it would command the company to state the opposite of its view as a definitive unequivocal act."[33] Furthermore, Warner-Lambert argued that the FTC order challenged a fundamental First Amendment assumption that "differing views are entitled to expression in the 'marketplace of ideas' " and that such assumptions must now be applied to the "economic marketplace . . . where there are two reasonable sides to a continuing controversy."[34]

The discussion of the First Amendment issues in the court of appeals decision in the Listerine case had been cursory. Therefore, although the court of appeals denied the petition for rehearing, the court's decision rejecting the rehearing developed with greater force and in more detail its position that the First Amendment permitted the FTC corrective advertising order as modified. A panel consisting of Judges Bazelon, Wright, and Robb rejected, 2-1, the petition for rehearing.[35] Judge Robb dissented from the decision denying the rehearing as he had dissented from the decision approving the FTC order with modification.

In his second opinion in the case, Judge Wright stressed the commonsense differences between commercial speech and other kinds of speech, differences which yielded commercial speech a "different degree of protection."

Wright emphasized that "it is only truthful claims which are protected under the First Amendment."[36] If it be said that current and future advertising to which the FTC affirmative disclosure applies is not false and deceptive, Wright replied that current and future advertising must be seen in context. What was essential was the need to rebut past advertising claims: "Advertising which fails to *rebut* the prior claims as to Listerine's efficacy inevitably builds upon those claims; continued advertising continues the deception, albeit implicitly rather than explicitly."[37]

Corrective advertising of the compulsory affirmative disclosure type found in the Listerine case was deemed to present no First Amendment problem because all the FTC had done was to require "certain statements which, if not present in current and future advertisements, would render those advertisements themselves part of a continuing deception of the public."[38] If an advertiser knows that at some time the FTC can not only require him to abandon a particular type of advertising claim but also require him to include specific disclaimers in future advertisements, such concerns impermissibly have a chilling effect also on fully protected truthful speech. Will the advertiser not hesitate to make "true" claims as well for fear they will be called false? In the Florida right of reply case, it was argued that if an editor knew he could be required to provide a foe with a right of reply, the original editorial might itself be chilled to the point of being cut altogether. Judge Wright said this was not a problem in this context because the truth of commercial speech is "more easily verifiable by its disseminator." Commercial speech was a hardier plant than other forms of speech because the profit motive was such an incentive as to make it unlikely that such speech would be "chilled by proper regulation and foregone entirely."[39] Wright then observed that if some chill is still left, that is a price that might have to be paid "if the interest of consumers in truthful information is to be served at all."[40] Advertisers would hardly be deterred from false and misleading advertising if the FTC could only force a cessation of the repetition of the falsity. The public would already have been damaged and deceived by the effect of the past false advertising.

Perhaps it will be said that all that the Listerine ad demonstrates is that FTC corrective advertising orders are still valid after *Virginia Pharmacy*. In one perspective, this may merely mean that the new First Amendment status of commercial speech may have been somewhat over-advertised. If, on the other hand, the new status of commercial speech and the new emphasis on mandatory corrective remedies are properly to be viewed in tandem, then perhaps it is possible to argue that the newly imposed barrier to corrective response with respect to the editorial and news columns have likewise been somewhat oversold.[41] If corrective information by advertisers is imperative for the protection of commercial consumers, such corrective information may be equally necessary in politics for political consumers, the voters.

Of course, the emphasis on corrective remedies in the commercial advertising context is related to counteracting the damage done from false and misleading advertising. Truth or falsity is deemed to be more immediately subject to proof in the commercial product than it is in the political platform area. This is probably true. But the two new developments of protecting commercial advertising and affording corrective remedies serve another objective as well - increasing the information flow to the recipient, the commercial consumer. The need of the political consumer for information is just as critical.

After the Florida right of reply case, the Listerine result is somewhat startling. In the former case, freedom of the press was declared to be freedom on the part of publishers of any "compulsion to publish that which 'reason' tells them should not be published."[42] Should a publisher's freedom from compulsion to publish be absolute but an advertiser's freedom from any compulsion to speak be limited? Certainly a new trend in First Amendment thinking is to accord the freedom of the press component of that Amendment a fuller protection than that accorded to its freedom of speech component. The result of such an approach is to give the media, protected by the freedom of the press clause, more constitutional protection than that afforded the non-press or the public under the freedom of speech clause.

Judge Wright furnishes a hint in the Listerine case that, at least as far as he is concerned, a remedy of mandatory publication even as applied to the print media may still be lively despite the Florida right of reply case. In the Listerine case, Wright relied on a 1951[43] Supreme Court decision which upheld "a judgment that a newspaper publisher, in an effort to destroy a competing radio station, had unlawfully refused to accept advertising from anyone who advertised on radio."[44] Wright noted that the Supreme Court had approved a federal district court order which mandated an Ohio town's daily newspaper "to publish each week for 25 weeks a conspicuous notice apprising the public of the terms of the judgment."[45]

On the same point - whether mandatory publication is entirely impermissible in the print media as applied to the broadcast media - it should be noted that the court of appeals specifically approved the same compulsory affirmative disclosure in both media. Judge Wright noted that in print media ads the affirmative disclosure had to be set in type at least as large as the type in which the principal text of the ad appears. Further, it was required that the type should be separated from the text in order to make it immediately visible. As for the broadcast media, the FTC required that during the audio part of the compelled disclosure Listerine TV and radio ads, "no other words, including music, may appear." Judge Wright commented approvingly on these specifications as follows:[46] "These specifications are well calculated to assure that the disclosure will reach the public. It will necessarily attract the notice of readers, viewers, and listeners, and be plainly conveyed."

In short, the FTC specifically compelled the manufacture of Listerine to make the required disclosure in both the print media and the broadcast media. Expression, therefore, was "compelled" with respect to a matter that will appear in the print media. To be sure, it was the advertiser not "the press" which was the recipient of the compulsion.

Although the Supreme Court frequently professes allegiance to the *Tornillo* doctrine which views the First Amendment as a barrier to compelling publication by the private press of that which it chooses not to print, the Court has very recently indicated approval of compelling expression. This approval, it should be emphasized, was noted in a public issue, rather than an advertising context.

In *Central Hudson v. Public Service Commission*,[47] the Supreme Court held that a New York Public Service Commission regulation which completely bars an electric utility from advertising to promote the use of electricity violates the First and Fourteenth amendments. The New York Court of Appeals held that governmental interest in prohibiting promotional advertising encouraging use of energy which would only intensify the present energy shortage was outweighed by the limited protected status of the commercial speech in question - advertising promoting the use of electricity. The Supreme Court reversed. In *Central Hudson*, the Court, per Mr. Justice Powell, observed that the New York Public Service Commission had not shown that something less than a total ban on advertising promoting consumption of energy would not have been sufficient to protect the governmental interest in conservation of energy. The Court suggested that the Commission could have attempted to regulate the format and content of the public utility's advertising. Mr. Justice Powell observed: "It [the New York Public Service Commission] might, for example, require that the advertisements include information about the relative efficiency and expense of the offered service, both under current conditions and for the foreseeable future."[48] Justice Powell stated that absent a showing that some measure of regulation falling considerably short of a total ban on advertising promoting use of electricity, the court cannot "approve the complete suppression of Central Hudson's advertising."[49] The suggestion here appears to be that the Public Service Commission might validly have mandated the inclusion of certain kinds of information in its advertisements disseminated by the Central Hudson Gas and Electricity Company. Mandating expression - at least in an advertising context - in the interest of information does not seem to be categorically forbidden by the First Amendment. Indeed, the suggestion in *Central Hudson* is that such a mandate would be entirely permissible.

The commercial advertising cases in general, and the Listerine case in particular, demonstrate that the recipient or consumer interest in information must be weighed along with the disseminator's interest in that information. The Listerine case is a situation where both the members of the consuming public and the advertiser were able to assert First Amendment claims. In the Listerine case, the state, desiring to provide necessary information for the consumer, afforded the consumer a remedy which, the advertiser contended, infringed his freedom of expression. The advertiser's interest in uninhibited expression was subordinated to that of the consumer's interest in full and accurate information. The process of weighing competing First Amendment interests exhibited in the Listerine case demonstrates a process which is increasingly absent where one of the First Amendment claims is a media or editorial autonomy claim. However, the arguments used in the Listerine case on behalf of the commercial consumer are no less vital when the claim of a political consumer is involved.

In those conflicts where each adversary has a First Amendment claim, some attention must be accorded to the power relationships of the parties. Similarly, the technology of the medium involved must be taken into account. Finally, the impact on the information process of the community which subordinating one First Amendment claim and preferring another will yield must be frankly and fairly assessed. The individual's interest in political information should receive as much encouragement from law as the individual's interest in commercial information is now getting.

If such a result was one of the consequences of the new commercial speech cases, the result would be a paradox. The new commercial speech cases brought the marketplace of ideas to the marketplace. It would only be fair if the mechanism for a true marketplace of ideas were first developed there.

RIGHTS OF ACCESS FOR AND RESPONSE TO PRINT MEDIA ADVERTISING: AN OVERVIEW

Despite its nominal burial, the distinction between commercial and non-commercial speech should prove enduring for at least three reasons. First, if the Florida right of reply case is read as applying only to the news and editorial columns but not to the advertising columns, then the possibility of constitutional recognition for a principle of non-discriminatory access to advertising is at least tenable. Second, the new constitutional status for commercial speech, grounded as it is in the consumer interest in communication, should aid the development of a First Amendment-based non-discriminatory right of access to print media advertising. Third, as we have seen, some of the language in the new commercial speech cases may be used to support the construction of a right of response to print media advertising. Recourse to either a right of access to advertising or a right of reply to advertising would, of course, be dependent on first designating the content of the material in question as commercial speech.

Some conclusions from the foregoing analysis are in order. Where public media are concerned, such as the car card space of a municipally owned rapid transit company, political speech in the form of political advertising must be viewed as protected speech under the First Amendment and the claims of such speech must be resolved by a principle of non-discriminatory access. One obvious route by which this result can be reached is by relying on the revolution in the judicial treatment of commercial speech. Under this approach, it can be argued that commercial advertisements, whether they propose a commercial transaction or whether they are entirely political in content, have reached a new measure of constitutional protection and cannot be banned as a class by the state, at least in a public place where use as a public forum is not inconsistent with its primary purpose. Under such an analysis, it would be possible for political advertising to make a generic, if not a specific, claim for public access.

Recent cases have continued to look with disfavor on prohibitions against entire categories of expression. In *Consolidated Edison* v. *Public Service Commission*,[50] the Supreme Court held that the First and Fourteenth Amendments were violated by a New York Public Service Commission ban on the use of "message" inserts accompanying electric utility bills. The inserts promoted the use of nuclear power as a way for the country to achieve energy independence. Speaking for the Court, Mr. Justice Powell made it clear that the First Amendment forbade the "prohibition of public discussion of an entire topic."[51]

The new First Amendment stature of commercial speech may yet bring new life to more populist conceptions of First Amendment theory. If a principle of non-discriminatory access to public media still endures, if no class of speech may be totally banned by the state, then the claims of political advertisers for access to public facilities have obtained a new vitality. The new thinking in the Supreme Court about commercial speech is at least in language, if not in heart, consumer-oriented. For once it is not the editor who is the addressee of the Court's First Amendment concern, but rather the recipient. The consumer is deemed to need to know the price of prescription drugs. A state prohibition on the communication of price information about prescription drugs is thus perceived as an affront to the consumer interest in information. This interest in commercial information, we are told, is now protected by the First Amendment. If a category of consumer advertising information such as the prices of prescription advertising cannot now be banned totally by the state, surely it should be more difficult than previously to argue that a category of advertising information such as political advertising can be banned as advertising.

This distillation of various principles from recent First Amendment case law suggests some guiding ideas for the contemporary status of a First Amendment-based right of non-discriminatory access for commercial advertising to the private press. The true spawning ground of editorial freedom, it may be argued, is by definition the news and editorial columns of the newspaper. In that particular terrain, therefore, it can more easily be argued that the claims of the public at large must be subordinated to the claims of the editor and the journalist. In the more open sections of the paper, such as the advertising columns, the competing interests of editorial autonomy and discretion appear less weighty when measured against the claims of the proponents and consumers of information. The greater hardihood of the content involved, the fact that a financial incentive stands to guarantee its appearance, may justify corrective measures for abuse. In other words, the porno exhibitor may have a right to buy an ad but the Legion of Decency or another exhibitor may have a right to buy space to disparage the porno exhibitor's product. The theory of the commercial speech cases is that there is no danger that the possibility of reply will intimidate the expression of advertising to the point advertising would prefer to remain silent. In this view, the commercial nature of the product to be advertised assures its toughness and its probable survival.

The claim of editorial autonomy merits careful scrutiny rather than the dutiful homage it so often receives. How can a newspaper publisher be held free from any duty imposed by the state to voice what another person believes while an advertiser may be compelled by the state to make "corrective" statements about his product which in all good faith he simply does not believe? To some extent, of course, the answer lies in the different contexts in which these problems arise. In one situation, political controversy is at stake. In another, the truth or falsity of commercial advertising is at issue. That does not entirely explain the difference in result. Partially, the result manifests a radical change in our constitutionalism in which the success of those who make identical First Amendment claims is increasingly dependent on their status. The blunt truth is that in our society, the individual who can claim a press card may be able to secure a larger measure of First Amendment protection than the individual or organization who cannot.[52] In short, the claim of editorial autonomy is essentially one of special status and special protection.

These developments mark a curious turn on the long road which began in 1964 in *New York Times* v. *Sullivan,* where in the interests of free expression, new limitations were placed on the law of libel in order to encourage the citizen critics of government. In the years since, we seem to be exchanging the more inclusive protection which was extended to "citizen critics," with all the individualistic flavor that term was properly meant to suggest, for a far more exclusive concept of protection which is increasingly limited to the press alone.[53]

It might be answered that in the case of editors and publishers, the corrective remedies are too often directed to matters of political content. The assumption appears to be that political speech is more fragile than commercial speech and, therefore, too much concern for verification or rebuttal in that context will chill the entire category of speech. Is this really true? In the new public law of libel generated by the *New York Times*

v. *Sullivan*[54] case, one reason it has been made more difficult for public personalities to sue for libel is that the court has been willing to assume that by office or notoriety they have waived or forfeited some of their rights to use the libel law by entering the public arena. Little concern has been expressed over the point that reducing the opportunities to use the libel law to vindicate reputation may limit the supply, or, worse, the quality of those who seek either political office or who may wish to take positions in the public life of ideas.

The source of the idea that political speech is more fragile than commercial speech is intimately related to the question of who is protected under the First Amendment. An example is found in the line of First Amendment libel cases which commenced with *New York Times* v. *Sullivan*. In those cases, editors, publishers, and journalists in general were members of the press and have been accorded a new measure of protection. It is now far more difficult as a result of the *Times* case and its offspring for public personalities to sue the press for libel. By the same token, political and public actors receive considerably less in the way of First Amendment protection.

In saying this, I do not refer to the fact that the capacity of such persons to vindicate their reputations is now diminished although, of course, that is true. I refer instead to the point that limiting one's ability to defend one's reputation effectively may chill willingness to speak or write on unpopular and controversial matters. Although concern over a chilling effect on the press has generated the most absolutist claims for editorial autonomy, the same concern is not often expressed for a chilling effect on other sectors of society.

Focus has been principally directed to the argument that the editor and publisher merit greater protection because if they are not afforded such protection, controversial expression on their part will be avoided. Surely this is, as yet, empirically an unverified proposition. As such, it is entirely too doubtful a theorem upon which to base important distinctions in terms of basic rights. If a justification for the difference in result between the Listerine case and the Florida right of reply case is sought along these lines, the following, admittedly satiric, summary of the law is suggested: advertisers will still advertise even if they must occasionally promulgate rebuttals to their own ads. Greed, it is assumed, will assure the future of advertising. But editors cannot be depended on to continue to editorialize if they must occasionally give space to a rebuttal. Their fear of a state-ordered reply is so great that they will retreat into silence. To attribute such timidity to media which include among their properties the greatest metropolitan dailies in the land would be absurd if the doctrine of the greater fragility of political speech were not as entrenched as it now is.

In a century which has seen millions die in the name of one political ideology or another, in an era where political precept has been approached as those in former times treated religious dogma, it is odd indeed to hear political expression called "fragile" and commercial speech called "hardy." Commercial speech is not deemed to be too weak for mandatory counter-argument. Indeed, the spokesmen for commercial speech are considered to be appropriate as vehicles for rebuttals to their own products. It is hard to see why editors alone should merit a status so sacred that they only should decide when a reply to their truths is in order.

In one of the most influential of First Amendment essays, Alexander Meiklejohn argued for absolute protection for political speech but only a reasonable measure of protection for other forms of speech.[55] To some, this present status of our law will be seen as conforming to this prescription. In my opinion, it does not. Contemporary First Amendment law is pursuing a different path. By identifying First Amendment freedom with absolute media freedom, the case for effectively voicing political ideas in the dominant media of expression as a matter of right is automatically lost.

The difference in result between the Florida right of reply case and the Listerine case turns the Meiklejohn approach to the First Amendment on its head. Presenting the consumer with commercial information is deemed so important that an advertiser may be compelled against his will to speak against his own advertisement. Political information, on the other hand, is deemed so fragile, and any state directive with regard to it so inherently menacing, that an editor cannot be compelled to give his opponent a reply. Moreover, as between the information rights of the reader to read the reply and the editor's claim of untrammeled autonomy, the editor must prevail. Such an approach is to assume that people care more about receiving full information about the commodities they purchase than about the direction and structure of the society in which they live. Perhaps such a harsh judgment is merited, but it is unfortunate that First Amendment theory should have been commandeered to play a part in making such a judgment a reality.

The rise of a new protected status for commercial advertising at the same time that mandatory corrective relief with respect to such advertising has also been deemed to serve First Amendment ends is bound to affect other First Amendment problems as well. The new commercial speech cases considered in this chapter have on the whole not focused on clashes between claims of individual expression or claims of consumer need for information against claims of editorial autonomy. On the whole, the cases involved either situations where the state banned an entire class of advertising or wished to protect the consumer by requiring the advertiser to provide him with information the advertiser was unwilling to convey. In either of the latter two situations, the media themselves were not required to publish against their will as was the advertiser in the Listerine case.

The problem of compulsory publication is what Mr. Justice Frankfurter used to call a non-Euclidean problem. Access to the press is not a problem which absolute theorems are likely to be able to resolve usefully. Just as an advertiser's claim of free expression merits careful consideration but not absolute acceptance, so claims for editorial autonomy merit the most serious consideration. It is in no one's interest that such claims receive an immediate and ritualistic type of absolute acceptance.

From an individualistic perspective, the full weight of First Amendment protection is now shifting from the political to the commercial sector. Whether a theory of First Amendment protection will ever shift to an individualistic dimension with respect to political speech is a question for the future. Nevertheless, the new commercial speech cases have already had an important impact. They have focused attention on the fact that the First Amendment protects individual consumers and readers and that its sole purpose is not to protect a single guild or industry. The present focus of the Court is on the individual interest in commercial information, but it is doubtful whether such a concern with providing the individual with information can stop with commercial information. In short, a First Amendment perspective which is directed to the citizen's need for full and accurate information cannot help but hasten the re-emergence of the irrepressible question of access.

Notes

1. See Schmidt, *Freedom of the Press* v. *Public Access,* 248-9 (1976). Professor Schmidt suggests that a "narrow contingent access statute" directed to anticompetitive refusals to deal that "would not impinge upon legitimate publisher autonomy" would be valid. But he expresses doubt about "the constitutionality of a similar access obligation aimed at political ads." Schmidt seems to support the view that access obligations for political ads would be unconstitutional on the ground that refusal of a political ad is "central to the autonomy of the press under the First Amendment." This position appears to be unnecessarily restrictive of public rights to political information. If the legislature were to command the editor to "prefer one political candidate to another," then perhaps press autonomy would be restricted in a First Amendment sense. But a requirement of fair treatment in a section of the paper which is by definition open to the public for a price, that is, the advertising columns, is surely in a different category.

In a monopoly newspaper situation where by definition it is not possible to have recourse to alternative sources for newspaper space, the case for increasing political advertising in a right of access would be particularly strong. Antitrust policy, sound trade regulation policy, and First Amendment concern for diversity all support strong arguments for applying access obligations to political advertising as well as commercial advertising. In addition, in fairness to Professor Schmidt it should be said that a new trend has appeared in First Amendment law since he wrote - the advent of a new First Amendment status for commercial speech. Oddly enough, this new development means that commercial speech has now outpaced political speech in terms of its First Amendment status.

2. 316 U.S. 52 (1942).
3. Id. at 54.
4. Id. at 55.
5. 418 U.S. 298 (1974).
6. See Erznoznik v. Jacksonville, 422 U.S. 205 (1975).
7. Packer v. Utah, 285 U.S. 105, 110 (1932), quoted in Lehman v. City of Shaker Heights, note 5, supra, at 302.
8. Lehman v. City of Shaker Heights, note 5, supra, at 302.
9. See Mississippi Gay Alliance v. Goudelock, 536 F. 2d 1073 at 1083 (5th Cir. 1976). See discussion of this case in Chap. 4, pp. 41-51.
10. Virginia State Board of Pharmacy v. Virginia Citizens Consumer Council, Inc., 425 U.S. 748 (1976).
11. Lehman v. City of Shaker Heights, note 5, supra, at 303.
12. Bates v. State of Arizona, 433 U.S. 350 (1977).
13. Id. at 364.
14. Florida Election Code, F.S. 104.38.
15. 418 U.S. 241 (1974).
16. Note 12, Bates v. State of Arizona, supra, at 364.
17. 421 U.S. 809 (1975).
18. Id. at 822.
19. Central Hudson v. Public Services Commission, 100 S.Ct. 2343 at 2364 (1980) (dissenting opinion of Mr Justice Rehnquist).
20. See Pittsburgh Press Co. v. Pittsburgh Commission on Human Relations, 413 U.S. 376 (1973).
21. See generally A. Kent MacDougall's thoroughgoing review of new developments to a new unwillingness to accept newspaper decisions refusing to sell space and time to advertisers. MacDougall, " 'Censorship'?: Advertising New Arena of Rights Battle," Los Angeles Times, Oct. 24, 1977.
22. See Virginia Pharmacy, note 10, supra, at fn. 24, p. 772.
23. See Bates v. State of Arizona, note 12, supra, at 383.
24. Id. at 384.
25. Feil v. FTC, 285 F.2d 879, 897 (9th Cir. 1960), cited in Bates v. State of Arizona, note 12, supra, at 383 fn. 37.
26. Feil v. FTC, note 21, supra.
27. Warner-Lambert v. Federal Trade Commission, 562 F.2d 749 (D.C. Cir. 1977).
28. Id. at 758. This point was argued by counsel for Amici, the Association of National Advertisers, Inc., and the American Advertising Federation.

29. *Id.* quoting *Virginia State Board of Pharmacy* v. *Virginia Citizens Consumer Council, Inc.,* 425 U.S. 748 at 771-2 n. 24 (1976).
30. *Id.* at 759.
31. See *Warner-Lambert* v. *Federal Trade Commission, cert. denied.* 435 U.S. 950 (1978).
32. See *Warner-Lambert Company* v. *Federal Trade Commission, Petition for Rehearing and Suggestion for Rehearing en Banc,* Civil Action No. 76-1138, filed Aug. 16, 1977, in the United States Court of Appeals for the District of Columbia, p. 2.
33. *Id.* at p. 5.
34 *Id.* Warner-Lambert made particular reference to a recent antitrust decision where the appeals court held that a lower court decree which ordered an organization of professional engineers to "state affirmatively that it does not consider competitive bidding to be unethical" was invalidly overbroad. See *United States* v. *National Society of Professional Engineers,* 555 F. 2d 978 at 984 (1977). Judge Leventhal observed for the court: "To force an association of individuals to express as its own opinion judicially dictated ideas is to encroach on that sphere of free thought and expression protected by the First Amendment."
This quotation, by itself, might indicate that no speaker or group of speakers would be forced to express views they did not share. However, its doctrine is far less thoroughgoing than it sounds because Judge Leventhal did approve that portion of the lower court arbitration order which prevented the Society of Professional Engineers from adopting any policy statement which described price competition as "unethical." In this view, consistent with the First Amendment, in order to implement the objectives of antitrust policy, an organization can be compelled to submit to a judicial dictate not to express a point of view it would like to express. To deny a speech which the speaker would like to make is, in this view, apparently less grievous than to compel speech which the speaker disbelieves. Similarly, Leventhal in the *Engineers* case thought it permissible for the federal court to require the Society of Professional Engineers "to publish an advice that its prior ruling has been rescinded in light of the court's decree that it was an unlawful interference with a legal right of the engineer, protected under the antitrust laws, to provide price information to a prospective client in advance of retainer." The Court of Appeals decision was affirmed. See *National Society of Professional Engineers* v. *U.S.,* 98 S. Ct. 1355 (1978).
35. *Warner-Lambert Company* v. *Federal Trade Commission,* 562 F.2d 768 (D.C. Cir. 1977).
36. *Warner-Lambert Company* v. *Federal Trade Commission.* Note 35, supra, at 769.
37. *Id.*
38. *Id.*
39. *Id.* quoting *Virginia Pharmacy,* note 10, *supra,* at 771-2 n. 24.
40. *Id.*
41. CF. *Miami Herald Publishing Co.* v. *Tornillo,* note 15, *supra.*
42. *Miami Herald Publishing Co.* v. *Tornillo,* note 13, *supra,* at 256.

43. See *Lorain Journal Co.* v. *United States*, 342 U.S. 143 (1951) discussed in *Warner-Lambert* v. *Federal Trade Commission*, note 27, *supra*, at 761 n. 60.
44. *Id.*
45. *Id.*
46. *Warner-Lambert Co.* v. *Federal Trade Commission*, note 24, *supra*, at 763.
47. *Central Hudson Gas & Electric Co.*, 100 S. Ct. 2343 (1980).
48. *Id.* at 2354.
49. *Id.*
50. 100 S. Ct. 2326 (1980).
51. *Id.* at 2333. The regulation of the New York Public Service Commission did not "fall within the narrow exceptions to the general prohibition against subject-matter distinctions." *Id. Lehman* v. *Shaker Heights*, note 5, *supra*, was specifically distinguished. In *Lehman*, a private party had sought a right of access to a publicly-owned facility. Consolidated Edison, on the other hand, was trying to use "its own billing envelopes to promulgate its views on controversial issues of public policy." *Id.* at 2334. The Court distinguished Harry Lehman's wish to use the car cards in Shaker Heights with Consolidated Edison's wishes to use its own billing envelopes: "But the Commission's attempt to restrict the free expression of a private party cannot be upheld by reliance upon precedent that rests on the special interests of a government in overseeing the use of its property." *Id.*

A challenging question might be asked about the *Consolidated Edison* case. Suppose the New York Public Service Commission had not banned the "message" inserts but instead required that the "inserts" could be distributed only if they allocated equivalent space to an opposing point of view? If an electric utility is so extensively regulated to have its action deemed quasi-governmental, such a requirement might be constitutional. On the other hand, if the action of the utility is not deemed "state action" in this context, then compelling expression on private property would probably, on *Tornillo* principles, be deemed constitutionally impermissible.

52. Mr. Justice Stewart delivered a lecture at the Yale Law School in which he argued that the First Amendment is designed to accord special protection to the press as an industry. See Stewart, 26 Hastings L.J. 633-4 (1975).

53. The theory of this new distinction appears to be predicated on the view that the press is the most effective check on abuse by government, and the checking of abuse by government is, or should be understood, as the primary function of this position, see Blasi, *The Checking Value in First Amendment Theory*, 3 American Bar Foundation Research Journal 523 (1977).

54. 376 U.S. 254 (1964).

55. See generally Meiklejohn, *Free Speech and Its Relation to Self-Government* (1960).

8

How Fair Should Investigative Television Be?: Appraising the Alternatives

Should a hard-hitting documentary on television be regarded as a one-sided editorial or as hard-hitting reporting? Should the fairness doctrine be applied to investigate journalism on television? These are enduring questions for contemporary television.

There are at least five approaches to the problem of investigative journalism on television. The first approach would be to hold that the fairness doctrine should be abolished in general and that investigative journalism, in particular, should be liberated from its confining strictures. In this view, the uninhibited exercise of investigative journalism by broadcasters with no duty to provide time for counterattack is the very definition of freedom of the press.

The second approach is to apply the fairness doctrine to investigative journalism and to require specific provision of response time for viewpoints opposed to that taken by the program in issue.

The third approach is to apply the fairness doctrine to investigative journalism, enforcing it not by a right of response but through the license renewal process. If a particular program is part of a pattern of imbalances, distortion, or propagandizing through documentaries, a public interest violation will be revealed sufficient to justify a conclusion that the licensee should not have his license renewed.

The fourth approach would be to hold that the fairness doctrine does not embrace investigative journalism. However, at this point the resemblance to the first approach ends. The fourth approach would attempt to meet problems of imbalance and need for reply through some provision for securing entry to television through a scheme of paid access.

The fifth approach would be to hold not only that the fairness doctrine embraces investigative journalism but that it mandates fairness in each documentary. Under this approach, if the network takes an avowed editorial position, such editorializing is entirely permissible and fairness doctrine obligations then attach. If the program is not a candid piece of editorializing but is an attempt to make a presentation of a controversial issue then such a presentation must be fair or balanced.

THE FIRST APPROACH: ABSOLUTE AUTONOMY

The first approach obviously has some advantages. Government is not involved in any role of content oversight whether that role involves an *in gross* oversight or whether it involves a minute content analysis of a particular program. The abiding defect of the first approach is that removing government efforts to require some fairness in television documentaries does not confer freedom of expression on the people. Similarly, this approach does not even endow the individual broadcast licensees with editorial freedom. The overwhelming bulk of such documentaries or investigative shows are produced by network television. Rhetorically, exempting documentaries from the fairness doctrine is the liberation of television from government. The abandonment of a minimal governmental role here results in endowing the heads of the three major network news departments with absolute editorial discretion. Editorial freedom is, of course, a fundamental First Amendment precept. Would we celebrate that freedom if there were only one editor? If there are just three editors, how much cause is there for additional celebration?

The choice is not between governmental oversight and editorial freedom. It is between the present system of minimal public oversight as opposed to no oversight over what network executives choose to do. In short, the first approach is attractive if we examine it in the rhetorical posture in which it is usually presented - a quarrel between two abstractions: journalistic freedom and governmental intervention. If we analyze the controversy in terms of the actual protagonists, we see it is a far different kind of battle: a minimal claim for accountability and fairness as opposed to untrammeled corporate power.

THE SECOND APPROACH: A RIGHT OF SPECIFIC RESPONSE

It is the second approach which really was at the heart of one of the more celebrated investigative journalism cases on television, the *Pensions* case.[1] On September 12, 1972, NBC broadcast a documentary, "Pensions: The Broken Promise." Although NBC newsman Edwin Newman did say on the show that not all pension plans were bad, over all, the program was a tough statement to the effect that the promise of pension plans had proved to be a sham for American workers. Richard Solomon, a Los Angeles actuary, objected to the program on the ground that the number of pension plans which had in fact failed to deliver was infinitesimal.

Solomon alerted Accuracy in Media, which filed a complaint with the FCC that NBC's pension show had violated the fairness doctrine. The FCC agreed. The FCC ruled that the sheer volume of the anti-pension statements merited the presentation of an opposing viewpoint on pension plans.[2]

Two years after the broadcast, a panel of the federal court of appeals in Washington, DC, reversed the FCC. The court stayed the FCC order that further opportunity for reply should be granted the pro-pension plan point of view. The panel declared that the editorial judgment of the broadcaster, if reasonable and made in good faith, should be maintained in fairness cases. The fact that the FCC would have reached a different editorial judgment itself could not justify a conclusion that the fairness doctrine was violated.

Then the court of appeals agreed to hear the case *en banc*, but the FCC filed a suggestion of mootness with the court of appeals on the ground that with the enactment of new pension legislation, the Employment Retirement Security Act of 1974, the case had become moot. Ultimately, the case was remanded to the FCC on the ground of mootness. All hope of obtaining a groundbreaking decision on whether the fairness doctrine applied to investigative journalism ended on April 19, 1976, when the Supreme Court refused to review the case.[3] Thus the *Pensions* case came to an end.

NBC could easily have given some response time to defend "good" working pension plans. Allocating some time on NBC's "Today" show for an opposing viewpoint would have been a painless way of providing program balance on the merits of private pension plans. But NBC chose to litigate. Perhaps, at a minimum, it hoped that litigating would persuade a court to rule that investigative journalism was not covered by the fairness doctrine. Perhaps NBC hoped that, at best, the court would accept the challenge presented by the network and rule that the fairness doctrine was entirely unconstitutional.

How could the network expect that the fairness doctrine would be declared unconstitutional after the Supreme Court had unanimously upheld it in *Red Lion* in 1969[4] and reaffirmed it, at least in passing, in the *CBS* case in 1973?[5] Two lines of distinction are possible. Each hinges on whether the fairness doctrine, upheld in *Red Lion*, should require a right of specific response to a particular program. *Red Lion*, it will be remembered, dealt on its facts with the personal attack rules, a fairness doctrine offshoot. On its facts, *Red Lion* stood for the validity of requiring a right of reply in broadcasting to a personal attack. Does *Red Lion* also embrace a right of issue response? Or to put it another way, if a particular side of an issue was presented, or advocated, in the course of a documentary, did the opposite of that position have to be provided? Is there a right of specific issue response?

Like so many media issues, the matter was curiously open. In the *CBS* case, the Supreme Court had refused to rule that the First Amendment required a general right of access to purchase time for editorial advertising. One line of reasoning behind the Court's decision in *CBS* was that diversity of opinion did not require such a ruling since the fairness doctrine served that end. But did the fairness doctrine require a balanced presentation overall of controversial issues of public importance? Or did it merely require a balanced presentation of each issue that broadcasting chose to cover? From the network point of view, a specific right of response had a dampening effect on investigative journalism. Rather than be compelled to provide time that certainly would otherwise not be made available to outsiders, the network might decide to avoid investigative journalism altogether. In the view of the network, the second approach, which the FCC itself followed in the *Pensions* case, was the approach which, quintessentially, violated the First Amendment. Is a network the owner's plaything? What is the line between journalism and propaganda? Is the unfettered dissemination by the network of propaganda the necessary consequence of First Amendment freedom? If so, this is a difficult and troubling conclusion to accept. If propaganda or even skillfully presented opinion has no counterpoise, do we have a true marketplace of ideas? Instead of a marketplace of ideas about pension plans we have a single stall, the NBC stall.

THE THIRD APPROACH: ENFORCING THE FAIRNESS DOCTRINE THROUGH THE LICENSE RENEWAL PROCESS

The third approach is the idea that one should resolve problems of propagandizing, imbalance, or unfairness in investigative journalism exclusively through the license renewal process. In this view, an overall assessment of whether a licensee has been "fair" at renewal time does the least violence to First Amendment concerns because you are not examining any specific program but merely asking one question: in a three-year period, did this licensee's programming provide a sufficiently balanced presentation of controversial issues of public importance so that one can say the licensee operated in the public interest? The very largeness of the question is deemed sufficient to redeem the inquiry from being mired in the considerations of specific programs. As a result, such an inquiry is, arguably, free from the taint of a specific content analysis which would violate the First Amendment.

Henry Geller's proposal rejecting a program-by-program assessment of fairness doctrine compliance and its associated remedy of providing a subsequent opportunity for response was commended by the court in the *Pensions* case as worthy of FCC consideration. The court did not require such an approach to fairness doctrine enforcement in that case. The FCC did reject the proposal in its *Fairness Report*. When that report was placed squarely before the federal court of appeals for review in 1977, the court ruled that the FCC had not erred in not adopting the Geller proposal: "We therefore conclude that the Commission is neither constitutionally nor statutorily *required* to return to its pre-1962 method of fairness doctrine enforcement."[6]

Of course, the fact that the FCC is not compelled to limit the fairness doctrine to the renewal context does not mean that it is not free to do so in the future. Similarly, Congress, at some future time, could direct the FCC to take such an approach. Also, it is clear that the Geller proposal struck some responsive chords in the first judicial panel which heard the *Pensions* case. Conversely, it is probably significant that the panel that reviewed the *Fairness Report*, consisting of Judges McGowan, Tamm, and Wright, is less likely to automatically genuflect at a broadcaster's assertions of First Amendment violation. However, the Geller idea that specific enforcement of the fairness doctrine on a program-by-program basis be abandoned is likely to prove a durable platform for fairness doctrine critics and thus the idea merits serious analysis.

It is a paradox that this third approach, the Geller approach, is defended as doing the least violence to First Amendment standards since it depends on a sanction which silences an offender forever. The second approach merely mandates a right of specific response to a specific issue. The broadcaster, under this approach, is still in business. The third approach, which would enforce the fairness doctrine exclusively through the license renewal process, uses the sanction the industry has for years, with good cause, called the "death penalty" - the sanction of denial of license renewal. The trouble with this sanction is that if it is taken seriously it has unnecessary overkill. The remedy for unfairness on television is fairness, not murder. Enforcing the fairness doctrine through the sanction of refusing to grant license renewal is literally murder: it destroys the broadcaster.

Oddly enough, the other defect of the third approach is that it may be too mild. Henry Geller, principal exponent of limiting fairness to the renewal context, says frankly that even if a large file of fairness complaints has been compiled against a broadcaster the station's renewal will not be in jeopardy:[7] "The FCC would not be concerned with having contrasting views broadcast on some issue years later, but rather with determining whether a flagrant pattern of violation is indicated - the *New York Times* v. *Sullivan* standard noted above. No conscientious broadcaster need fear review with a standard so heavily weighted in his favor." By referring to the *New York Times* v. *Sullivan* standard, presumably what Geller means is that by analogy to the public standard law of libel, there should be no liability unless it can be shown that the broadcaster's programming has been presented over a three-year period in reckless disregard of whether the programming is in compliance with the fairness doctrine. As thus candidly described, using the renewal context as the exclusive means of fairness doctrine enforcement is unlikely to be a realistic incentive for fairness doctrine compliance. Moreover, as Henry Geller is again frank to concede, such an approach itself would not be directed to requiring the presentation of opposing viewpoints.

The danger with making the only sanction for fairness compliance denial of the license renewal application is that it is likely to be deemed so drastic by the FCC that it will never be used. If the license renewal process is to be the only vehicle for enforcement of the fairness doctrine and that process is in fact never used to deny a licensee renewal for fairness doctrine violations, then the fairness doctrine will be rendered a mere hortatory command devoid of force or importance.

There is still another defect with attempting to enforce the fairness doctrine solely through the license renewal process. In terms of a major mission of the fairness doctrine, the encouragement of a vigorous and fair debate among opposing viewpoints, reliance on the renewal process is incapable of furnishing any immediacy or assistance to the struggle of competing ideas. It would take three years before a licensee would be told with any force that there was any defect in its overall presentation of controversial issues.

In 1977, when the court of appeals ruled that the FCC in its *Fairness Report* proceeding had not erred in not adopting what I have labeled the third approach, the Court repeated, with apparent approval, the FCC's concern that "the proposed renewal assessment could not be made without inquiring into individual complaints, inquiries which often are made on the basis of stale records."[8] The Court, citing the *Fairness Report*,[9] stated that it agreed with the FCC that limiting appraisal of fairness doctrine compliance to the renewal process context "would deny the Commission the ability "to remedy violations before a flagrant pattern of abuse develops".[10]

A particular exercise in distortion, slanting, or biased presentation of a particular issue would never be able to be immediately corrected by a listener or viewer on complaint to the FCC. Immediate correction could come only if a licensee himself felt that he had been overzealous in the presentation of a particular issue on a program. In such circumstances, in order to ward off an attack at license renewal time on a fairness ground, a licensee might conclude that some right of response to an opposing viewpoint was in order. To build hopes of encouraging responses to one-sided presentation of issues on broadcasting on expectations that broadcasters on their own will search out opposing viewpoints is, in my view, unrealistic.

Former CBS newsman Fred Friendly, on the other hand, has contended forcefully that efforts by broadcasters rather than government to secure rebuttal and counter-speech are both possible and preferable.

Television critics have consistently and rightly stressed the need for the development of rebuttals to television. Former FCC Commissioner Nicholas Johnson wrote a book on the subject significantly titled *How to Talk Back to Your Television Set*. Friendly suggests that the time has arrived for "an Op-Ed page of the Air."[11] The mechanism for such a page is not outlined in detail. Assuming that the networks would be willing to make the allocation of time for such a venture that would make it meaningful, can such ventures be relied on as an adequate substitute for the fairness doctrine? Friendly is right when he highlights what broadcast journalists must do to make such a project work. There must be a significant allocation of broadcast time as well as a commitment to a "search for eloquent, effective, diverse voices of dissent, capable of holding the attention of broadcast audiences."[12] Finally, broadcast journalists must be sensitive to the fact that no op-ed page of the air can work unless broadcasters refrain from trying to have the last word.

Rebuttal techniques that are in the custody of broadcasters are attractive from the point of view of minimizing government interference with broadcast journalism. Such an approach is entirely faithful to the concept, increasingly asserted by broadcast journalists, that programming decisions are editorial decisions and that the First Amendment extends to broadcasters absolute protection over editorial decision-making.

It is at this point where the solution of leaving rebuttal to television entirely in broadcast hands fails. It does a disservice to the frank recognition of the tension in our First Amendment theory between media rights and public rights to attempt to pretend conflict can be resolved at the altar of editorial autonomy. Such an approach resolves the controversy entirely in favor of media rights. The fairness doctrine imposes some public obligations on the media. Its very existence is a challenge to the inviolability of editorial autonomy and it is precisely on that level that the fairness doctrine should be defended. The broadcast networks are too powerful and too closed a world for the public to be satisfied with their view of diversity and dissent. Other agencies for accountability must of necessity be used. For example, in the *Pensions* case, NBC tried to defend fairness or the balance of its *Pensions* show by preparing an exhibit of the comments on the program of twenty-five newspaper TV critics in order to show what various media thought the show was really about.[13] On the whole, the media critics thought the show was effective and commendable. But actuary Richard Solomon, who had experience with pension plans and AIM, a conservative media citizen group with values different from those of NBC, disagreed. The point is not that the media critics who agreed with NBC were wrong or that AIM was right. The point is that public rights cannot be left for protection to those who work in and write about the media.

THE FOURTH APPROACH: PAID ACCESS AS AN ALTERNATIVE TO ROBUST, UNINHIBITED INVESTIGATIVE JOURNALISM

The fourth approach to the problem of fairness doctrine and investigative journalism is that the fairness doctrine should not be applied at all to investigative journalism. Unlike the first approach, this alternative would try to deal with the problem of imbalance in investigative journalism by requiring some mandatory corrective relief to be imposed governmentally. The gist of this approach is that relief should proceed by way of access rather than the fairness doctrine.

In the CBS case, the Supreme Court refused to rule that the First Amendment required as a general proposition that the networks could not have a policy of refusing to sell any time for the presentation of particular viewpoints. On the other hand, the assumption of the fourth approach is that the fairness doctrine would not apply to investigative journalism. The assumption of the Court in CBS is that the balanced discussion of ideas on television does not require a First Amendment-based right of access since an administrative law doctrine of fairness at present performs the same function. The fairness doctrine has the additional grace (perhaps saving grace) of leaving the choice of spokesman and the selection of issues which merit response for an opposing viewpoint to the broadcaster. If investigative journalism were specifically exempted from the fairness doctrine, would the constitutional case for a First Amendment right of access to television be stronger? The Court's opinion in CBS does not answer this question, but it is clear that its decision does not betray any real affection for a constitutionally imposed, that is, judicially created, right of access. Yet the Court did say that if the FCC had mandated that the networks could not have a policy of refusing to sell time to outsiders for the presentation of editorial viewpoints it would have been a different case. Presumably, in such circumstances a right of access would have to be analyzed in terms of whether the language of the Federal Communications Act of 1934 was sufficiently broad to permit the FCC to forbid the network from excluding from television any presentation of ideas which do not originate with the network. In the CBS case, the Court refused to rule that, absent a specific FCC declaration of policy, the public interest standard prohibited the networks from imposing a ban on the sale of time for the presentation of ideas to outsiders, even if one of the "outsiders" was then the major political party in America, the Democratic party.

Furthermore, the fourth approach prompts another question. If the choice is between access and fairness in broadcasting, is access the preferable alternative? In CBS, Chief Justice Burger urged as an argument against recognition of a First Amendment-based right of access the problem that only the rich would be able to buy time on television. This prompted Nicholas Johnson's famous remark in the FCC determination of the *CBS* case that he thought that was the case already. However, if access is the only alternative, how can we be sure that when the opposing viewpoint to an investigative journalism effort is poorly financed, a response will actually surface? It is one of the merits of the fairness doctrine that it has been held both by the FCC and the Supreme Court that if the person personally attacked on broadcasting cannot afford time to respond, then free time must be made available. This approach has been utilized with respect to controversial issues as well. Illustrative is John Banzhaf's success in winning free time to argue against smoking when cigarette advertising was still a reality on television.[14]

If, with respect to a subject covered by investigative journalism, the only way to secure response is through the purchase of time, real debate about such issues may never occur. The fairness doctrine is more serviceable in this regard.

THE FIFTH APPROACH: MUST EACH DOCUMENTARY BE FAIR?

Must fairness in a television documentary be achieved within the confines of the documentary itself or should it be achieved through some follow-up programming? It will be recalled that the remedy afforded by the FCC in the *Pensions* case was a request that at some future time the opposing viewpoint should be given some opportunity for expression. Judge Tamm, on the other hand, who supported the FCC decision in the *Pensions* case, nevertheless suggested at one point that a balanced presentation of the controversial issue examined should be achieved within the documentary itself. In his first opinion in *Pensions* - a dissent - Tamm reasoned along the following lines: if a program is not labelled as an editorial, then it falls into a news report such as an "investigative or documentary report." Tamm argued that "in the presentation of a so-called investigative or documentary report I believe that there is a legally enforceable obligation on broadcasters to present a report in which all conflicting positions and viewpoints are fairly portrayed."[15] Tamm believes that investigative television journalism has a tendency to propagandize and that the fairness doctrine mandate of balance is a necessary corrective:[16] "The investigative reporter, regardless of his initial motivation, too often reaches a point where objectivity disappears and he becomes an ardent advocate for a particular point of view or position ... There is no doubt but that embellishment, color and opinion often prove to be more interesting than objective presentation of both sides of an issue of public interest but is such a discharge of the responsibility of the telecaster to give a fair picture and a presentation of all points of view?"

As has been earlier observed, Judge Tamm made these observations in his first opinion in the *Pensions* case and appears to have dropped the idea that fairness is required in each documentary by the time of his second opinion in that case. The second opinion does not refer again to that position. Whether Judge Tamm is or is not committed to such a position, consideration of the idea is useful since it impels some reflection on the nature and purpose of public issue programming such as television documentaries. Regardless of how much or little support there is at present for such a notion, does it make sense to require fairness in the presentation of each documentary? In the fracas over "The Selling of the Pentagon,"[17] CBS did in fact give time in later programming for spokesmen for Herbert and for the military. Should the producers of "The Selling of the Pentagon" have provided Herbert with his own time segment on that program to make use of as he wished?

The difficulty with trying to solve fairness problems in documentaries by insisting on fairness within a particular documentary itself is that it is probably a futile objective. If a news department of a network is sufficiently exercised about a social evil that it does a documentary to expose the evil, should the network be obliged to portray with equal force and flair the spokesmen and views of those identified with the very "social evil" being investigated? The debate that results from such efforts is likely to be stilted, and perhaps in the end, still one-sided. In the *Pensions* case the NBC staff itself spoke of the need to include "fairness filler" on the *Pensions* plan show. When the effort to secure balanced presentation is thought of as "fairness filler" by those who are entrusted with furnishing balance, there is not much basis for faith in the integrity of an effort to provide balanced presentation within the confines of a single documentary.

Providing fairness on an overall programming basis is open to some of the same objections that arise out of an effort to secure fairness within the documentary itself. The same audience that saw an NBC documentary at 10:00 p.m. may not see the rebuttal follow-up on the *Today* show at 8:00 a.m. a week later. Similarly, suppose CBS did give time to Congressman Hebert of Louisiana to defend the House Armed Services Committee and the Pentagon point of view? What match was an old Capital Hill warhorse like Congressman Hebert for the sleek network personnel who have had a whole documentary to themselves to present the opposite view? Moreover, the documentary to which Hebert responded maximized the whole range of technical capability that is quite justly associated with a group as experienced and sophisticated as CBS News. Congressman Hebert is no match in media charisma for Roger Mudd. The problems of the private person who is the representative of an opposing viewpoint who does not have whatever aura public office brings are even greater. Even at best, then, a rebuttal by a non-media personality television documentary is inherently unequal. The choice that is in issue is not between a perfect response to a particular presentation of an issue and no response. The choice is between some imperfect response or no response.

In my view, if we are to conclude that the fairness doctrine should apply to investigative journalism, it would appear that requiring a later programming opportunity for opposing viewpoints when a complaint is made about imbalance in a specific documentary is the preferable remedy. This approach provides a reasonable recourse for the complainant and at the same time is far less obstructive to investigative reporting. Enforcement of the fairness doctrine by providing a later opportunity for response still assures some fidelity to the doctrine's constitutionally-related premise: the encouragement of vigorous debate. If the widest access for controversial ideas is a public right, as the Supreme Court declared in *Red Lion*, assuring some direct redress to a complaint and some possibility of related opportunity for response appears to be sensible and sound.

INVESTIGATIVE JOURNALISM ON TELEVISION: SOME CONCLUSIONS

Why is the first alternative - no fairness doctrine and unfettered editorial discretion - not the best alternative?

"60 Minutes," widely acclaimed as television's best regular news magazine, provides an answer. On Sunday night, May 1, 1977, "60 Minutes' " Mike Wallace interviewed David Frost about Frost's forthcoming interview with Nixon. Wallace asked Frost why the interview of the century was not being carried on the networks. Frost replied that ABC, CBS, and NBC each refused to buy the show. Wallace then asked a spokesman for each of the networks why they did not want the show. NBC refused it because it did not have enough money. Mike Wallace was incredulous. NBC, which bought the rights to the Moscow Olympics for millions, did not have enough money. Was Herb Schlosser, of NBC News, sure it was not that the subject did not attract them? "No," said Schlosser, "[we] would show Attila the Hun if there was an audience for it."

Why did CBS not want the show? Well, said Richard Salant, the head of CBS News, CBS did not pay people to be interviewed. Or at least they did not do it any more, said Salant with a bitter reference to a payment by CBS to Haldeman to appear on CBS. As for ABC, they would not even negotiate with Frost.

What did Frost think about it all? Although never known previously for his concern for access to the media, Frost said he was greatly troubled about the impact of the network shut-out on diversity of opinion.

Decisions on who can secure admission to public affairs or news programming on network television are essentially lodged in the sole discretion of the heads of the network news departments. When asked about the fact of this concentration of power, Richard Salant of CBS conceded there was some force in this criticism, but that he did not know what could be done about it. Then Salant returned to the analogy beloved by the networks. Networks were like newspaper editors. They were only doing what the *New York Times* did when it decided what was fit to print. The ground chosen by the networks to resist efforts for more diffusion of authority in deciding what wins entrance into network television is editorial discretion. The First Amendment is designed to protect editors, and heads of the nation's news departments are editors. Unfortunately, there are only three of them.

I have set forth five approaches for dealing with the resolution of the problems of investigative journalism: (1) abolish the fairness doctrine and confer on the broadcast journalist the same unfettered editorial discretion enjoyed by the print media journalist; (2) apply the fairness doctrine to investigative journalism on television by means of a right to a subsequent presentation of a viewpoint opposed to that taken by the program; (3) apply the fairness doctrine to investigative journalism but limit enforcement of the doctrine solely to the renewal process; (4) refuse to extend the fairness doctrine to investigate journalism but nevertheless try to cope with problems of balanced presentation and distortion in investigative journalism through a scheme of paid access for opposing viewpoints; (5) require that the fairness doctrine apply to investigative journalism and that each documentary try to make a balanced presentation of the issues examined within the confines of a single program. When we set out to appraise these alternatives, the first seems unrealistic. Although broadcasters have tirelessly suggested to Congress that the fairness doctrine should be abolished, and occasionally there appears in the Congress a champion of this view such as Senator Proxmire in the Senate and Congressman Van Deerlin in the House, Congress seems as little disposed now as ever to abolish the fairness doctrine.

Similarly, the fourth altnerative dealing with problems of imbalance and distortion in investigative journalism on television through a paid access route seems unrealistic. The broadcast networks have made known their hostility to selling time for the presentation of social and political viewpoints and the Supreme Court of the United States has held that they are not obliged as a First Amendment matter to provide such paid access. Furthermore, the FCC has thus far refused to rule that the public interest standard of the Federal Communications Act mandates that the networks sell some time for purposes of providing for access for viewpoints that otherwise might not be presented by the networks.

The fifth alternative, insisting on balanced presentation in the confines of each documentary, seems unsatisfactory as well. All that is likely to be accomplished by insisting on such an objective is a kind of perfunctory admission that there might be some merit to an opposing viewpoint; for example, "There are some nice pension plans too." This is the kind of damnation with faint praise with which Edwin Newman closed the pensions show.

This leaves two alternatives: enforcing the fairness doctrine either through the license renewal process or through requiring presentation in a later program of an opposing viewpoint to that taken by the documentary in question. Of these two, which is preferable?

What will limiting fairness doctrine enforcement to the renewal process actually achieve? Will it lead to programming which, overall, reflects the balanced presentation of controversial issues of public importance? Probably not. Why? Primarily because as a sanction it is both too weak and too powerful. Suppose fairness *is* made a factor in the renewal process? If the license renewal process in the FCC continues to operate in the future as it has in the past great weight will be accorded by the FCC to past performance and the investment of the incumbent licensee. Relegating the fairness doctrine to the renewal process is, therefore, unlikely to have a deterrent effect sufficient to stimulate the recalcitrant to compliance. If broadcast licenses are renewed in the future with the same methodical regularity which has characterized FCC behavior in the past, consigning the fairness doctrine to the renewal process may well be the equivalent of consigning it to oblivion.

Why is the remedy of mandating specific opportunities for the presentation of opposing voices often rejected on First Amendment grounds as an intrusion on broadcaster freedom by the same persons who suggest as a sanction for imbalance in program presentation the complete destruction of the licensee through the sanction of refusing to renew the license at renewal time? Seeking to enforce the fairness doctrine through a discretionary license renewal policy hardly frees the broadcast journalist from the possibility of having day-to-day editing decisions influenced by fear of adverse governmental reaction. To the contrary, such policies appear to me to make every editing decision fraught with ultimate consequences. The editing decision is thus transformed into a situation where in a controversial matter (and by definition in fairness doctrine cases we are concerned exclusively with controversial issues of public importance) the broadcaster stands to risk his license. This approach maximizes, rather than reduces, the influence of government intrusion into broadcast journalism.

If enforcement is intended to be serious and rigorous rather than *pro forma* and ritualistic, limiting fairness doctrine enforcement to the renewal process will endow the government censor with a weaponry of a far more ultimate and destructive character than that involved in an FCC order to provide opportunity for the presentation of opposing viewpoints in subsequent programming.

Although the renewal process should not be the exclusive domain for fairness doctrine enforcement, it should also, I think, be made clear that fairness violations can still appropriately figure in renewal proceedings as they have done in the past. The fairness doctrine does no less violence to the First Amendment rights of broadcasters if it is confined to renewal proceedings. A fairness violation should not constitute the basis for refusing to grant a renewal application unless the evidence discloses, in the most persuasive fashion, insensitivity to the need to provide the audience with the meaningful presentation of conflicting views on issues of public importance. In the *Brandywine-Main Line Radio* case, a station run by Dr. Carl McIntyre lost its license on these grounds. If a future analogue to that case were to arise, I would hope that a different result would ensue and that the fairness doctrine would not serve as the ground for license renewal. A heavy-handed approach to the problem of balanced presentation should not result in the sanction of an enforced total silence on the offending broadcaster through the sanction of denial of the license renewal application.

A specific duty to comply with a requirement to give an opportunity for presentation of opposing viewpoints seems to me to be at least a remedy which in some degree relates to the problem. It is non-punitive as far as the broadcaster is concerned and it adds to speech as far as the public is concerned. This was the objective of the FCC approach to the pension plan program. The licensee is free in his own way, and to a considerable extent in his own time, to provide an opportunity for an opposing viewpoint. It cannot be stressed enough that this sanction is in no sense an equal time sanction. The broadcaster need not offer time equivalent to the length of the documentary. The fact that one is the complainant with respect to a particular fairness doctrine complaint does not mean that the complainant will be selected to give the presentation of the opposing viewpoint. Dates of presentation, length of presentation, content of presentation, and selection of those making the presentation of a viewpoint in opposition are all left to the discretion of the broadcast journalist. The only obligation that the broadcaster has under such an approach is to offer some time for another viewpoint on the issue in controversy. Such an approach still responds mightily to the powerful claims of editorial autonomy but it also responds with equal force to the claims of free and open debate.

Notes

1. See *National Broadcasting Co., Inc.* v. *FCC*, 516 F.2d 1101 (D.C. Cir. 1974).
2. See 44 FFC 2d 1027 (1973).
3. *Accuracy in Media, Inc.* v. *FCC*, 96 S. Ct. 1664 (1976). Even though

the *Pensions* case was mooted, the assessment of Judge Wright as to the ultimate significance of the *Pensions* case in a subsequent communications case is perceptive and accurate: "The Pensions judgment was ultimately vacated after enactment of pension reform legislation ... but the numerous opinions filed in the case stand as important statements of the views of members of this Court on the knotty issues involved in application of the fairness doctrine." See *Straus Communications, Inc.* v. *FCC*, 530 F.2d 1001 at 1008 (D.C. Cir. 1976).

   4. *Red Lion Broadcasting Co.* v. *FCC*, 395 U.S. 367 (1969).
   5. *Columbia Broadcasting System, Inc.* v. *Democratic National Committee*, 412 U.S. 94 (1973).
   6. *National Citizens Committee for Broadcasting* v. *FCC*, 567 F.2d 1095 at 1116 (D.C. Cir. 1977).
   7. Geller, *The Fairness Doctrine in Broadcasting: Problems and Suggested Courses of Action* 51 (1973).
   8. *National Citizens Committee for Broadcasting* v. *FCC*, note 6, *supra.*
   9. *The Handling of Public Issues under the Fairness Doctrine and the Public Interest Standards of the Communications Act*, 48 FCC 2d 1 at 18 (1974).
   10. *National Citizens Committee for Broadcasting* v. *FCC*, note 6, *supra.*
   11. Friendly, *The Good Guys, the Bad Guys and the First Amendment* 227 (1975).
   12. *Id.*
   13. See *National Broadcasting Co., Inc.* v. *FCC*, note 1, supra, at 1147-51. The exhibit is marked as Exhibit B in the Court's opinion.

   In the *Pensions* case, Judge Leventhal made special use of this exhibit. Leventhal summarized his view of the exhibit as follows: "In general, the reviewers' appraisal of the nature of the program are consistent with NBC's editorial judgment." 516 F.2d 1101 at 1126. The FCC refused to import any significance to the exhibit. However, Friendly believed the FCC should have given the exhibit some consideration with respect to the views of the critics on whether the program was about all pension plans, as contened by AIM, or was merely about some abuses in some pension plans, as contended by NBC. Leventhal apparently believed the reviews supported the NBC view. There would be no fairness violation if this were true. It seems odd to prefer the judgment of TV newspaper critics over that of the FCC on what is essentially a question of whether the fairness doctrine has been violated. This is particularly true when the TV critics did not even know that their comments were to be used for such purpose nor is there any indication that the subject matter of the program for fairness doctrine purposes was on the mind of a single reviewer when he wrote.
   14. See generally *Banzhaf* v. *FCC*, 405 F.2d 1082 (D.C. Cir. 1968).
   15. *National Broadcasting Co., Inc.* v. *FCC*, note 1, *supra*, at 1154-5.
   16. *Id.* at 1154.
   17. See generally S. Edward Foote, *id.*, CBS, and Congress, "The Selling of the Pentagon Papers," *Educational Broadcasting Review*, Winter 1971-2, p. 127.
   18. *Brandywine-Main Line Radio, Inc.* v. *Federal Communications Commission*,

473 F.2d 16 (D.C. Cir. 1972). I believe the *Brandywine* case was essentially a group defamation case in disguise. It must be conceded that the case now stands as precedent for the proposition that a penalty for fairness doctrine non-compliance can be license denial at renewal time. As such, the case, if improperly extended, is a precedent capable of considerable mischief. See Barron, *Freedom of the Press for Whom?*, pp. 199-208.

9

The Cross-ownership Case and the Trouble with Judge Bazelon's Conversion

Judge David Bazelon, a federal appellate judge whose impact on contemporary broadcast regulation has been enormous, has beaten a remarkable retreat from the views he once held on the fairness doctrine.[1] Increasingly, he has seen the fairness doctrine as a threat to First Amendment freedom rather than a vehicle for its enforcement. Broadcasters, not surprisingly, have welcomed his conversion. Judge Bazelon may prove to be a troublesome convert to the broadcaster cause, because his concern for the promotion of diversity of opinion in the electronic media has not changed. What has changed is his view on the best means to achieve that goal. Judge Bazelon has apprently become converted to the view that the cause of assuring diversity of opinion in the broadcast media will be better served by substituting a tough diversification of ownership rule for the fairness doctrine. In *National Citizens Committee for Broadcasting* v. *FCC*, the United States Court of Appeals for the District of Columbia was required to resolve a problem arising out of concentration of control of media ownership in the United States.[2] Judge Bazelon, one-time fairness doctrine champion, wrote the opinion in the case, joined by Judge Aubrey Robinson and Judge Skelly Wright.

As the culmination of a long, convoluted, and inconsistent approach to the problem of newspaper ownership in the broadcast media (the so-called cross-ownership problem), the FCC in 1975 set forth some new rules on cross-ownership which offended media interests who thought the rules went too far and citizen groups who thought they did not go far enough.[3] First, the rules prohibited the formation or transfer of newspaper-broadcast combinations in the same community. The same rules, however, preserved existing newspaper-broadcast combinations except for sixteen communities where the only daily newspaper and the only television or radio station in the community were under common ownership. In such communities, there was a total local media monopoly. Therefore, the FCC rules provided that the owners would have to choose between the paper and the station and divest one of them within five years.

If these new rules are considered in the light of the fairness doctrine, what is their significance? The fairness doctrine appears to be under siege. Although it probably will survive, it is still a question of how much of the vigor in fairness doctrine application displayed by the FCC in the late sixties and early seventies will endure. Certainly there has been a concerted and not altogether unsuccessful effort to portray the fairness doctrine as a menace to broadcast journalism. This post-Watergate war on the doctrine prompts a question: should the major legal obligation of broadcasters, the duty to make a balanced presentation of controversial ideas, be abandoned for a diversification of ownership policy? The FCC cross-ownership rules represent a new regulatory response to the dangers of media concentration and the virtues of diversity of opinion. How much wallop in fact do the cross-ownership rules really pack? They do not apply to most existing combinations. In fact, as Judge Bazelon said, ninety per cent of existing combinations were grandfathered under the rules.

Putting these developments together - a weakening zeal for the fairness doctrine and a new diversification policy - what do they promise for the future? They suggest that radio and television are going to be required to provide less in the way of public access and response than ever before. Yet, in the main, existing broadcasters are going to be allowed to retain their existing levels of concentration of control. Moreover, it is going to be more difficult than ever for new entrants and would-be competitors to gather the economic muscle to challenge the existing broadcasters. The new entrants would be prevented by law from acquiring the same media clout as the existing competitors. New entrants, unlike present broadcaster incumbents, would be denied the right to own newspapers and broadcast outlets in the same community. If this was to be the emerging pattern for broadcast regulation, Judge Bazelon, in his opinion for the federal court of appeals in the *National Citizens Committee* case, objected to it. The court of appeals upheld the FCC order adopting the cross-ownership rules banning the future formation or transfer of jointly owned newspaper-broadcast station combinations in the same community. However, the court of appeals significantly altered the order by ruling that the FCC erred in its attempt to "grandfather" most existing newspaper-broadcast combinations. The court of appeals held that divestiture should be required except in those situations where evidence in a waiver proceeding clearly showed a particular cross-ownership situation to be in the public interest.

The original FCC rules were eventually reinstated by the Supreme Court, which unanimously rejected the attempt by the federal court of appeals, led by Judge Bazelon, to obliterate media cross-ownership today rather than leaving it as a hope for realization in the future.[4] In this chapter, I shall first discuss Judge Bazelon's opinion in the federal court of appeals because it exhibits so well the motivations and difficulties which attach to efforts to use diversification of ownership policy as a means of avoiding the difficult issues raised by a communications policy which insists on establishing mandatory procedures for the fair ventilation of important and controversial issues. At the outset, it should be pointed out that an attempt to break up existing cross-ownership combinations involves a brave, almost heroic, effort. When the FCC confronted the cross-ownership problem, that is, common ownership of a major newspaper and a VHF television station, cross-ownership was most intense in the nation's largest and richest markets. Judge Bazelon notes that in 1970 when the FCC undertook its study of cross-ownership: "There were 94 newspaper television combinations, of which 34 were in the top 50 markets, and 52 in the top 100."[5] In 1975, 79 of these newspaper-television combinations were still intact. The bravado of the direct judicial assault by the federal court of appeals on existing ownership patterns in the media was tempered by a careful allowance by that court of a procedure whereby broadcasters could apply for waiver of the cross-ownership ban.

Signs abound in the court's opinion in the *National Citizens Committee* case that diversification of ownership in the broadcast media is seen as a more preferable way to accomplish diversity of opinion. Judge Bazelon conceded that the personal attack and political editorializing rules which were upheld in the *Red Lion* case were "salutary." He then remarked: "Nevertheless, the fairness doctrine may well mark the outer limits of a permissible diversification policy which relies on direct government control over the content of broadcast programs."[6]

Bazelon's opinion in *National Citizens Committee* is fascinating because it shows the dilemmas presented to any liberal and sensitive judge or social critic who is interested in encouraging diversity of viewpoints on broadcasting and who, at the same time, doubts that law can be very helpful in requiring journalists to be fair. Freedom from legal obligation to present diverse viewpoints may satisfy a puristic view of the First Amendment, but it cannot guarantee or even promise the reality of the presentation of diverse viewpoints on broadcasting. The paradox for the critic or judge with a passion for diversity of opinion is that the same concerns which make him suspect government attempts to mandate diversity of opinion lead him to favor yet another form of government control: restrictions on newspaper-broadcast station cross-ownership. Judge Bazelon frankly avows that his present views on the necessity for breaking up cross-ownership stems from his disenchantment with the fairness doctrine as the vehicle for securing diversity of viewpoint in broadcasting.[7]

> [T]he Constitutional difficulties with promoting diversity through speech restrictive means highlight the virtue of the prospective crossownership rules. The prospective ban is an attempt to promote diversity without government regulation of or supervision over speech. The rules attempt to promote vigorous public debate not by imposing restrictions on broadcasters, but simply by permitting more to be heard. Of course, there is no guarantee that the prospective ban will increase diversity in all cases. . . .

When Judge Bazelon says a tough approach to cross-ownership will permit "more to be heard," does he mean that more groups and individuals from *outside* broadcasting will be heard *on* broadcasting? If greater public access - with consequent greater diversity of opinion - is his purpose, how do we know that increasing the number of owners will increase the variety of persons and issues presented on television? In this area, as in so many others in communications law and policy - like the fear of chilling effect in the question of whether journalists should be compelled to reveal their sources - no persuasive empirical base is ever offered to justify the most far-reaching changes in the law. The hope that diversity of opinion will follow from atomizing media ownership is approached more as a matter of faith than of proof. This diversity-through-diversification dogma is voiced by Judge Bazelon:[8]

> It is not unreasonable for the Commission to assume that the licensing of an independent, rather than an affiliated station, offers greater hope of providing the community a new voice and to incorporate that assessment in its licensing policy. The First Amendment seeks to further the 'search for truth.' Surely that search will be facilitated by government policy that encourages the maximum number of searchers.

Judge Bazelon objects to the fairness doctrine because it reflects a governmental effort to encourage debate. Such an effort, he feels, is suspect. But a governmental effort to encourage the "maximum number of searchers," that is, increasing the number of owners of media outlets, is apparently not suspect. Yet a deconcentration of media ownership policy trespasses on broadcaster freedom to the point of eliminating the broadcaster. As a result of the policy some owners will have to choose between their television station or their newspaper.

Judge Bazelon has occasionally been enthusiastic over the kind of diversity of opinion cable television may some day deliver. Fulfilling the promise of cable would in this view destroy the rationale for the hated distinction between the reality of regulation for the broadcast media and the reality of no regulation for the print media. The whole premise of broadcast regulation - the scarcity of the frequencies - would then come tumbling down: "Alleviating scarcity would not only eliminate the need for promoting diversity, it would also presumably eliminate the need for all licensing save the necessary to prevent interference." In that happy day, "broadcasting would no longer present unique problems requiring unique regulation."[9] Cable's capacity to produce this diversity seems far off indeed.[10]

Is a diversification of ownership policy more likely than cable policy, or reliance on the fairness doctrine, to maximize diversity of opinion in broadcasting? The American Newspaper Publishers Association argued that limiting the opportunities of newspaper owners to own broadcast stations "unconstitutionally conditions the First Amendment right to publish a newspaper." The argument raises an interesting point. Why is governmental action in one field maximizing diversity of opinion permissible when other governmental action having less impact on the property rights of a publisher is impermissible, that is, a right of reply statute?

Judge Bazelon defended a ban on newspaper-broadcast station combinations against First Amendment attack by the following argument: "The ban neither mandates nor prohibits what may be published. It only forbids the formation of co-located combinations the Commission has determined do not serve the public interest. Of course, in serving the public interest the ban may indirectly affect the economics of publication, but the First Amendment does not provide a shield against this." Bazelon observed that the claim by newspaper publishers that the ban on co-located newspaper-broadcast station combinations is a violation of the constitutional guarantee of freedom of expression is ironic: "The prospective ban is an attempt to enhance the diversity of information heard by the public without on-going government surveillance of the content of speech."[11]

The fairness doctrine is also designed to enhance diversity of information without restricting content. Yet this has not prevented Bazelon from expressing grave doubts about the constitutional validity of the fairness doctrine as well as the enduring quality of the Supreme Court's affirmation of it in *Red Lion*.[12] Similarly, the argument that right of reply legislation *added* to speech, thereby enhancing diversity of opinion, did not save the Florida right of reply statute from a declaration of invalidity by the Supreme Court. Of course, Bazelon would argue that the crucial distinction is that the enforcement of the fairness doctrine involves continuous governmental supervision of the content of speech whereas enforcement of a diversification of ownership policy does not. But is a diversification of ownership policy such as the ban on co-located combinations not open to the same claim?

Judge Bazelon impliedly concedes that this is true by quoting from the transcripts of the Nixon tapes as follows: "The main, main thing is *The Post* is going to have damnable, damnable problems out of this one. They have a television station . . . And they're going to have to get it renewed."[13] At the time these statements were made by Nixon to Haldeman, there was little danger under existing broadcast law, at least in a determination which proceeded under the merits, that the *Post* TV station license in Washington, WTOP, would not have been renewed. Nevertheless, a government-induced renewal attack on the *Post*'s TV license motivated, as the transcript suggests, by the most bitter and unacceptable ideological considerations, was plausible. Under broadcast law as it existed at the time that the taped conversation took place, ownership by a television station of a newspaper in the same community was at least a demerit on renewal. We have seen other situations where existing broadcast law suddenly did a 180-degree turn and swerved suddenly in a direction directly opposite to past broadcast law. An example of the dramatic suddenness with which FCC law can change was the 1976 FCC decision, which for the first time found an exemption in the equal time statute, for a non-broadcaster-sponsored debate between the presidential candidates of the two major parties, thus permitting the TV Ford-Carter presidential debates.[14]

In Bazelon's view, raising the possibility that diversification policy can be administered to serve the ends of ideology rather than competition has a message for newspaper publishers. It tells them that the susceptibility of broadcasting to regulation is the reason newspaper publishers should not open themselves "to intimidation by affiliation with a broadcast station."[15]

The irony is that the rule Bazelon mandates in the newspaper-broadcast station combination case also leaves newspapers "open to intimidation." The Court of Appeals in *National Citizens Committee* holds that "divestiture is required except in those cases where the evidence clearly discloses that cross-ownership is in the public interest."[16] In other words, one could petition to have a particular cross-ownership combination spared. Allowing a petition for waiver procedure whereby some existing cross-ownership combination could be "grandfathered" still made it possible for government to favor some combinations and disfavor others. How can we be sure that the ultimate determination that an existing cross-ownership is not in the public interest will not turn on inadmissible factors analogous to those in the Nixon-Haldeman conversation about WTOP? If the Bazelon approach to newspaper-broadcast station co-located combinations had been law, existing combinations would surely have sought to avoid divestiture by petitioning the FCC that it be deemed a combination that is serving the public interest.

At least in a fairness context we have the issue squarely articulated.

One party claims the broadcaster has not given overall balanced presentation or that a particular presentation has been particularly one-sided. What is at issue is at least spread on the table. The unique vulnerability to law of broadcasters which distinguishes them from their colleagues in the print media does not lie, as their spokesmen in convention assembled are often prompted to suggest, in the fact that they are subject to the legal obligations which flow from the equal time rule, the personal attack rules, and the fairness doctrine. Rather, the unique legal vulnerability of broadcasters lies in the fact that the broadcaster's license is viewed as an entirely different species of property from the newspaper publisher's newspaper. The abiding distinction between the publisher and the broadcaster is that the broadcaster's interest in his station is not contemplated in the law as a form of property. When the broadcasters protested divestiture as a remedy for co-located newspaper-broadcast station combinations, Judge Bazelon gave the following rejoinder:[17]

> Divestiture, to begin with, is a misleading term in this context. It implies that the broadcaster has that which the Communications Act specifically states he does not have - an interest in the license beyond its expiration date - and that he is being forcibly deprived of a vested right. A licensee must apply for renewal of his license every three years and the Commission is to grant renewal only if it finds that it is in the public interest to do so.

Thus, even if the fairness doctrine and the equal time rule were all repealed, the legal status of the broadcaster would still be vulnerable as long as he is licensed. This is the great dilemma of broadcasting. Broadcasters in the main purport to wish for an end to regulation such as the fairness doctrine. On the other hand, they are not sure they wish to see an end of licensing. The broadcaster view here is less clear. It is said that regulation should be retained only to prevent electronic interference. Is it not clear that what most broadcasters really want is an end to regulation which exacts obligations from them with respect to the audience they serve? Yet at the same time they wish to retain the regulation whereby they are licensed and would-be entrants are kept out. Regulation in the form of licensing that promises safety is welcomed. Surely a demand for regulation without obligation is too self-serving to be acceptable to society as a whole. Surely government cannot "grandfather" forever the existing participants in a regulated industry against outsiders at no cost. If the scarcity rationale that broadcasters profess to disparage were abandoned and free entry were a possibility, would it be welcomed? If it would not, then the protestations against the assaults of government on the electronic media should be approached for what they are - arguments devoid of fundamental merit.

Cross-ownership in the media should be restricted and discouraged but the potential achievements of this or any other aspect of diversification of ownership policy should not be exaggerated. One example may illustrate. Commercial VHF television stations, whether owned independently or by a newspaper, in the main must feed at one of only three network stalls. The late Judge Leventhal observed that the "evils of communications controlled by a nerve center of government loom larger than the ends of editorial abuse by multiple licensees who are not only governed by the standards of their profession but aware that their interest lies in long-term confidence."[18] Note that Judge Leventhal spoke of the hope that "editorial abuse" will be better redressed by multiple licensees.

Unfortunately, in the network context the opportunities for abuse, editorial or otherwise, are hardly reduced by large numbers. Broadcast licensees may be "multiple" but there are only three major broadcast networks - ABC, CBS, and NBC. Nevertheless, Judge Leventhal's remark is indicative of a new mood which expects from diversification policy far more than it is likely to be able to deliver. Even if existing cross-ownership patterns were radically altered, network dominance of the content of independently owned television stations would not be reduced. Network dominance of broadcast content makes any effort devoted solely to breaking up media ownership patterns unlikely to have much tangible effect on broadcast content. The point is that even a tough diversification policy - which a ban on existing cross-ownership certainly represents - is itself insufficient to promote or assure diversity of opinion in broadcasting. Diversification policy is an important weapon for the establishment of public rights in broadcasting but it cannot adequately serve as an exclusive regulatory philosophy.

Judge Bazelon and his colleagues tried to restructure the present world of American broadcasting so that in each community the only newspaper would not own a major television station in that community. It was a useful, if unsuccessful, step in seeking to make a decisive break with the dominant pattern of the contemporary mass media in the United States - the steady linking together of more and more media outlets in fewer and fewer hands.

It was a brave, and essentially doomed, attempt. All the legal skill that media wealth could buy was certain to be aimed directly at a massive effort to overturn the decision in the Supreme Court. Apart from the freedom of expression issues with which we are chiefly concerned, the decision presented serious administrative law questions. It was hardly clear whether a court could itself order an administrative policy which the agency with the direct authority to develop policy had specifically refrained from requiring. The petition for waiver procedure was a necessary aspect of the court of appeals decision if the ban on present cross-ownership was to stand. Otherwise, even cross-owerships that were performing in a superior way would have fallen with no chance for survival. On the other hand, the waiver procedure was the Achilles heel of the court of appeals decision in the cross-ownership case because it gave a pre-eminent role to the exercise of government discretion when the exercise of government discretion in media matters was precisely the phenomenon - according to the policy premises of the decision - which was to be avoided at all costs. In addition, the waiver procedure with its potential for time-consuming and expensive inquiries into virtually every existing cross-ownership combination promised little immediate change in ownership patterns. Furthermore, the safe exit for media interests affected by the cross-ownership decision was simply to encourage trades. A newspaper in one city would sell its television station in that city to a newspaper in another city. In short, the immediate promise of the decision seemed to promote nothing so much as the further enrichment of the Washington, DC, communications bar - assuming that further enrichment was possible.

Perhaps this is too bleak a reading of what would have ensued if the order banning existing cross-ownerships had stood. Some important consequences of Judge Bazelon's decisions have already been realized. A good illustration was the post-appeals court decision of a trade of television stations in Detroit and Washington, DC. A momentum for breaking up cross-ownership was encouraged by the Bazelon decision. The Supreme Court decision made it clear that the trade had not been necessary. Nevertheless, the Washington *Post*, which had been a partner in the Detroit-Washington television station swap, editorialized:[19] "That the Supreme Court might have required the Washington Post Company to sever its link with WTOP encouraged the swap of stations now under way, but the transaction stands on its own as good public policy. If the presumption about diverse sources of information has any validity - and we believe it does - the trade of stations will serve both Detroit and Washington. That, in turn, will be good for those who own the stations."

If my reading of Judge Bazelon's decision is correct, he hoped to make a bargain with broadcasters - to offer liberation from the fairness doctrine in exchange for a tough diversification of ownership policy. It has now become clear that Bazelon's hopes for an overall tough diversification policy, particularly in the cross-ownership context, will not be realized.

The media sought and obtained review of the federal court of appeals decision in the cross-ownership case. When the case was decided by the Supreme Court in June 1978, *Broadcasting* magazine, the industry trade journal, crowed: "Supreme Court sides with crossowners."[20] *Broadcasting*'s estimate of the decision was a fair one. While the federal court of appeals had affirmed the FCC order imposing a prospective ban on the future initial licensing or transfer of co-located community owned newspaper-broadcast combinations in the same community, the court of appeals' alteration of the original FCC order shook media management and lawyers around the country.

The court of appeals had refused to "grandfather" existing co-located combinations and ordered the adoption of regulations requiring the dissolution of all existing combinations that did not qualify for waivers. The FCC had ordered divestiture of only sixteen existing co-located combinations on the ground these were "egregious" cases because the combination involved the community's sole daily newspaper and either the only radio or the only television station in the community. The court of appeals had held that, under federal administrative law, restricting divestiture to just the sixteen situations mentioned was arbitrary and capricious. The Supreme Court rejected the attempt of the federal court of appeals to attempt across-the-board "trust-busting" in the communications field. The Supreme Court upheld the original FCC regulations, including the divestiture requirement in the sixteen specified communities. The FCC desire to "grandfather" the present pattern of media cross-ownership, now embedded in American communities, had been affirmed by the Supreme Court.

The puzzle of the cross-ownership decision was that, like the *Miami Herald* decision, it was unanimous. The Supreme Court in *Miami Herald* spoke of concentration of ownership of the media as a serious problem. The Court did so once again in the cross-ownership case. But break-up of media cross-ownership patterns in the same community was apparently not going to be the solution for problems of concentration of ownership any more than recognition of a right of access appeared to present an attractive solution in the *Miami Herald* case.

In the corporate speech case, the Court through Mr. Justice Powell rejected the contention that "the state may control the volume of expression by the wealthier, more powerful corporate members of the press in order to "enhance relative voices" of smaller and less influential members."[21] Powell, citing the *Red Lion* decision, indicated that application of such a proposition in the broadcast media would contradict "basic tenets of First Amendment jurisprudence." As for the print media, this notion had been rejected in *Miami Herald* case despite the fact that "allegations were there made and substantiated of a concentration in the hands of a few of 'the power to inform the American people and shape public opinion,' and that the 'public has lost any ability to respond or contribute in a meaningful way to debate on issues'."[22] In short, the Supreme Court is aware of the problem of concentration of ownership but the existence of an enormous imbalance in terms of concentration of ownership is not regarded in itself as a First Amendment violation.

Since the prospective ban was designed to "increase the number of media voices in the community" and not to restrict or control the content of free speech, the federal court of appeals had concluded that the ban would not violate the First Amendment rights of newspaper owners. The media took vigorous exception to this position. They contended that restricting newspaper entry into the broadcast industry was a violation of the First Amendment because it denied the full exercise of free expression rights to a sector of society.

Mr. Justice Marshall, speaking for the Court, was not persuaded. For rebuttal he turned straight to the *Red Lion* principle, another unanimous communications case, where the Court had held that there is no "unabridgeable First Amendment right to broadcast comparable to the right of every individual to speak, write, or publish." In order to enhance the volume and quality of coverage of public affairs - in the unique context of the broadcast media, modes of regulation might be permissible "where similar efforts to regulate the print media would not be."[23] The same populist theory of the First Amendment that had been used in *Red Lion*, where the media argued that any restraints on media exercise of rights of expression were impermissible, was relied on in the cross-ownership case:[24] "Requiring those who wish to obtain a broadcast license to demonstrate that such would serve the 'public interest' does not restrict the speech of those who are denied licenses; rather it preserves the interests of the 'people as whole . . . in free speech'."

In the cross-ownership case, as in the *Miami Herald* case, the Supreme Court was obviously puzzled and troubled by the continuing pattern of concentration of ownership in the media. One consitutional law scholar, Professor Randall Bezanson, has suggested in an insightful article that massive media may be necessary to cope with massive government. Are the forces of concentration of ownership, the repeated pattern in one city after another of either oligopoly or monopoly, in media ownership a needed counterweight to government? The very lack of pluralism in media ownership may have a new functional and correctional utility in the age of the positive state.

Elsewhere in this book I have criticized the decision of the Supreme Court in the *Miami Herald* v. *Tornillo* decision by saying that it had two ends and no middle. The missing middle of the opinion relates to the reason for the rejection of the access arguments. Similarly, in the cross-ownership case there is no attempt by the Supreme Court to provide a First Amendment rationale for preserving cross-ownership.

A good part of recent writing on freedom of the press has been concerned with trying to justify the reality of unparalleled press power by providing a reinterpretation of the First Amendment. Randall Bezanson's provocative thesis is that "the press serves ends that may not be incompatible with the current structure of the communication media." Bezanson observes that "the capacity to reach the public might be unavailable absent oligopolistic strength."[25] This analysis is in sharp contrast to the traditional critique that concentration of ownership in the media is irreconcilable with the marketplace of ideas rationale for free expression. Professor Bezanson frankly concedes that there is no competitive marketplace and then adds that perhaps that is not a bad thing.

There is a certain invigorating quality to an attempt to make a virtue out of oligopoly. In this view, neither the press nor the Supreme Court should have a guilty conscience about the steady pattern of centralization in media ownership. In a challenge to this author's view that concentration of ownership is a danger to any real marketplace for ideas, Professor Bezanson writes:[26] "From this perspective, Professor Barron's analysis is less forceful as either a criticism of the present structure of the press or a justification for governmental regulation. Indeed, the very attributes of monopolistic power and lack of responsiveness to competing views that he specifically criticizes may be positive characteristics of the press under the Burger view. Centralization of power may equip the press to scrutinize and counterbalance the increasingly pervasive influence of expanding government. In this regard, the Burger view of the press function, which underlies the new free press theory, may be the more realistic theory."

Certainly, a theory of the press that sees it as an increasingly centralized corporate power source is realistic in the sense that it is descriptive. Whether it is an adequate, tolerable, or desirable theory is another matter. One virtue of a theory of the press as desirably monopolistic is that at least it provides a theory for the new legal developments which give new constitutional sanction to the powers and structure of the institutional press. In both the *Miami Herald* case and the cross-ownership case, there is clearly no enthusiasm about existing patterns of monopoly and oligopoly in the dominant media. Yet there is little willingness to confront the problem of media cetralization in terms of what it means for the present and future understanding of freedom of the press. In the *Miami Herald* case, the Court concludes basically that it is more important that the press should be free than that it be fair. *Miami Herald* also included a disturbing reminder from Mr. Justice White that "freedom [for the press] does not carry with it an unrestricted hunting license to prey on the ordinary citizen."

The Bezanson thesis certainly provides a rationale for the result in the cross-ownership case. Yet the thesis is basically troubling. Its roots are entirely evident. They grow out of the merited appreciation for the press role in Watergate in curbing government excess. Could a weak and struggling newspaper have dared to undertake the role assumed by the Washington *Post*? Even giving these considerations their due, it is doubtful that media monopoly should still be regarded as a virtue. Such a theory reflects an unacceptable acquiescence in a view that the important - if not the exclusive - antagonists in our society are government and the media. Such a perspective necessarily assigns too passive a First Amendment role to the ordinary citizen. Effective opportunity for individual expression and individual self-realization surely should be at the focal point of any adequate First Amendment theory. It is an anemic First Amendment theory that views individual citizens as dim figures on the free expression landscape. The press clause of the First Amendment should not be read as a warrant for viewing the present centralizing structure of the media as cast in constitutional cement.

The press has demonstrated the capacity to ferret out and correct abuse in government, but the reward for that undoubted service cannot be removing the institutional press from any legal obligation to that society. No constitutional armor should be placed on existing trends in media centralization and ownership. We should not be too quick to abandon efforts to secure debate and dialogue and to strengthen individual voices in our society. To succeed in such efforts, we cannot rely entirely on the role of the institutional press.

A theory of freedom of expression which has as its primary focus protection of the great newspaper chains and broadcast networks can too easily degenerate into media apologetics. A theory of freedom of expression where large media corporations are the only heroes is both suspect and unhappily underinclusive.

The Supreme Court in the cross-ownership case gave particular attention and approval to the creation by the FCC of regulatory techniques designed to secure diversification of ownership which have as their source policies which emanate from the First Amendment rather than the antitrust law. Interaction between the regulatory pattern in the broadcast media and the non-regulatory pattern in the print media can hardly fail to influence each other. Indeed, Professor Bollinger has argued[27] that these conflicting patterns of regulation should influence each other more than they now do. Alternate regulatory approaches are particularly evident in the cross-ownership context. There, by definition, the same owners possess media properties which are highly regulated with respect to the broadcast part of the combination and largely unregulated with respect to the print part of the combination.

The Supreme Court, in the cross-ownership case, rejected the contention of the National Association of Broadcasters that the FCC did not have authority under the Federal Communications Act to use its licensing authority over the broadcasting industry to promote diversity in an overall communications market where those regulated include the print as well as the broadcast media. The Court said curtly:[28] "This argument undersells the Commission's power to regulate broadcasting in the 'public interest'."

Vindicating FCC jurisdiction over a media entity which owns both broadcast and print properties may some day, in the hands of a more sympathetic judiciary, provide a basis for building a right of access to the print media component of a broadcast newspaper combination. The requisite state action would presumably be furnished by the authorization in the cross-ownership case of FCC jurisdiction, consistent with the First Amendment, over media ownerships whose joint print-broadcast properties are being subjected to direct FCC regulation. Such extended approaches to state action, or course, go far beyond any mode of constitutional interpretation which the present property-minded Burger Court is likely to undertake. The rejection in the cross-ownership case of the argument that broadcast-press combinations were placed by the First Amendment beyond FCC regulation may acquire greater significance as the media concentration phenomenon intensifies - as it is expected to do as the century goes on.

A deepening of the present pattern of concentration of ownership may bring different approaches to the present tendency to acquiesce in existing patterns of a continuous linking together of the major media properties of the nation. In a superb Washington *Post* study, rare to be published in a major newspaper which is itself part of one of the nation's leading communications empires, William Jones and Laird Anderson concluded in July 1977 that in "two decades, virtually all daily newspapers in America will be owned by perhaps fewer than two dozen major communications conglomerates." Jones and Anderson write:[29] "Given current laws and economic conditions as well as an apparent inability to challenge many media acquisitions under current antitrust laws, the rapid concentration of press power in the hands of a few giant companies appears inevitable."

The Court was emphatic in the cross-ownership case in stressing that diversification policy serves First Amendment as well as antitrust values. The Court referred with approval to the remark in the CBS case that the " 'public interest' standard necessarily invites reference to First Amendment principles."[30] In CBS, it will be remembered, the Court was very careful to say that the First Amendment did not require that the networks refrain from maintaining a policy of refusing to sell editorial advertising. The Court said it expressly did not decide the issue of whether the FCC had authority to promulgate access regulations under its authority to regulate in the public interest. Cross-ownership, on First Amendment grounds, may still be a factor in renewal proceedings apart from proof of monopolization. Mr Justice Marshall said in the cross-ownership case:[31] "And even in the absence of a competing applicant, license renewal may be denied if a challenger can show that a common owner has engaged in specific economic or programming abuses."

It is important to recognize what the Supreme Court in the cross-ownership decision does and does not do. It accepted the FCC "grandfathering" of existing co-located combinations, but present co-located combinations are not "grandfathered" forever. Licensees involved in such combinations still must come up for renewal under the terms of the Federal Communications Act. Lack of diversification of ownership can still be asserted as a demerit in petitions to deny and in comparative hearings. This possibility is doubtless what prompted former FCC Commissioner Nicholas Johnson, more in despair than in anger, to comment after the Supreme Court's decision in the cross-ownership case that all that was left to citizen groups fighting against concentration of ownership in the media was "guerrilla warfare."[32]

On its facts, the cross-ownership case is a defeat for any immediate change in patterns of ownership and cross-ownership in - as the Supreme Court was perfectly willing to concede - the most influential media: mass circulation daily newspapers and television stations. From the point of view of citizen access and the goal of deconcentration of ownership in the media, however, the decision can be given a nonetheless somewhat hopeful reading. It is still possible at least to continue to wage war in FCC proceedings and in the lower courts toward the end of overturning existing patterns of ownership and cross-ownership in the media.

The Court stressed that existing combinations would be subject to challenge by competing applicants to the same extent that they had been prior to the FCC regulations. The Court then commented: "That is, diversification of ownership will be a relevant but somewhat secondary factor." Further, at least by implication, Marshall said to citizen groups that they still could rely on the weapon of the petition to deny.[33]

The Supreme Court showed particular displeasure with the conclusion of the federal court of appeals that the FCC should impose an across-the-board divestiture rule on the ground that existing co-located newspaper-broadcast combinations did not serve the public interest. Although prepared to agree that a diversification of ownership furthered statutory and constitutional policies, the Court denied that the FCC was required to find that there was a presumption against existing co-located newspaper-broadcast combinations. The Court believed that under FCC law diversification of ownership policy was not the preeminent consideration when determining whether an existing licensee should be renewed. In such circumstances, FCC concern over loss of local ownership, over whether new owners would perform as well as old ones, whether losses of existing owners would result from forced sales, and whether losses from divestiture would "discourage future investment in quality programming" were all considerations to which the diversification of ownership factor could be appropriately subordinate.

The Supreme Court rejected the conclusion of the federal court of appeals that the Commission acted unreasonably in "treating existing newspaper-broadcast combinations more leniently than combinations which might seek licenses in the future." The Supreme Court believed that the FCC refusal to break up most of the existing newspaper-broadcast combinations was reasonable. Why was the refusal reasonable? The Court in reply recited the reasons the FCC had offered in defense of its regulations. Break-up of existing combinations would result in the loss of "the stability and continuity of meritorious service" provided by newspaper owners as a group. Particular newspaper owners who had provided good service would be unfairly prevented from continuing to broadcast. Economic dislocations, the Court continued, might prevent new owners from obtaining the capital to maintain existing levels of quality in local programming. Furthermore, "local ownership of broadcast stations would probably decrease."[34] Seventy-five per cent of all existing newspaper-television combinations were owned by local interests. The FCC feared that breaking up the combinations would only have the result that local interests would trade stations with out-of-town owners. Just the whiff of a new FCC cross-ownership brew prompted the Washington *Post* to trade its television station for one in Detroit.

Both the National Association for Broadcasters and the American Newspapers Publishers Association argued that the FCC regulations at issue in the case unconstitutionally constituted a forfeiture since a newspaper would have to forfeit the right to publish a newspaper in order to receive a broadcast license. Justice Marshall pointed out that no one had to forfeit anything because even under the regulations a newspaper owner could acquire a broadcast license for a station in another community. It is not clear from this whether Marshall is suggesting that a flat ban against ownership by a newspaper of any broadcast station would be unconstitutional. The comment does point to the problem that even the co-located combination rule as applied by the court of appeals did not prevent dominance in the nationwide media market by a few owners even if there was a diversity of ownership in a particular community. Does the cross-ownership decision place a blessing on swapping stations? No consideration is given in the decision to whether ownership by a media combine of a single media outlet in a large number of separate markets has adverse consequences for the opinion process. Is domination of the media by a few large combines any more desirable than domination of a single market by a cross-ownership combination?

A question the Court does direct its attention to is: do we know that a ban on cross-ownership will provide better programming? The problem is that we may know the contrary. Justice Marshall pointed out that the FCC in a study of co-located newspaper-television combinations revealed that "in terms of percentage of time devoted to certain categories of local programming" the co-located stations had shown an

" 'undramatic but nonetheless statistically significant superiority'."[35] Marshall quoted former FCC Commissioner Ben Hooks, who, while dissenting from the FCC regulations generally, had concurred in the FCC's decision not to require across-the-board divestiture of existing co-located combinations.[36] "As I contemplate the superior performance of many newspaper-owned stations . . . and speculate on the performance of some unknown successor, my conditioned response yields a 'a bird in the hand is worth two in the bush' philosophy. Opponents of divestiture ask: Why require divestiture for its own sake of a superior broadcaster, with experience, background and resources, for an unknown licensee whose operation may be inferior. Can we afford, through wide-scale divestiture, to experiment with a dogmatic diversity formula: and, after the churning has ceased, who will profit - the news owners or the public?"

On balance, how should the cross-ownership decision be viewed from the point of view of limiting the concentration of ownership in the media? While not exactly putting the Court's imprimatur on existing patterns of ownership in the newspaper and television business, the decision is in the main supportive of those patterns. Thus, the Court is careful to point out that while diversification of ownership is a relevant factor in the context of license renewal well as initial licensing, the past performance of the incumbent - whether he had other media ties or not - is "the most important factor in deciding whether to grant license renewal and thereby to allow the existing owner to continue in operation."[37] Further indication of disinclination to upset the present media ownership applecart is that the Court went out of its way to say that an incumbent licensee who has rendered meritorious service "has a 'legitimate renewal expectancy' that is 'implicit in the structure of the Act' and should not be destroyed absent good cause."[38]

The Supreme Court has refused to walk a straight line in assaying the overall implications of concentration of ownership in the media. Although imbalance in media ownership is permissible, the assertion of public rights, particularly in a broadcasting and cross-ownership context, even though the combinations involve newspapers, is equally permissible. When corporate power and individual rights are antagonists and public claims for diversity of opinion clash with media claims for free expression of opinion, it is perhaps to be expected that tension, ambiguity, and imprecision will be the end result.

The June 1978 Supreme Court refusal to require an across-the-board break-up of existing newspaper-television combinations demonstrates the enormous difficulties that are involved in attempting to secure some rough equality in communicating power between the public and the broadcaster through an effort directed primarily to concentration in the media. In the case of the broadcast media, the truth, however bitter it may be for broadcasters, is that government cannot be banished from broadcasting. Suppose, for example, the Supreme Court had approved the double-barreled diversification policy which Judge Bazelon had advocated - a refusal to "grandfather" existing co-located combinations combined with a procedure for waiver for those combinations owners who could show that the public interest demanded continued operation? Even if the Supreme Court had been disposed to accept this approach, government would hardly have been exiled from critical decisions affecting broadcast journalism. The FCC, and later the courts, would have still had to weigh the merits of each petition for waiver from the strictures of a cross-ownership ban just as in a fairness context the FCC, and the courts, have to weigh the merits of a fairness claim. The great difference is that in the former context the stakes are infinitely higher; then what would be at issue is the license to operate as a broadcaster.

The folly of Judge Bazelon's strategy of exchanging the fairness doctrine in favor of a primary reliance on a diversification and divestiture policy is demonstrated by what happened in the cross-ownership case. Little on the immediate legal horizon now gives much encouragement to an overall restructuring of existing patterns of ownership and cross-ownership in either the print or broadcast media. To substitute a diversification of ownership policy for the fairness doctrine in the hope of at last securing diversity of ideas in the media is unlikely to yield much except the surrender of public rights to the balanced presentation of ideas. The cross-ownership case illustrates that there is enormous reluctance to undertake, and enormous difficulty in undertaking, an unscrambling of the great broadcast media egg. Judge Bazelon's conversion from the fairness doctrine to a strict diversification policy has failed to attract converts on the Supreme Court. There is little inclination there to set in motion any legal earthquakes which would send tremors in the managerial or legal circles which now keep a steady and experienced eye ever open for the constant acquisition of new media properties - preferably with a distant location. The real trouble with Bazelon's apostasy from the fairness doctrine[39] is that despite the profound and genuine concern for free and untrammeled expression which motivated it, diversification policy is simply not an adequate alternative - at least as an exclusive remedy - to assure and promote diversity of opinion or to minimize the role of government in broadcasting. As long as it remains a central premise of First Amendment law in the broadcast field that both the public and the broadcaster have a claim to First Amendment rights, then the realization of those public rights will have to be anchored in the fairness doctrine.

Diversification of ownership in the broadcast media has now been left as a goal for the future, not as an agenda for the present.[40] At tomorrow's party a new equity is promised for broadcasting, but all the tickets have already been given out. The real message of the cross-ownership case is that if you already have a ticket (own a broadcast station), you will probably get to keep it. When the legislative scheme for the regulation of communications satellites finally was agreed upon, the late Congressman Emmanuel Celler was heard to mutter that AT&T, having escaped regulation on earth, was now to escape it in the celestial sphere as well. For the existing broadcast-television combinations throughout the land the cross-ownership decision represents still another development in the steadily accelerating trend of removing the present structure of media ownership beyond the law - at least here on earth.

Notes

1. See Judge Bazelon's impassioned dissent, severely critical of an application of the fairness doctrine, in *Brandywine-Main Line Radio, Inc.* v. *FCC*, 473 F.2d 16 (D.C. Cir. 1972). See also Bazelon, *FCC Regulation of the Telecommunications Press*, 1975 Duke L.J. 213.
2. *National Citizens Committee for Broadcasting (NCCB)* v. *FCC*, 555 F.2d 938 (D.C. Cir. 1977).
3. *Second Report and Order*, 50 FCC 2d 1046 (1975), as amended upon reconsideration, 53 FCC 2d 589 (1975).
4. *FCC* v. *National Citizens Committee for Broadcasting* (NCCB), 436 U.S. 775 (1978).
5. *N.C.C.B.* v. *FCC*, note 2, *supra*, fn. 11 at 945.
6. *Id.* at 950.
7. *Id.*
8. *Id.* at 950-1.
9. *Id.* at 950 fn. 31.
10. See *Midwest Video* v. *FCC*, 571 F.2d 825 (8th Cir. 1978), where the FCC imposition of a compulsory access channel obligation on cable systems operators was invalidated on First Amendment grounds. Despite the much-touted technological multi-channel capacity of cable, cable operators seem as allergic to public access obligations as commercial broadcasters.
    In *FCC* v. *Midwest Video*, 99 S.Ct. 1435 (1979), the Supreme Court affirmed the Eighth Circuit, and ruled that the mandatory public access cable rules were invalid under the Federal Communications Act. The Court, per Mr Justice White, relied for this result on sect. 3(h) of the Federal Communications Act which declares that broadcasters shall not be treated as common carriers. In the Court's view, this provision was fundamentally inconsistent with the imposition of access requirements on cable systems. The Court tried to narrow its holding, however, by proclaiming its continuing allegiance to the *Red Lion* decision. Furthermore, the Court took pains to point out that the question of "whether less intrusive access regulations" would be valid was not before the Court.
11. See *N.C.C.B.* v. *FCC*, note 2, *supra*, at 954.

12. See *Brandywine-Main Line Radio, Inc.* v. *FCC*, note 1, *supra*.
13. Quoted in Judge Bazelon's opinion in *N.C.C.B.* v. *FCC*, note 2, *supra*, at fn. 49 p. 954. Taped statement of Richard Nixon to H.R. Haldeman and John Dean, 15 Sept. 1972, quoted in Senate Select Committee on Presidential Campaign Activities, Final Report, S. Rep. No. 981, 93d Cong., 2d Sess. 149 (1974).
14. *Chisholm* v. *FCC*, 538 F.2d 349 (D.C. Cir. 1976).
15. *N.C.C.B.*v. *FCC*, note 2, *supra*, at p. 954.
16. *Id.* at 966.
17. *Id.* at 962.
18. *NBC* v. *FCC*, 516 F.2d 1101 at 1133 (D.C. Cir. 1975).
19. Editorial, "The Newspaper-Television Link," *The Washington Post*, p. A 22, June 16, 1978.
20. See *Broadcasting*, cover page, June 19, 1978.
21. See *First National Bank of Boston* v. *Bellotti*, 435 U.S. 765 (1978).
22. *Id.* at 791 fn. 30.
23. *FCC* v. *N.C.C.B.*, note 4, *supra*, at p. 800.
24. *Id.*
25. Bezanson, *The New Free Press Guarantee*, 63 Virginia L. Rev. 731 at 774 (1977).
26. *Id.* at 775.
27. Bollinger, *Freedom of the Press and Public Access: Toward a Theory of Partial Regulation of the Mass Media*, 75 Mich. L. Rev. 1 at 37 (1976).
28. *FCC* v. *N.C.C.B.*, note 4, *supra*, at 794 (1978).
29. From the series by Jones and Anderson on press concentration, *The Washington Post*, July 24, 1977, pp. 1 and 3.
30. *FCC* v. *N.C.C.B.*, note 4, *supra*, at p. 795, quoting *Columbia Broadcasting System, Inc.* v. *Democratic National Committee*, 412 U.S. 94 at 122 (1973).
31. *Id.* at 809.
32. See *Broadcasting*, note 19.
33. *FCC* v. *N.C.C.B.*, note 4, *supra*, at p. 809.
34. *Id.* at 804.
35. *Id.* at 807.
36. See *Second Report and Order*, 50 FCC 2d 1046 at 1109 (1975) quoted in *FCC* v. *N.C.C.B.*, note 4, *supra*, at pp. 807-8 fn 28.
37. *FCC* v. *N.C.C.B.*, note 4, *supra*, at p. 806.
38. *Id.* at p. 805.
39. In the period since the Supreme Court decision in the cross-ownership case was decided, Judge Bazelon has had occasion to express himself on the fairness and access concepts as applied to broadcasting. Have his views on these matters changed owing to the refusal of the Supreme Court to adopt his more thoroughgoing approach to the cross-ownership problem which would have applied a ban to existing as well as future cross-ownerships? It appears that Judge Bazelon's disenchantment with the fairness doctrine does not extend to the access concept to the same degree. For him, the usefulness of a limited right of access appears to depend on the extent to which the particular communications forum at issue is technologically limited or not. Thus, a limited right of access might be constitutionally impermissible in the case of cable

with its multi-channel capacity but would be permissible in a VHF television market.

In *CBS* v. *FCC*, 5 Med. L. Rptr 2649 (D.C. Cir. 1980), Judge Bazelon held that the First Amendment was not violated by a provision of the Federal Communications Act (sect. 312(a)(7)) vesting federal candidates for office with an affirmative right of access to broadcast air time. Conceding that elsewhere he had "questioned the 'scarcity' rationale as a justification for regulation of the broadcast media," *id.* at 2665, fn. 114, Judge Bazelon nonetheless used that rationale to uphold the claim of the Carter Mondale Presidential Committee that the FCC had been correct, relying on sect. 312(a)(7), in ruling that the three television networks had erred in refusing to make available a half hour of television time to the Carter-Mondale Presidential Committee in early Dec. 1979. Judge Bazelon observed that "the 'scarcity' rationale is most valid when applied to television." *Id.* Furthermore, he reasoned that broadcast journalism was not interfered with in *CBS* v. *FCC, supra,* since journalistic discretion was not restricted. Instead, sect. 312(a)(7) reallocated or transferred a segment of air time from the television candidate to the political candidate: "This kind of limited allocation of the airwaves does not constitute an unwarranted incursion on editorial matters." *Id.* at 2665.

In *CBS* v. *FCC, supra,* Judge Bazelon expressed sympathy for a limited access claim at least where Congress had specifically authorized such a claim. However, in a recent fairness doctrine case, *American Security Council Education Foundation* v. *FCC,* 607 F.2d 438 (D.C. Cir. 1979), Judge Bazelon returned to the theme that there were "substantial constitutional perils inherent in the fairness doctrine." *Id.* at 459. He observed that whatever benefits the fairness doctrine "may have generated in diversity have been undercut by the tendency of the fairness doctrine to suppress coverage of controversy altogether." *Id.* Thus, it appears that Judge Bazelon is still disenchanted with the fairness doctrine. His opinion in the *CBS* v. *FCC* case can perhaps be understood by his insistence that a reallocation of time from the broadcaster to the political candidate does not involve the same intrusion on broadcast journalism that the fairness doctrine does: "Applying the fairness doctrine to daily news coverage poses a serious threat to the independence of the broadcast press." *American Security Council Education Foundation* v. *FCC,* 607 F.2d 439 at 459 (D.C. 1979). Indeed, Bazelon pointedly reminds us that the *Red Lion* decision had suggested that the fairness doctrine could be re-examined "if experience should demonstrate that the doctrine failed to promote diversity." *Id.* at 460 fn. 10.

40. For a view of the cross-ownership case which sees it almost as the death knell of an effective and vital diversification of ownership policy, see Yasser, *Federal Communications Commission* v. *National Citizens Committee for Broadcasting: The Ultimate Media Hype,* 67 Kentucky Law Journal 904 (1979). Professor Yasser believes that if diversification policy is left to the FCC it will never become translated into meaningful regulatory action. At this point, he observes that "the only chance for a rational communications policy is with Congress." *Id.* at 925.

10

Through an American Looking Glass: Law and Press in Britain

One of the most delicate relationships in any free society is that between the press and the law. How much press involvement with law is it possible to have and still have something that may honestly be called press freedom? It is surprising that the claim of immunity from law, associated with medieval kings, should have been adopted by so contemporary an institution as the modern mass media. The theory has reappeared to some degree in the United States. It is perhaps an understandable development. When state-controlled media are the rule throughout most of the world, when the UN is asked to endorse complete state control of the media, and when that control is defended as the very definition of freedom of the press, it is not surprising that the proper antidote to press censorship should be considered absolute press immunity from law.

In Britain the idea that the press should be relatively immune from legal constraints is far less stridently urged than is the case in the United States. British journalists and lawyers are somewhat divided on whether the different legal status of their press as compared to that of the United States is desirable. Index of Press Censorship editor Michael Scammon says he tells British journalists: "You think you have a free press. You don't know what a free press is."[1] In a telling phrase, Harry Evans, editor of the *Sunday Times*, has called the British press a "half free press."[2]

There is a major structural difference, and there are at least three substantive differences between press law in the United States and press law in the United Kingdom. The structural difference is, of course, that there is no constitutional protection for the press in the United Kingdom such as is found in the Constitution of the United States. In Britain, to speak of constitutional protection for freedom of the press is, essentially, to make a moral appeal and an appeal to the historical tradition of keeping legal restraints on the press at a minimum. To say that an institution is protected by the moral and historical traditions of the nation is hardly to downplay such protection. The protection of the unbroken, if unwritten, practice of freedom may be worth far more than the protection provided by a written constitutional guarantee.

At the same time it must be recognized that in Britain, as a strictly legal matter, the domain of press freedom may be sharply curtailed at any time by an Act of Parliament. The same potential for repressive legislation exists in the United States; but in the United States the theory, and, in the main, the practice, is that the judiciary stand ready to do battle with such a legislative assault on freedom of the press by reliance on the sword of the Constitution. So it is that in Britain press freedom stands in a more exposed state than in the United States.

The vulnerability of the British press to such legislative assault has now been recognized at least in part in the call for the protection of a written constitution. On this point, Lord Hailsham made a considerable stir in the United Kingdom by saying that "the absence of any legal limitation on the powers of Parliament has become quite unacceptable."[3] This structural difference has other consequences as well. Constitutional interpretation of the First Amendment by the American judiciary has shrunk the domain of statutory and common-law intrusions into press freedom to a far greater extent than has been the case in the United Kingdom.

I mentioned at the outset three substantive differences between the press law of the United Kingdom and the press law of the United States. These three differences are found in the law of contempt, the law of libel, and what may be called, for lack of a happier term, the law of national security, the range of problems which in the United Kingdom are usually discussed in the context of the Official Secrets Act. All three branches of the law are legal restraints on the press of the most fundamental character and in each area, in both the formal statement of the law and in its execution, the British law operates with greater severity upon the press than does the American.

Although law works more directly on the press in Britain than in the United States, the press is no less influential in Britain than in America. A basic question must be whether in terms of boldness, liveliness, and robust debate, the voice of the British press is softer or duller than our own. The answer to this question to me is clear. The British press is no less dynamic than our own, with one exception: the treatment of politicians and people in public life is far gentler than is the case in the United States. The reason for this gentility has nothing to do with the compassion of British journalists. There is no reason to suppose that they take any less pleasure in publicizing the infirmities of their politicians than their American counterparts. The reason for the mildness with which the British press treats officialdom lies entirely in the severity of the English law of libel.

Occasionally the power of the press in Britain is minimized, as it sometimes is in the United States. The late newspaper magnate Cecil King[4] berates the tendency to give too much credence to the influence of mass circulation newspapers. King speaks of the *Daily Mail,* founded in 1896, and of the *Daily Mirror,* founded in 1903, as follows:[5] "Of these two papers, Lord Northcliffe, their founder, said that the *Daily Mirror* was for those who couldn't think; the *Daily Mirror* for those who couldn't even read! In those early days, the *Mirror* was bought as a picture paper, a companion paper to other newspapers which published very few illustrations of any kind." It is a curious phenomenon that Britain still has tabloids whose capacity to influence events may be scoffed at, although whether such scoffing is merited is another question.

On the whole, the press is as powerful a force in British society as the American press is in the American society. When Lord Hailsham unleashed a considerable furor with his plea for a written constitution in Britain, he remarked that he considered the press more influential than the constituent unit of British government, the House of Lords, to which he belongs. The influence of the House of Lords on government "is far weaker than that of the senate in other countries, like America, and is arguably less persuasive than powerful leading articles in the *Times,* or even a good edition of *Panorama* (a weekly television show)."[6]

An area where British and American concerns about press problems converge is with respect to the decline in competition in the UK in the national press and in the United States in the metropolitan press. (The problems raised by the continually intensifying patterns of concentration of ownership media in the United States are dealt with in Chapter 9 of this book.) Paradoxically, the expense and the long-term economies of scale involved with the advent of new technology in the newspaper business has accelerated the decline in newspaper competition. Steadily rising labor costs have been another factor. The advent of television and the decline in newspaper readership is another. Moreover, big advertisers wish to reach the largest audience. Therefore, they are "inclined to go for the papers with the largest sale and ignore the others." The result is hardly surprising: "So the big get bigger and the weak get weaker." In 1971, Cecil King predicted that the London morning daily newspapers "will one day be nearer four than their present nine."[7]

King's prophecy seems near the mark. In January 1977, Lord Beaverbrook's beloved *Daily Express* switched to tabloid size in order to survive. With the London evening papers, the chances for survival are no better. The *Standard* and *The Evening News* fight a daily and losing battle with the

London traffic in a valiant effort to get their papers to the commuter on his way to the tube. The bemused commuter is increasingly indifferent as to whether the evening paper is there because the television news awaits at home. Moreover, if he is driving home, he will already have gotten an hour of news on his auto radio. In Britain, as in America, the refrain is the same: how can the number of daily newspapers in Britain be kept from diminishing? Lord Goodman has suggested subsidies to the press from government. The tremendous interest stirred in Britain over who would acquire the financially troubled *Observer* shows the desire to arrest the steady attrition in the country's national newspaper. (Lord Goodman was Chairman of the Board of Trust of *The Observer*.)

Requests for government subsidy from press circles would be startling in the United States. Although government intervention in favor of the press to alleviate the restrictive efforts of the antitrust laws has been accomplished through the efforts of the American Newspaper Publishers Association, press subsidy is not considered respectable in newspaper circles in the United States. But press subsidy has been seriously studied in Britain.

The Labour Party and some unions suggested "that successful papers should be made to share their advertising revenue with unsuccessful ones, to keep the press diverse."[8] The Royal Commission on the Press, in its Final Report issued in the spring of 1977, rejected the proposals for subsidizing the press in the interests of preserving diversity:[9] "In particular, we are strongly against any scheme which would make the press, or any section of it, depend on government through reliance on continuing subsidies from public funds. We are also opposed absolutely to the establishment of any public body which could, or might have to, discriminate among publications in such a way as to amount to censorship in the sense of preferring to support some publications and not others. Subsidies would make the continuance of publications contingent upon government's willingness, or in difficult times, its ability to maintain them." Whether the Royal Commission's rejection of subsidies is the last word on the point remains to be seen.

Another remedy, often discussed in connection with the problems presented by monopoly and common ownership of multiple media outlets, is a right of access to the media. Rights of access to the media and claims of direct participation to the press of the public have had a tumultuous recent history in the United States in the case of the print media. In the case of the broadcast media, these aspirations are given some expression through law in the form of the fairness doctrine and the equal time rule. There are some faint echoes of this movement in contemporary Britain as reflected by the BBC's "Open Door" program or by a special column in the *Sunday Times* which roughly corresponds to the op-ed page in the *New York Times*, but it is all very minor.

Where British law and American press really present a sharp contrast is the different resolution which British law makes with respect to conflicts between individual and media rights. Since the individual's interest in reputation is protected so sternly in Britain, British law succeeds in protecting this aspect of human personality and dignity more satisfactorily than our own. In the sense that the rigor of the protection curtails press freedom we are confronted with a society, equally civilized, where openness in government and in human affairs is not perceived as a paramount value as, increasingly, it is in American society. Why is openness valued less in Britain? In a story prepared for *The Washington Post* on the Official Secrets Act, Reginald Maudling is quoted by Bernard Nossiter as describing Britain as an "instinctively private, discreet and secretive society [where] there has been little spontaneous acclaim for the virtues of the Fourth Estate, and still less tendency to construct an accepted theory of journalistic rights."[10]

Why do the rigorous legal controls on the press in Britain not stir mutiny in the British press? Certainly any attempt to reproduce their counterpart in the United States would meet with immediate resistance. Why the difference? Is it a case of a different society having different primary values? Is it a case of the prisoner having become fond of his chains?

Some tentative hypotheses may be suggested. In British journalism, the variegated nature of freedom is better understood and more widely championed than is the case with American journalism. In the United Kingdom, the law of free expression is not perceived simply as a matter of ensuring that in the perpetual and natural quarrel between the media and the government the law should strive to give the benefit of the doubt in cases where press freedom to publish is at stake to the media and not to the government. The latter presumption is a desirable one but making it does not resolve all problems of free expression.

How best to secure free expression is now one of the most difficult problems a free society faces. In this terrain, just claims are not in harmony but in conflict. Examples of such conflicts include the right of free expression on the part of the media and the right of individual self-expression on the part of those who have no direct access to the media, the right of the public to know and the right of individuals to privacy, reputation, and dignity. To be able to see that in the power of a single newspaper to speak there is great freedom and great protection, particularly against the ceaseless claims of the state, is perhaps the single most important perception which any society can make. To be able to see that untrammeled expression may be accompanied by the helpless silence of those attacked or by a shame and humiliation that can never be remedied is equally important.

THE LAW OF LIBEL AND BRITISH JOURNALISM: A DIFFERENT ATTITUDE

Unlike the case in the United States, the hand of libel law lies heavy on English journalism. It is not only the sexy and raucous *Mirror* that is required by the constant threat of the writ to make every journalistic decision a legal one. Anthony Whittaker, legal adviser to the *Sunday Times*, which in international prestige is on a par with *Le Monde*, *The New York Times*, *The Washington Post*, and the Zurich *Neue Freie Presse* told me he was responsible for reading the entire paper for possible offense to the law of libel, contempt, and the Official Secrets Act.[11] Whittaker performs this task from ten to five, but the eye of the law does not then shut upon the *Sunday Times*. Night lawyers, in the form of junior barristers, come in every evening and check the paper for the three Grand Inquisitors of English journalism, the laws of libel, contempt, and Official Secrets.

American newspapers simply do not have a lawyer on the premises in the English sense. To be sure, an American columnist like the late Drew Pearson employed a full-time lawyer to read his daily column each day prior to its publication. American dailies, great and small, do, of course, have legal counsel, sometimes house counsel, but for many newspapers it would be considered incredible that every story be read by a lawyer prior to publication. Yet this is the practice with some of the most important of Britain's great national newspapers. As former British publisher Cecil King puts it: "A situation which requires the *Daily* and *Sunday Mirror*, for instance, to employ some fifteen barristers whole and part time to keep out libels is hard to defend."[12] In the editorial offices on the second floor of the *Evening Standard* building in London the lawyer's office is right next to the office of the editor, Charles Wintour. Major stories are carefully checked with legal counsel before they are committed to print. Every story, whether by directive of the editor or not, is read by the legal office prior to publication.

Yet for all the rigor of the legal control on the press, British journalism is surprisingly unrebellious. Wintour observed he was just as astonished by the disclosure of the journalistic practices by the government after seeing the Watergate movie *All the President's Men* as he was by the depiction of the conduct of government officials. "At no time," he marveled, "was the office lawyer brought into discussion during *All the President's Men*."[13] Wintour expresses a fairly characteristic view:[14]

> The laws of the land, although far more restrictive than those of the United States, are not so harsh that a newspaper is prevented from doing its job properly. A newspaper is free to report the news of the day; it is free to comment on the news; it is free to carry out deeply probing investigations into social and financial scandals; it is free to run political, economic, environmental or social campaigns. It is free

to hold a mirror up to British life and to stare at any part of it as long as it chooses.

Yet even Wintour mentioned that the problems libel law presented to American journalism were as nothing compared to the restraint presented by the libel law to the British press. Wintour referred to the practice of former Prime Minister Harold Wilson, who brought writs against the press whenever attacks appeared which displeased him, which was nearly all the time. In the United States, of course, the opportunities for public personalities to sue for libel are severely restricted. English law, unlike American law, simply makes no distinction between public and private figures. Most of the writs brought by Prime Minister Wilson against press critics were settled out of court, to be sure, but they were settled to Wilson's advantage. In Wintour's view, the total discretion of the jury in assessing damages, and the uncertainties as to what verdict in terms of damages the jury will ultimately arrive at were the most disturbing aspects of English libel law.[15] Criticism of English libel law is certainly mild, particularly in view of the success which libel lawyers enjoy in Britain at the expense of media defendants.

John Whale of the *Sunday Times* expressed the view that libel law was a kind of necessary scourge for English journalism: "Libel law is restraint, of course, but it is a force for accurate journalism."[16] The libel law ensured that "you can prove what you print."[17] In Whale's view, the English libel law was not a malign influence on the press: "The libel laws are not an inhibition to the bad. The laws of contempt and of confidence are, of course, in a different category."[18]

At least one editor does not find that the libel law requires him to live side by side with lawyers as is the case with the daily newspapers. In the view of Anthony Howard of *The New Statesman,* English libel law makes "no trouble [for the press] unless you make a mistake."[19] Howard said he was not in constant consultation with counsel concerning the proof of stories about to be published. Only the doubtful article is referred to counsel and then Howard himself decides whether to publish, and sometimes does against the advice of counsel. In Howard's view, when one weighs the major substantive restraints on English libel law, the principal offender is evident: "Contempt is a more serious restraint than libel."[20]

While in America it is not surprising to find a lawyer defending the libel law, it is usually rare in America to find a libel lawyer defending the libel law. In England, lawyers and journalists both are more likely to accept the view that injury to reputation merits legal protection than in the United States. Illustrative are the views of an English solicitor with considerable experience in libel matters, Michael Rubinstein. When I visited him in his office in Gray's Inn, he described the role of the solicitor at least from the perspective of advising the libel complainant. Rubinstein represents clients who not infrequently skirmish with the press, such as actress Vanessa Redgrave. He does a great deal of informal negotiation with the press on behalf of his clients: "Most libel suits don't go to court. They are settled out of court."

A typical scenario is the following. Something is printed about a client. Rubinstein is informed by the client that the story or statement is untrue. He describes what happens thereafter:[21] "The paper is confronted with the facts and usually a correction will follow. An apology is different. To apologize for libel may expose oneself to damages if a libel suit is brought. Most papers would rather correct than litigate a libel matter due to the great expense of such litigation."

The very severity of the English law of libel is an incentive to such "voluntary" correction by the English press, to a greater extent than is perhaps the case with the American papers. Rubinstein is of two minds about English libel law. He does not wish to abolish the law of libel: "Papers are too often irresponsible and inaccurate."[22] On the other hand, he feels people are not typically much damaged by libel. When I asked him what in his opinion would be the single best remedy for libel law reform, his reply reconciled his apparently ambivalent views on the English libel law: "Limit libel damages to a relatively small sum provided they get a rapid and honorable apology." This suggestion comports well with Rubinstein's admiration for the approach taken by Scottish law to libel: "In Scotland they barely know claims for damages. Nominal damages are the rule. Therefore, they rarely sue."

Similarly, his colleague Anthony Whittaker, legal adviser to the *Sunday Times*, does not wish for the repeal of the English libel law: "Libel law is no bad thing. Libel is a severe discipline."[23] By severe discipline, Whittaker means that the libel law is a way of insisting on evidence for what is said. When Whittaker reads an article which appears to raise a real risk of a libel suit, he asks if there is any evidence to support it. The decision to publish is of course an editorial decision, but the lawyer's question is viewed by many of his colleagues on the staff as a spur to journalistic performance.

What is the response of the press to the rigors of the English law of libel? Is the press in the United Kingdom campaigning for reform of the libel law? Is it bitter at the instant self-surveillance it must engage in in order to avoid the issuance of a libel writ? The answer on the whole to these questions is that the British press is not working very hard to relax the English law of libel. An understanding of why this is so may come from considering the views of a solicitor who has a great impact on British journalism, Lord Goodman.

On a fall day in 1976 I was ushered into the offices of Goodman, Derrick & Co., solicitors, and thus to the chambers of one of Britain's most knowledgeable libel lawyers, for an audience with Lord Goodman, a large, impish, and delightful man who had recently, and memorably, served as Chairman of the Newspaper Publishers Association and who was soon to become Master of University College, Oxford. "So you wish to know what I think of the law of libel? Why, I think it is exemplary. That is what I think about it." He quickly assured me he was not jesting. "If a man can prove truth he has a complete defense. If a man can prove fair criticism, he has a complete defense." What indeed was there to fear from such law?

Lord Goodman did not agree that a person is not entitled to any aid from the law in protecting reputation. Similarly, he did not see why a person should have to be prepared to forfeit his reputation as the price of entering public life or pursuing a public career. He thought the American law, at least insofar as it affected "public" plaintiffs, put the burden on the wrong person. Why, he asked, should the victim of the attack have to prove there was no reasonable basis for the libel? As a matter of fact the American law of libel, at least vis-à-vis the public personage, is even more unfair since proof of negligence on the part of the "public" libel plaintiff will not lead him to victory. Such a plaintiff must show that the libel defendant published with reckless disregard or indifference to the truth or falsity of what was charged, a most difficult burden to carry.

What of the chilling effect on publication presented by a law of libel that is permitted to retain its common-law vigor? Lord Goodman's view was that speech which is an unsubstantiated attack on individual reputation should be inhibited. With respect to the argument that the very existence of the libel law discouraged debate, he emphatically disagreed. Newspaper files were not filled with stories which would be published were it not for fear of an oppressive libel law. Newspaper publishers may indeed, he said, wish to "fly a kite" (publish a story about something they are not able to verify). This, in his view, was no reason that the law should hold publishers harmless if their kites fell on their heads. Newspapers, he contended, should be inhibited from publishing that which would jeopardize reputation unless they were sure of the truth of what was published.

I pointed out to him that his views were extraordinary, that his equivalent in America, the head, let us say, of the American Newspaper Publishers Association, would hardly share his views. He said he realized this, but remarked that he and others had marveled during the Watergate crisis not so much at the behavior of government as at the behavior of journalism. He reflected in wonderment on *All the President's Men* and said that the incidents there recounted of invasion of individual privacy and attempts to suborn witnesses astonished him.[24] Newspaper publishers should have fortitude and should not expect to be immunized from law and responsibility.

Lord Annan, chairman of the committee which wrote the *Report on* the *Future of Broadcasting* (the Annan Report) has said of his friend Lord Goodman: "He knows that if you care passionately about liberty in one aspect, you are going to have to admit that liberty in another sphere is less important."[25] The simplicity of this observation may not attract the attention it deserves. For example, in the debate over press coverage of criminal proceedings in the United States, how often is it said that there is no conflict between the rights of free press and fair trial. Yet the truth is that the conflict is present and is invariably resolved by preferring one set of rights over another. Lord Goodman has been praised for seeing these tensions.

From an American point of view, it is remarkable to find the British law of libel praised by a lawyer who has served as chairman of the Newspaper Publishers Association. In Lord Goodman's view, in Britain today "we are better now than we were in the eighteenth century in the area of protecting the reputation of innocent people."[26]

Goodman rejects the proposal that "there should be added to the defences of truth and fair comment on a matter of public concern a further defence that, although the statement made in the event turned out to be untrue, it was believed to be true on reasonable grounds at the time of publication."[27] He recited the arguments in favor of recognition of this defense. This consisted mainly in the argument that fear of libel litigation prevented the dissemination by the press of information which was in the public interest despite the fact that there was a reasonable basis for believing the information to be true. Nonetheless he protested against relaxing the rigors of the English law of libel in this regard. In his view, a publication which is an unsubstantiated attack on individual reputation should be inhibited. In Goodman's view, the law of libel helps preserve freedom in a free society. As he states it: "The freedom from being traduced is as much a freedom as the freedom to criticise."[28] The substance of these observations is not remarkable. What is remarkable is their source. Can anyone imagine the head of the American Newspaper Publishers Association defending the law of libel and press freedom with such even-handedness?

For Lord Goodman, the only real deficiency of the English law of libel was in the costs of litigation which could, if one lost, be ruinous. There was nothing in the English law of libel, he declared, which should deter newspapers from publishing that which in fact should be published. He made this observation, he said, as one who had worked with newspapers for many years during his professional life.

In Lord Goodman's view, the changes in the American law of libel which began in the mid-1960s were unsatisfactory. The effect of these changes made it virtually impossible, in his view, for people in American public life to sue for defamation. Moreover, the reason suit was not brought was unlikely to be understood by the ordinary public. The public person did not sue because he would not win, but the ordinary newspaper reader and member of the public did not know that. The public knew nothing of the revisions in the law of libel. As far as the public which had been exposed to the original libel was concerned, the reason the public victim of defamation did not sue was because the libel was true. (The distinction between a matter that although false was not published in reckless disregard of truth or falsity and a matter that was false and was knowingly published despite its falsity was too treacherous and subtle for the popular mind.)

With more sophisticated readers, of course, more understanding can be expected with respect to the impact of the libel law on what appears in the press. For example, in a London symposium on financial journalism, Patrick Hutber of the *Sunday Telegraph* remarked that the libel law was no barrier to readers of City (or financial) news. Hutber commented: "I don't say X is a scoundrel. I merely write: 'Despite his efforts, X has never been received into the inner confidence of the City'." Alex Brummer of *The Guardian* agreed. "The reader does get the message." In other words, the reader is frequently able to penetrate the euphemisms Fleet Street invents to circumvent the libel law. Hutber observed, however, that the exuberant carelessness of the stories in the scandal-exploiting magazine, *Private Eye,* was "making it difficult for all of us to continue to use euphemisms." Hutber observed that a standard phrase in City journalism is as follows: "Of course, there is no suggestion that X knew anything about this." "Now," said Hutber, "when we *say* this, we risk being believed." Even despite these clear admissions of the restrictive consequences of the libel law on journalism, no real antagonism was voiced against that body of law.

Adam Hopkins of the Sunday Times asked of his City journalist colleagues: "Don't you ever come across a story which you know morally to be true but you can't prove to be true?" Hutber and Brummel, for the *Daily Telegraph* and *The Guardian* respectively, both answered that one should not publish until one knows the story to be true. Or as Brummel put it, "the law of libel is no threat. The law of libel is something financial journalism can live with."[29]

To what should we attribute the quite different attitudes toward libel law which are found on the opposite sides of the Atlantic? American newspaperman and London correspondent, Bernard Nossiter, offers three reasons: First, Britain never experienced an American Revolution. Second, it has a different approach toward authority, and third, there is no written constitution. Furthermore, Nossiter tried to explain the larger protection vis-à-vis the libel law enjoyed by the British public person in Britain compared to that found in the United States by recalling the remark made to him by a British MP whom he was investigating for a story involving a conflict of interest: "We view the politician as citizen; we don't pay them that much."[30]

Anthony Howard furnishes other reasons for the attitude of British journalism toward the libel law. "Why," I asked him, "was the British Press so timid?" The overall reaction of English journalists, I told him, might be expressed as follows: "The law of libel is bad. Let's not change it." Howard replied that this was not quite so. "There is some objection. But you are asking how house-trained is the British press? It is pretty house-trained." Howard listed some of the reasons for this. The status of journalists is lower than in the United States. "We have no equivalent to Walter Lippmann or Joseph Alsop. A foreign secretary calls up a press lord. Our politicians are friendly with newspaper proprietors, not journalists."[31]

Howard found another reason in the greater ideological divisions found in British society. Journalists did not object to legal controls on the press in Britain because the press is so distrusted politically. There is real hostility, he observed, to the media by the Labour party rank and file. This is because the representation of labor by the largely Tory press is negative. Also, the number of labor voices in the press has steadily declined.

In the parlance of American constitutional law, we would say the British law of libel encourages media self-censorship and chills expression, particularly in the core area of critcism of officialdom. For British libel lawyers like Lord Goodman, however, this view is too indifferent to the fate of the victim to warrant acceptance:[32] "There may be circumstances in which the public interest demands that a man's reputation be risked *pro bono publico,* but in such cases it is unreasonable to ask that, if a newspaper is sufficiently convinced of its facts to be prepared to seek to destroy a man's reputation, it should be prepared to accept the financial responsibility if it perpetrated so gross an error? 'Publish and be damned' is a brave and worthy slogan: 'publish and let your victim be damned' is of more dubious moral quality . . ."[33]

To insist on absolute liberty for yourself may mean that you have diminished the liberty of another. This dilemma of liberty is widely understood in British law and journalism. This realization was more widely understood in the United States a generation ago than it is today. Absolute liberty for journalism may have costs in terms of individual freedom. This is a truth that some American journalists and some civil libertarians are not always willing to concede. It is strange that there are not many civil libertarian media critics on the American scene today who express the view that questions of press freedom and individual freedom are not always either/or propositions.

At the same time that American law has taken major steps to remove obstacles to press efforts to report and monitor government activity by the press, American law has also moved to place new legal obstacles in the path of individual efforts to secure redress against the press. In the United Kingdom, on the other hand, individual rights and press rights are still much more likely to be viewed by British courts as rights of equivalent stature. British law, for example, has not modified the law of libel in order to make press publication of inaccuracy less hazardous, as has been done in many contexts in the United States.

When American press law is compared with British press law, one comes away with a desire to carry over to British law some of the passion for open government and uninhibited press publication of government activity found in recent American law. On the other hand, one wishes that it were possible to persuade American courts to share some, if not all, of the concern that British courts provide for individual rights when they are gravely damaged by a particular press publication. In a word, the British press law is too deferential to government and the American press law too inclined to prefer publication whatever the costs to particular individuals.

Notes

1. Conversation with Anthony Whittaker, Oct. 13, 1976.
2. See Harold Evans, "The Half Free Press," in *The Freedom of the Press,* the Granada Guildhall Lectures, 1974 (London: Hart-Davis, MacGibbon 1974) 21-47.
3. Lord Hailsham, Dimbleby Lecture, "Elective Dictatorship," *The Listener,* Oct. 21, 1976, p. 496.
4. Cecil King modestly described himself as follows: "For many years, I controlled the largest group of mass media in the world, playing a large part in building up the *Daily Journal* from a journal on the verge of bankruptcy to a paper that is read daily by half the adult population of Great Britain." Cecil King, *Without Fear or Favour* (London: Sidgwick & Jackson 1971) 189. King was chairman of Daily Mirror Newspapers Limited and Sunday Pictorial Newspapers Limited, 1951-63, and of the International Publishing Company, the world's largest publishing combine, 1963-8.
5. *Id.* at 197.
6. Hailsham, note 3, *supra,* at 497.
7. See King, note 4, *supra,* at 200.
8. "State Aid Ruled Out," *The Sunday Times,* Nov. 21, 1976, p. 4.
9. Royal Commission on the Press, Final Report, p. 112, July 1977.
10. Bernard Nossiter, *The Washington Post,* Feb. 23, 1976.
11. Conversation with Anthony Whittaker, Oct. 13, 1976.
12. See Cecil King, *Without Fear or Favour,* 215. King was not, as many

British newspaper people are, stoic about the law of libel: "I think it will eventually be seen that the Press and television must be freed from the bugbears of both the law of libel and the Official Secrets Act; that libel damages must be limited to the actual damage done; and that 'Official Secrets' should include only those that endanger the security of the state." *Id.* at 216.

13. Conversation with the author, Oct. 27, 1976.
14. C. Wintour, Pressures on the Press: An Editor *Looks at Fleet Street* (London: André Deutsch, Ltd 1972) 254.
15. Conversation with Charles Wintour, Oct. 27, 1976.
16. Conversation with John Whale, Sept. 30, 1976.
17. *Id.*
18. *Id.*
19. Conversation with Anthony Howard, Nov. 18, 1976.
20. *Id.*
21. Conversation with Michael Rubinstein, Nov. 4, 1976.
22. *Id.*
23. Conversation with Anthony Whittaker, Oct. 13, 1976.
24. All references are to a conversation with Lord Goodman, Sept. 17, 1976.
25. Preface, Goodman, *Not for the Record: Selected Speeches and Writings* (London: André Deutsch 1972) 10.
26. Goodman, note 25, *supra*, at 25.
27. *Id.* at 24.
28. *Id.* at 23.
29. All the references are to a symposium on "The City and The Press: A Crisis of Confidence" at Portland Hall, School of Communication, Polytechnic of Central London, Nov. 17, 1976. The participants were Patrick Hutber, *Sunday Telegraph,* Alex Brummer, *The Guardian,* J. Dundas Hamilton, Stock Exchange Chairman, and Adam Hopkins, *Sunday Times.*
30. Conversation with Bernard Nossiter, Nov. 10, 1976.
31. Conversation with Anthony Howard, Nov. 18, 1976.
32. Goodman, note 26, *supra*, at 24.
33. *Id.* at p. 10.

11
The Future for Media Law in the 1980s*

What can we expect from media law in the eighties? When one reflects on the fact that fifty years ago the very term "media law" would have seemed a strange one, we begin to realize both the youth of media law and the growth of the media in this country.

ACCESS BY THE MEDIA TO INFORMATION

One issue is the question of access to information for the press. By the press I mean both the broadcast and print media. How much of government activity should be open to the press? The Freedom of Information Act has helped to make some public records available to the press so that it, in turn, may make those materials available to citizens. Certainly government documents should as a rule be open and accessible. This generality is easy to state, but it is difficult to apply such a proposition in a specific context. Compulsory openness is not necessarily the friend of record-keeping. Consider an example. Secretary of State Kissinger made notes of his telephone conversations while he was in office. After his service was completed, he donated these notes to the Library of Congress. Should these notes now be made available to the press as "agency records" within the meaning of the Freedom of Information Act?

The Supreme Court held, for a variety of reasons, that such "records" were not available to the press.[1] Much of the Court's opinion was directed to technical questions of interpretation of the Freedom of Information Act.

This result can be defended for reasons apart from the necessity of protecting the confidentiality of the executive decision-making process. The result of the Kissinger case is sound from the point of view of history. To insist that everything be made public is sometimes, paradoxi-

---

* This chapter is based on an address which I delivered at the Glassboro Conference on Media Law, Glassboro State College, Glassboro, New Jersey, May 5, 1980.

cally, to make things more secret. If the Secretary of State knows that the notes of every conversation he makes are ultimately going to be available to any journalist who seeks them under the Freedom of Information Act, we may expect that the Secretary of State, unless he is unusually dense, will simply not make any notes of his telephone conversations. As a result, not only contemporary society but history itself is cheated with respect to the events of a particular time.

If immediate disclosure is not threatened and notes need not be made publicly available until after a period of years has passed, as is often the case, at least history will know what happened. When everything must be made public, the consequence is that routes of secrecy are developed which are truly impenetrable. The central fact about all First Amendment issues is that they do not respond to an absolutist approach. Absolutism always has a heroic and intoxicating quality. But absolutism in First Amendment problems is, like absolutism in other contexts, too likely to be indifferent to competing values. The point is that First Amendment issues, like most human problems, as Justice Frankfurter taught long ago, cannot be solved by "uncritical libertarian generalities."[2] They can be solved best by the difficult weighing of rights in conflict.

Certainly access to public records is important and claims for access to public records by journalists should receive great weight, but such claims cannot always prevail. Is it not odd that the same media spokesmen who argue that the First Amendment gives them an absolute right of access to all public records and even information about private lives often argue with equal intensity that the First Amendment gives the public no right of access to the media? This is indeed a paradox. It is argued that there is absolute access *for* the media but no right of access for the public *to* the media.

Of course, there is a right of access to information which is enjoyed by the media and private individuals. In *Stanley* v. *Georgia*,[3] the Supreme Court of the United States said there was a First Amendment right to receive information. In the great journalist privilege case, the *Branzburg*[4] case, the Supreme Court again said there undoubtedly was some First Amendment protection for the information-gathering process. This doubtless is true, but the key word is "some." Some protection is, of course, quite a different matter from absolute protection.

The argument that press privacy is absolute but that a right of privacy for government or for the individual is qualified or non-existent is unpersuasive. The media cannot say, on the one hand, that no one can ever know their sources and, on the other, that the sources of governmental decision-making, even in the most sensitive matters, must be known to everybody.

Similarly, some in the media are quite ready to argue that their editorial decision-making processes are inviolate. Yet these same people often believe that the innermost thoughts of a hitherto unknown family suddenly faced with tragedy is fair game for the roughest questions in order to satisfy the curiosity of viewers on the six or eleven o'clock TV news. In the law of the 1980s, absolute claims for protection for news gathering by the media are not likely to prevail uniformly. Nevertheless, these claims will occasionally receive, as they ought to, important protection. Thus, we have seen in the *Richmond Newspapers* case[5] a retreat from the interpretation of the 1979 *Gannett*[6] case suggesting that criminal trials may be closed to the press. On that front the Court held that the criminal trial, as distinguished from the pre-trial suppression hearing or the preliminary hearing, should always be open to journalists unless the circumstances are exceptional.

The decision in *Chandler v. Florida*[7] in January 1981 leaves it to the states to decide whether their criminal courts can be televised. But the Constitution as a barrier, *per se,* to the coverage of state court criminal trials has now been removed. The defendant's consent should have been made a prerequisite to televising coverage of a criminal trial. A defendant should not be subjected to a form of punishment - publicity - which the state has not required prior to any finding of guilt.

In summary, the law of the 1980s is slowly moving to grant some measure of the protection to press claims for access to information that has been extended to press claims for freedom to publish. Freedom to publish, of course, continues to merit the highest degree of protection as far as our court system is concerned. The court system will have to confront the reality of television more directly than it has in the past. But the fact that there is no constitutional barrier to covering court procedures should not lead us to yield too quickly to claims by big media to information of a confidential variety. When media seek to review matters potentially hurtful to individuals, such as the nature of adoption, juvenile, and divorce proceedings, or matters disruptive of the government process, such requests should be treated skeptically by the courts.

If one sector of society in the interest of information has a right to know everything, then surely the claims of the rest of society to privacy can hardly keep from being endangered. The press is rightfully celebrated as the tribune of the people, but it must be careful not to become, in its claims to access to information, a new Grand Inquisitor.

ACCESS BY THE PUBLIC TO THE MEDIA

There is another side to the access question. I have focused on the problem of access to information, that is, requests for information to governmental records by the press. What about another kind of access - requests by the public for access to the media? The movement for a right of access to the print media which took on real strength in the late

1960s is currently quiescent. Looked at from the beginning of the 1980s, it does not appear that that situation will change. The development of a legal right of reply to the print media in this country is still far off. What of the electronic media? May we expect that the justly celebrated freedom to publish or not to publish which print journalists enjoy will be speedily applied to the electronic media? All the signs show that the broadcast media are seen as properly subject to a greater measure of obligation with respect to providing the public access to broadcasting than are the print media.

Network or broadcast licensee decisions about what should and should not be broadcast will continue to be examined in a manner quite different from print media decisions about what to publish or what not to publish. An example of this reality is the decision of the federal court of appeals which unanimously affirmed the FCC's holding that the three television networks had violated the provisions of the Communications Act by refusal to sell time to President Carter's campaign committee in the fall of 1979.[8] The case was written by Judge Bazelon, a judge who, as shown earlier, has been increasingly sympathetic to the First Amendment claims of broadcast journalism. The Carter-Mondale Presidential Committee, relying on Section 312(a)(7) of the Communications Act requiring broadcasters to afford "reasonable access" to federal candidates, had requested a half hour of network time to air a documentary designed as the launching pad for President Carter's re-election campaign. Section 312(a)(7) is an example of an affirmative governmental effort to make freedom of expression a reality.

One of the great communications issues of our time is whether freedom of expression should merely be interpreted to protect the rights of those who have a forum in which to speak. Given the imbalance in communicating power in this country, we need to develop procedures whereby those who own forums have some obligation to open them to others. As Judge Bazelon put it, "Section 312(a)(7) makes a tremendous positive contribution to the cause of freedom of expression."

Bazelon made some additional comments that merit reflection in the Carter-Mondale case. He said that in television we deal "with a medium devoted exclusively to communications - and one which by all accounts is *the* medium of communications for most of our society." This is a very important comment. The idea that television is *the* medium of communication for most of our society is at root the basic distinction between the First Amendment treatment of the broadcast media and the print media. In the *Pacifica Broadcasters*[9] case involving obscenity and broadcasting, the Supreme Court said: "Of all forms of communications, it is broadcasting that has received the most limited First Amendment protection."

This may be true in the context of the regulation of obscenity. From the point of view of access to the media, however, I would argue that broadcasting law is more responsive to the original intention of the First Amendment than is the law affecting the print media. Broadcasting law is also more faithful to First Amendment values than is the law governing the print media. In broadcasting, people who do not own media still have some opportunity to answer back. In broadcasting, to some extent, dialogue is a matter of right and not of grace.

The usual rationale for justifying the many distinctions in the legal treatment of the print and broadcast media is that after all there is a technological limitation in the spectrum and only so many can be licensed to broadcast, whereas there is no such limitation with respect to newspapers. This is an odd thesis when one reflects on the fact that in most of our cities there are at least three VHF television network affiliates and only one daily newspaper. The real basis of broadcast regulation is that television is *the* medium of communication. Broadcasting and television particularly are subject to public obligation not because of a technical scarcity argument, but because of the social impact of television.

In a medium as powerful as television we insist on dialogue. Any society committed to debate and to the free interchange of ideas is properly reluctant to allow such an important medium to be the toy of any group of journalists no matter how responsible and intelligent. When the President of the United States, running as a candidate, seeks television time, the opportunity to secure such time cannot be entirely left to the commercial programming wishes of the controllers of broadcast journalism. Or, as Judge Bazelon put it in the Carter-Mondale case, "it is difficult to contend that the limited appropriation by government of the available spectrum for use in forming the electorate is constitutionally unacceptable."

When we speak of problems of access to the media, we speak of a world which the Framers did not know. Jefferson certainly spoke of newspapers that were difficult and irresponsible, but he did not know of media that were to rival governments in terms of wealth, importance, and prestige. The dilemma of the Carter-Mondale quarrel with the networks, or with the quarrel between Pat Tornillo and the *Miami Herald*, is that in these cases we are not presented with the paradigm First Amendment situation - a state desire to censor - but rather a modern censorship situation - a media desire to censor.

Unhappily, we are used to government attempts to restrain expression, but we are at a loss to deal with media efforts to accomplish the same end. Our law of libel makes it possible to deal with media irresponsibility, but our law - at least in the print media - is inadequate to deal with media restraints on expression. In the *Tornillo*[10] case, the Court assumes that the First Amendment has ordained that the press should be free rather than that it should be fair. Ultimately, we will come to see that it is possible for the press to be both fair and free. Fairness can be achieved without endangering press freedom.

Present patterns of media concentration of ownership and power are neither healthy for the country nor for the press. In the end, some public rights of entry into the private press will have to be recognized if the media are to escape the skepticism and suspicion with which they are viewed at present by large sectors of the public. Great business corporations, other than media corporations, have learned that sharing power is not the end of power but rather its security and future. These developments are in the distance. In the short run, the mode of legal control that the media must grapple with is not a law of reply, but rather the law of libel.

LIBEL AND MEDIA ACCOUNTABILITY

The law of libel continues to be volatile. At present, it serves two functions. One is its traditional function of recompensing injured reputation. The other and newer function is the utilization of the law of libel as a means of securing media accountability. This second function is particularly important in the case of the print media, where modes of accountability such as the fairness doctrine and the equal time rule (applicable to broadcast media) do not exist. This accountability function is, I think, demonstrable. The Court is, for example, extremely reluctant to depart from that accommodation between the interest in freedom of publication and the interest in safeguarding reputation which was struck in the *New York Times*[11] case in 1964.

Recent decisions show that the Court thinks that it has gone about as far as it should in limiting the law of libel in order to expand the untrammeled freedom to publish. Freedom to publish is an indispensable freedom. Our courts and our society at large properly believe that of all First Amendment interests this is certainly the most important, the most worthy of defense. Yet there is an increasing unwillingness to exalt the freedom to publish to the point that it menaces without hope of redress other competing values, such as privacy or reputation.

Our law of libel says that if you are a public figure or a public official you must expect to some extent to be occasionally wounded by the stings and arrows of outrageous debate. Even when these wounds are the result of a false statement, liability should not necessarily befall the media defamer. We do not want journalists to be insurers in every statement that they make of the absolute accuracy of what they publish. Journalists have deadlines. The wire service is a minute-by-minute activity. We cannot expect to make all journalists into research historians or scientists, nor should we. The duty to investigate must not be set at so high a level that newspapers fear to publish the ordinary and vital affairs of society.

At the same time, if what the press publishes concerning a public figure or public official is false, and if the publication was published knowing that it was false, then the new protections that the First Amendment is said to demand of the law of libel should not be applicable. As Mr. Justice Brennan once said, calculated falsehood does not merit First Amendment protection. May we probe the minds of journalists to find out if, when they published something which turned out to be false, they knew it to be false in the first place? Or should we attach to such deliberations the cloak of editorial privilege? The Court has recently refused to create a doctrine of editorial privilege in those circumstances. We have made it more difficult for public figures or public officials to sue the media for libel unless what has been said about them was either knowingly or recklessly false. We have made it more difficult to sue because, in the name of the First Amendment, we want to encourage criticism of those who take part in the give and take of public life. In this respect, our law of libel has become quite protective of the press. The imposition, however, of yet an additional requirement that media libel defendants should be able to claim editorial privilege when asked about their state of mind would surely set the balance too heavily against the individual interest in reputation. At least such was the conclusion of the Court in the case of *Herbert* v. *Lando*.[12]

The law of libel properly used should not be seen as a menace to a free press. It is a protection. At present, the public knows that if the print and broadcast media say something that is knowingly false they may have to respond in damages. Popular knowledge that the press cannot abuse its freedom to publish in an unlimited way is a great protection for the press. The libel law assures in the public mind some sense of authenticity for what we read in the paper or what we see on television.

Whenever there is talk of absolute freedom for any one group, we have to be extremely cautious. Absolute freedom for one group is too often bought at the price of freedom of others. There have been remarkable changes in the law of libel during the past twenty years. It is far more difficult for someone in the public limelight to successfully sue the media today than it was, say, thirty years ago. This is a salutary result. Those who choose to participate vigorously in the public life of our times should not be able to enter the vortex in order to have their say and yet be able at the same time to punish their foes with a libel suit when they are attacked. On the other hand, we must always be mindful that there is a fundamental inequality in communicating power in the nation. Even public figures and public officials who have chosen the public life ought not to be without some recourse to protect their reputations when the publication is knowingly false. This balance between reputation and expression which the Court struck nearly twenty years ago in *New York Times* v. *Sullivan* is likely to continue. Unless there is a great deal more diversity of ownership in the media, unless the great newspaper chains and broadcast networks suddenly find themselves coping with new competition, they will continue to be seen as they are now: as mighty forces in our society, which, like mighty forces in any society, should not be left entirely without some measure of legal control.

DIVERSITY OF IDEAS THROUGH CABLE?

There is considerable discussion in communication circles about the great potential for diversity which will flow from development of direct satellite broadcasting and the continuing rise of cable television. The hope is that these new media will provide new communications outlets and thus rapidly render the concerns about the need for alternatives to network programming outdated and overstated. This is the traditional American hope that continued progress in technological engineering will make social engineering unnecessary. Cable has not performed as advertised. Cable, it is true, is now only in its early adolescence. It shows no promise as yet of providing the diversity and the variety which many of its advocates hoped for at its birth. Most of our cable systems merely offer the subscriber the advantages of differences in network scheduling among the same network affiliates in different communities. This is, of course, not to be scoffed at. The point is that cable has yet to develop a voice of its own. Why? The dominant media are in the best position to finance development of new media. It is contrary to human experience to expect that those who profit greatly by a threatened technology will seek greatly to enhance the attractiveness of the threatening technology.

The much-vaunted capacity of cable brings to mind Henry David Thoreau's statement about the telegraph: "We are in great haste to construct a magnetic telegraph from Maine to Texas; but Maine and Texas, it may be, have nothing important to communicate." If we measure the contribution of cable from what it has been able to say in its own voice,[13] we shall have to conclude that it has not said very much. Ted Turner's new cable network, new uses for direct broadcast satellites, and the FCC's long overdue decision to free cable of the exclusivity rules indicate that the cable audience soon will be larger than ever before. Whether the growth of the cable will fragment the audience of the great commercial broadcast networks or expand that audience is uncertain. Cable must yet manage to show that it has a voice of its own. Furthermore, the ownership of cable should be kept distinct from the ownership of broadcasting if cable is to become an authentic and unique communications voice. This is not to say that cable will not yet radically change all broadcast communications.

New communications technologies will continue to flourish in the eighties. But we should be skeptical about claims that these new media will greatly or quickly diminish the importance and power of the established prestige media - the great metropolitan daily newspapers and the great broadcast networks. Alternative modes of communication, such as public broadcasting, and the development of new commercial networks, as well as cable systems that really do their own program originating should, of course, be encouraged. We should not expect them in any immediate way to steal the thunder of the dominant media. This means that we should be very careful of claims that the dominant media should be completely without any measurable legal control on the ground that their days are numbered and that their power is overstated.

SUMMARY

Recently, the Supreme Court recognized a First Amendment status for corporate speech.[14] As a result, business corporations through their access to large sums of money are in a position to compete with corporations with access to great media outlets to influence opinion. Now, both business corporations and media corporations have been placed constitutionally in a roughly equivalent position to influence, indeed perhaps to dominate, the opinion process. In a sense, this achieves a measure of equivalence in communicating power within the corporate realm between the business corporations and media corporations.

How do we achieve any semblance of equivalence in communicating power between the public and the media? How do we, in an age when mass communication media encompass the nation - indeed the world - give voice to our own citizens? Governments can command a voice, but how can the ordinary citizen find a tongue? The public knows it appears to the media as all eyes and ears but no mind.

New technology may solve some measure of the problem. In the largest respect, we must look to law in the weighing of competing rights for a good deal of the solution. We must begin to frankly recognize the great conflict that exists - the great disparity in communicating power - between the freeom of speech of the public and the freedom of press of the media. We must begin to understand that the meaning of freedom of expression is not exhausted by according protection to the media although such freedom is of great importance. We must also understand that the perspective of the First Amendment is not elitist and exclusive, directed to the press alone, but that its perspective is, instead, individualistic and humanistic, and extends to all our people.

Notes

1. *Kissinger* v. *Reporters Committee for Freedom of the Press*, 100 S.Ct. 960 (1980).

2. See concurring opinion of Mr Justice Frankfurter, *Dennis* v. *United States*, 341 U.S. 494 (1951).

3. *Stanley* v. *Georgia*, 394 U.S. 557 (1969).
4. *Branzburg* v. *Hayes*, 408 U.S. 665 (1972).
5. *Richmond Newspapers, Inc.* v. *Virginia*, 100 S.Ct. 2814 (1980). See Chap. 3, note 23.
6. *Gannett Co., Inc.* v. *De Pasquale*, 99 S.Ct. 2898 (1979).
7. *Chandler* v. *Florida*, 101 S.Ct. 802 (1981).
8. *CBS, Inc.* v. *FCC*, 629 F. 2d 1 (1980). This decision was resoundingly affirmed in a six to three decision of the Supreme Court in an opinion by Chief Justice Berger (*C.B.S., Inc.* v. *FCC*, 101 S.Ct. (1981)). The Chief Justice stated: "Section 312(a)(7) represents an effort by Congress to assure that an important resource — the airwaves — will be used in the public interest. We hold that the statutory right of access, . . . , properly balances the First Amendment rights of federal candidates, the public, and broadcasters."
9. *FCC* v. *Pacifica Foundation*, 438 U.S. 726 (1978).
10. *Miami Herald Publishing Co.* v. *Tornillo*, 418 U.S. 241 (1974).
11. *New York Times Co.* v. *Sullivan*, 376 U.S. 254 (1964).
12. 99 S.Ct. 1635 (1979). See generally, Chap. 5.
13. *First National Bank of Boston* v. *Bellotti*, 438 U.S. 907 (1978).
14. See *FCC* v. *Midwest Video*, 99 S.Ct. 1435 (1979) where the Supreme Court affirmed the Eighth Circuit's decision invalidating FCC regulations which would have imposed a mandatory obligation on cable system operators to devote a channel to public purposes. It should be noted, however, that Judge Bazelon pointed out in *CBS* v. *FCC*, note 8, *supra*, that the *Midwest Video* decision was based entirely on statutory grounds and that the "Supreme Court reserved consideration of a generally available affirmative right of access to cable television."

Epilogue

The contemporary struggle for possession of the First Amendment is intense, and its intensity is undiminished by the fact that the battle is fundamentally theoretical. The dominant approach of our law to problems of free expression has been romantic. Particularly romantic was the unexamined assumption that the removal of governmental restraint on the press would automatically encourage the wide dissemination of disparate viewpoints to the citizenry at large. The Holmes marketplace of ideas view rests on the hope that the unobstructed dissemination of information, rich in variety and contrariety, will enable the individual decision-maker, the ordinary citizen, to make informed judgments. Collectively the exercise of these individual judgments provides the mechanism which, in an ultimate, if not an operational, sense governs the nation.

The marketplace of ideas theory, both as metaphor and as a vehicle for implementation of conventional democratic theory, has become inadequate and inaccurate as even a symbolic description of contemporary First Amendment controversies. The twentieth-century reality, unanticipated by the optimistic mind of the eighteenth-century Englightenment which developed the First Amendment, is that an open marketplace of ideas will not necessarily result if the intrusive hand of government is kept at bay. Private economic forces and technological change have warped the First Amendment marketplace model both as metaphor and as reality.

To the extent that access theory had ever been designed to replace the marketplace of ideas theory in order to thrust the individual and his claims to rights of expression into the new and pervasive world of corporate media, the access theory now appears restorative of older First Amendment approaches, rather than, as has sometimes been perceived, a radical break with First Amendment tradition. In First Amendment theory, as apparently in so many other areas of American intellectual thought, a post-Watergate revisionism has appeared. For these new revisionists, media power is not a curse but a blessing. The enduring foe in this view is government. A powerful enemy merits a worthy foe. In this view, the press *should* be powerful because the purpose of press power is to curb the rising power of government.

In 1975, Mr. Justice Stewart gave a lecture at the Yale Law School which was significant because it exemplified an increasingly dominant mood in First Amendment law and theory. He declared that alone among the Bill of Rights, "the Free Press Clause extends protection to an institution." In this view, the constitutional recognition of freedom of the press is not the means to some larger end, such as effectuating democratic decision-making, aiding in the process of individual self-realization, assuring the variety and diversity of opinion, encouraging debate, or securing a marketplace of ideas - but an end in itself. As Justice Stewart put it, "the publishing business is, in short, the only organized private business that is given explicit constitutional protection."[1]

To see protection of the press alone as the primary purpose of the constitutional guarantee of freedom of the press is to think in terms of conferral of a special status on a sector of our society - the institutional press. The implication of Justice Stewart's view is that journalists are a special constitutional caste in our society.

Similarly, in a major critique of Alexander Meiklejohn's theory that the First Amendment should be seen as the instrument of individual self-governance, Professor Vincent Blasi writes: "My point is not that self-government presupposes a commitment by the electorate which seems unrealistic in our age of low voter turnouts and impoverished political discourse."[2] In Blasi's view, the self-governance approach to First Amendment understanding is open to a more fundamental defect:[3] "The Meiklejohn vision of active, continued involvement by citizens fails to describe not only the reality but also the shared ideal of American politics." Moreover, we are told that that "vision does not provide a secure basis for interpreting the First Amendment." What view does provide such a secure basis?

Blasi finds in the power of the press to curb excess or abuse by government the key to a secure basis for contemporary First Amendment interpretation. He describes this curbing function, or "checking value in First Amendment theory," as follows: "The central premise of the checking value is that abuse of official power is an especially serious evil - more serious than the abuse of private power, even by institutions such as large corporations which can affect the lives of millions of people."[4] Admittedly, more is to be feared from government than from the corporate media, but this does not mean that First Amendment theory cannot be made sufficiently eclectic to guard against abuse by the corporate media as well. In fairness to Blasi, he would provide legal redress against the media for private individuals although he might not do as much for public personalities.[5] "Narrowly drawn rights of reply contingent on personal criticism of the person seeking access should not be held to violate the First Amendment when the person criticized is not a public official."

Abandoning the goal of effectuating individual self-governance is unlikely, however, to leave much room for development of new means of legal redress for individuals victimized by media abuse. A First Amendment theory preoccupied with the media role in serving as a brake on abuse of power by government is a theory where, almost by definition, a First Amendment focus on individul rights is likely to be so muted as to be insignificant. Indeed, Blasi extols as a virtue of the checking function approach to the First Amendment the fact that it will be unnecessary for the individual to have to play a part in securing First Amendment values.

In Blasi's First Amendment regime, the individual may opt out. Matters of self-governance should be left to experts - the media.[6] "The checking value is premised upon a different vision - one in which the government is structured in such a way that built-in counterforces make it possible for citizens in most, but not all, periods to have the luxury to concern themselves almost exclusively with private pursuits." There is a difficulty with this analysis. Just as indifference to the actions of government by the citizenry tend to corrupt government and encourage it toward excess, assigning the task of providing accountability for government primarily to the media is likely to encourage a similar excess. Republics flourish and endure when the citizen participates, not when he opts out.

In the past few years, in the wake of Watergate and in the light of newly-won media immunities from law, the extent to which the present structure of American mass communications departs from the open marketplace of ideas model is now being analyzed, not as in the quite recent past, as a cause for anxiety and concern, but as a matter for celebration. Indeed, the increasing tendency of the American mass media to acquire monopolistic or quasi-monopolistic tendencies is now being praised as necessary to do battle with government.[7] Unhappily, such a theory fails to give enough attention to the individuals caught in such Armageddons.

Disappointment at seeing the collapse of the marketplace-of-ideas metaphor which has inspired so much of the judicial literature of freedom of expression is not in itself surprising. Normally, it would be expected that some agenda for reform would accompany such disappointment.

The remoteness of the media from the ordinary individual, like the remoteness of the ordinary individual from government, is now to be used not to give new protection to the individual but to justify the acquisition of new power by the centralization and concentration of ownership in the media. Surely this is to worship the chains that bind us and to build a First Amendment theory not on hope but on pessimism. A society so riven with pessimism and self-doubt that it can only be redeemed by corporate power agglomerations forever sniping at the equally unattractive agglomeration of governmental power has lost the need for a First Amendment.

Post-Watergate First Amendment theory is largely an effort to wrest away from the individual what little grasp he has left on possession of the First Amendment. We are left with two most unattractive protagonists - big government and big media. The new and destructive assumption is, increasingly, that the role of the individual in a regime ordered by the First Amendment is properly peripheral. This is a doctrine which will not only fail to achieve freedom of expression but which will write its epitaph.

The rise of the idea that the institutional press should be the central protagonist in First Amendment protection, and, at least by implication, the individual a peripheral one, has had ample encouragement. In 1964, the *New York Times* v. *Sullivan* case made it very difficult for elected public officials to recover damages in libel. Yet here the focus was still on the "citizen critic" of government rather than on the media defendant. There soon followed a remarkable expansion of that case. The consequence was a limitation on the reputational rights of private individuals so long as they were prominent.[8] The result was a radical incursion, on constitutional grounds, into the traditional law of libel and a greater insulation for the press from the penalties of libel law than ever before in the history of American journalism. In 1974, in the *Gertz* case, there was a strong suggestion in the Court's opinion that *media* defendants merited and were afforded a particular protection from the law of defamation that other libel defendants might not enjoy.[9] The focus on the "citizen critic" had entirely dimmed.

Most important, the decision of the Supreme Court in *Miami Herald Publishing Co.* v. *Tornillo* constituted the conferral of a special status on the press.[10] In that conflict between the right of free expression of a labor leader and the newspaper's right not to publish, the free speech claim was in effect held to be subordinate to the free press claim. Tobias Simon and I, as lawyers for Pat Tornillo, head of a teachers' union, argued for an inclusive theory of First Amendment protection. Tobias Simon, a life-long civil libertarian and labor leader, was shocked at the audacity of the *Miami Herald*'s refusal to allow its victim, his client, Pat Tornillo, to answer its editorial attacking him. The *Herald,* in turn, was shocked at the audacity of anyone who would dare to assert their free expression rights ahead of those asserted by the press.

Dan Paul, a lawyer for the Miami *Herald* and a civil libertarian, argued in his brief: "The First Amendment gives newspapers freedom to advocate their own views undeterred by any requirement to meet a governmentally imposed standard of 'fairness'."[11] In support of this proposition, Paul quoted Mr. Justice Stewart for the proposition that "the First Amendment's guarantee of a free press . . . gives every newspaper the liberty to print what it chooses, free from the intrusive editorial thumb of Government."[12]

Symptomatically, each side in the *Miami Herald* case was able to find appropriate support for its position in the writings of the nation's most distinguished First Amendment scholar. Counsel for Tornillo quoted the following passage among others from Professor Emerson:[13] "There are other devices for protecting the individual that are not only consistent with a system of freedom of expression but that would strengthen and vitalize it. The most significant is a right of reply ... It [a right of reply] is particularly applicable in the case of the press where abandonment of the libel action would be felt the most." Counsel for the *Miami Herald*, on the other hand, strongly emphasized the following passage from Professor Emerson which in turn had been relied on by Mr. Justice Douglas in his separate opinion in the case of *Columbia Broadcasting System, Inc. v. Democratic National Committee*:[14]

> any effort to solve the broader problems of a monopoly press by forcing newspapers to cover all "newsworthy" events and print all viewpoints, under the watchful eyes of petty officials, is likely to undermine such independence as the press now shows without achieving any real diversity.

Here indeed was a case of First Amendment rights in conflict.[15] In such conflicts is it inevitable that one claim must necessarily be triumphant and the other abandoned? Is it not possible in such circumstances to weigh on a case-by-case basis competing claims, in the light of different contexts, with the result that an access claim will be preferred on one occasion and a freedom to publish claim on another?

Benno Schmidt has analyzed the tension in First Amendment theory which has been provoked by the access problem in involving a clash between a historical First Amendment tradition of publisher autonomy and an instrumental approach to the First Amendment designed to serve the "utilitarian goal of diversity of expression."[16] At least theoretically, he says, such a clash would appear to require a reconciliation of "the values of autonomy and diversity."[17] If such a reconciliation were seen to be an appropriate - and possible - task for First Amendment interpretation, Schmidt describes how such an endeavor would be undertaken:[18] "The aim of analysis would be to determine which 'publishers' should be protected from access so that the values of autonomy can be best preserved. Conversely, analysis would have to determine which other 'publishers' should be made accessible to serve the goal of diversity. Rights of access would have to be allocated to particular publishing units in such a way that the aim of diversity would be served to the maximum, but jeopardy to the values of autonomy would be kept to a minimum." It is exactly such an approach to access problems which one may wish had been undertaken by the Supreme Court in the *Miami Herald* case.

Just as in the reverse discrimination case, *Regents of the University of*

California v. *Bakke*, the white medical student was permitted to go to medical school while the edifice of affirmative action was kept alive,[19] so, in the long run, it might have been wiser in the *Miami Herald* case for the Court if it had decided in favor of the publisher while keeping the legal edifice of access to the press alive. Instead, by deciding, so unreservedly, for editorial or publisher autonomy, the Court has itself occasioned a constant need continuously to reject press claims asserting a special status for the press.

Thus, in the 1978 term, the Court refused to hold that an ordinary business corporation's rights of free expression could be tampered with to a larger extent than the state would be allowed to tamper with the rights of a media corporation. In a claim for media inspection and copying of presidential tapes which had not been disclosed to the public and which were in the custody of the court, the Court rigidly resisted the argument that the press had a special claim for access to such materials:[20] "The First Amendment generally grants the press no right to information about a trial superior to that of the general public."

Similarly, in a 4-3 decision, the Court rejected the contention that the news media were entitled to special First Amendment rights of access to a jail. Chief Justice Burger responded that "the media has no special right of access to the Alameda County jail different from or greater than that accorded the public generally." Citing *Miami Herald*, the Chief Justice said that "editors who inspect a jail may decide to publish or not to publish what information they acquire." He denied that the "decisions of this Court or the First Amendment" support a contention that "media personnel are the best qualified persons for the task of discovering malfeasance in public institutions."[21] The victory of the *Miami Herald* over *Tornillo* was important. It is doubtless encouraging for the press to be told that it is free and does not need to be fair. But in silencing Tornillo, how much new, and more important, protection was lost?

The notable resolution of that conflict was a unanimous decision in favor of the press. Little wonder that Mr. Justice Stewart, and others, have since concluded that the press should be viewed as a special branch of government endowed by the First Amendment with special and unique privileges. For me, the irony was that I had hoped the *Miami Herald* case might be the vehicle of new public rights to the private press. The contrary happened and the *Miami Herald* case instead ushered in a new doctrine of editorial privilege. This new emphasis has had an impact in every area where journalism encounters law. This impact is found in virtually every chapter of this book.

Each chapter has focused on a point at which law intersects with journalism. The ultimate question in each is the extent to which the press should be subject to law.

For many in the media today, the exclusive office of the First Amendment is to make the press the last citadel of laissez-faire. In this post-Watergate era, arguments have been made that a special status should be conferred on the press, and that the press should be regarded as a branch of government with a special assignment to curb and expose excess and abuse in the other branches of government. Such a view can properly marshal powerful arguments in its support. Its defect is that it may take too tunnel-visioned a view of the nature of the antagonisms and antagonists in our society.

In this century of the positive state, we are properly mindful to endow the press with enough constitutional armor to withstand the assaults of the state. We should also be mindful that there are tensions as well between individuals and the press. In matters of reputation, access, and reply, as I hope the chapters of this book illustrate, the press and the individual sometimes are not allies but foes.

The individual has come increasingly to see big media as not very different from big government. With respect to government, however, our whole constitutional tradition is replete with modes of oversight and self-correction. These processes are inherent by virtue of the division of American government into three separate branches. The whole system of checks and balances promises some hope of relief for the individual in an unequal contest with government. Battles between the individual and the media, however, appear increasingly unequal.

The new chairman of the Federal Communications Commission, Charles Ferris, in his inaugural speech to the National Association of Broadcasters told them a flattering truth: "Broadcasters have the power to give access to competing ideas." Then he told them a truth they were less eager to hear: "You [the broadcasters] can expect that the Congress, the courts, and the commission will continue to require that you do not deny the public access to those ideas."[22]

It is sometimes said that the press should have no special burdens and no special privileges. This argument is deceptively attractive. The press has already received important new privileges in the form of a relative immunity from libel law and in the new immunity from having to satisfy any claims of access or reply to the print media. When we consider the actual plight of a libel plaintiff who wishes to defend a reputation inaccurately tarnished, we see - particularly in the case of a prominent libel plaintiff - how difficult it is to protect a claim for reputational integrity against a claim of free publication.

The trouble with the argument that the press should not be specially burdened or specially privileged is that we never know the starting point of such an argument. If the press is to receive no new privileges, this still does not dispose of the question whether existing doctrines of press privilege flowing from *New York Times* or *Miami Herald* are so dislocative of the First Amendment accommodations which preceded them that any future effort to give weight to a free speech or access claim is doomed from the outset. The reputational interest of the libel plaintiff is considered to be of equal dignity to the editorial sanctity claim of the media defendant. If one may use theological terms for constitutional controversies, freedom of the press is an important value but not a divine one.

The English experience shows a concern for the individual in conflicts between the individual and the press to which both American law and press are increasingly insensitive. On the other hand, the English experience shows a preference for government in conflicts between the media and government which is often inimical to freedom of expression. This observation highlights for me the following conclusion. In the excitement about decisions such as those involving the Pentagon Papers, the Watergate affair, our law may be so preoccupied with the problems engendered by clashes between the media and the state that inadvertent but nevertheless significant damage may be done to the individual who finds himself in less famous but no less serious clashes with the media.

Is it possible to have freedom of the press and yet require some measure of fairness and public participation in the processes of a free press? The view expressed in this book is that it is. The First Amendment, including the clause guaranteeing freedom of the press, is a people's amendment. Freedom of the press does *not* belong, in the largest sense, to the newspaper or to the broadcast industry. It belongs to the people.

The various collisions between individual and media freedom discussed in this book basically are designed to give new force not to a new idea but to an old one. In a free society, no sector within it, particularly a powerful sector, should aspire to be beyond the law. Mr Justice Frankfurter expressed it well more than thirty years ago:[23]

> Power in a democracy implies responsibility in its exercise. No institution in a democracy, either governmental or private, can have absolute power. Nor can the limits of power which enforce responsibility be finally determined by the limited power itself . . . In plain English, freedom carries with it responsibility even for the press; freedom of the press is not a freedom from responsibility for its exercise.

Notes

1. See Stewart, *Or of the Press*, 26 Hastings L.J. 631, 633-4 (1975).
2. Blasi, *The Checking Value in First Amendment Theory*, 1977 American Bar Foundation Research Journal 523 at 561.
3. *Id.* at 562.
4. *Id.* at 538.
5. *Id.* at 627.

6. *Id.* at 562.

7. See discussion of this point in the chapter on cross-media ownership problems in this book, Chap. 9, pp. 147-8, particularly in relation to Bezanson, *The New Free Press Guarantee,* 63 Virginia L. Rev. 731 at 774-5 (1977). It should be emphasized that although Professor Bezanson thinks that concentration of ownership may have some positive aspects from a First Amendment view, he is very careful to reject claims for a special status for the press as a general approach of First Amendment problems. In my view, finding First Amendment significance in centralization of the media is itself a way of according the press a special status.

8. 376 U.S. 225 (1953).

9. *Gertz v. Robert Welch, Inc.,* 418 U.S. 323 (1974).

10. 418 U.S. 241 (1974).

11. See brief for appellant, The Miami Herald Publishing Co., *Miami Herald Publishing Co.* v.*Tornillo,* Supreme Court of the United States, No. 73-797, October Term 1973, No. 73-797, p. 13.

12. *Id.* at 14, quoting *Columbia Broadcasting System, Inc.* v. *Democratic National Committee,* 412 U.S. 94 (1973).

13. Emerson, *The System of Freedom of Expression* 670 (1970) quoted in brief for appellee, Pat L. Tornillo, Jr, *Miami Herald v. Tornillo,* Supreme Court of the United States, No. 73-797, October Term, p. 11.

14. Emerson, *The System of Freedom of Expression* 671 (1970), quote in brief for appellant, note 11, *supra.*

15. In oral argument to the Supreme Court in the *Miami Herald* case, I portrayed - unsuccessfully - the case to the court as one of First Amendment rights in conflict.

16. Schmidt, *Freedom of the Press* v. *Public Access* 35 (1976).

17. *Id.* at 35-6.

18. *Id.* at 36.

19. 438 U.S. 265 (1978).

20. *Nixon* v. *Warner Communications,* 435 U.S. 589 (1978).

21. *Houchins* v. *KQED,* 438 U.S. 1 (1978).

22. Remarks of Charles D. Ferris, Chairman, Federal Communications Commission before the 56th Annual Convention of the National Association of Broadcasters, reprinted in *Broadcasting,* Apr. 1978.

23. See *Pennekamp* v. *Florida,* 328 U.S. 331 (1946).

Table of Cases

Accuracy in Media, Inc. v. FCC, 44, 123
American Security Council Education Foundation v. FCC, 154

Baker v. F & F Investment, 57
Banzhaf v. FCC, 104, 129
Bates v. State Bar of Arizona, 16, 96, 98, 104, 105
Bigelow v. Virginia, 16, 99
Brandywine-Main Line Radio, Inc. v. FCC, 3, 134, 137
Branzburg v. Hayes, 12, 56, 57, 61, 71, 174
Brown v. Commonwealth, 57

Caldero v. Tribune Publishing Co., 57, 71
Calero v. Del Chem. Corp., 65
Carey v. Hume, 57
Central Hudson v. Public Service Commn., 100, 111
Central South Carolina Chapter, Society of Journalists v. Martin, 34
Cervantes v. Time, Inc., 57
Chandler v. Florida, 175
Chicago Joint Bd. v. Chicago Tribune Co., 24
Chisholm v. FCC, 142
C.B.S., Inc. v. Democratic Nat'l Comm., 2, 3, 55, 56, 61, 64, 65, 69, 70, 73, 123, 124, 128, 129, 187

C.B.S., Inc. v. FCC, 154, 176, 186
Communication of United Church of Christ (Office of) v. FCC, 24
Consolidated Edison v. Public Service Commn., 113
Curtis Publishing Co. v. Butts, 62, 63, 65

Democratic Nat'l Comm. v. McCord, 57
Dennis v. United States, 174
Dun & Bradstreet, Inc. v. Grove, 104

Edwards v. Nat'l Audubon Soc., Inc., 64
Erznoznik v. Jacksonville, 92

FCC v. Midwest Video, 141, 181
FCC v. N.C.C.B., 60, 86, 139, 146, 148-154
FCC v. Pacifica Foundation, 64, 176
Feil v. FTC, 105
First Nat'l Bank v. Bellotti, 66-68, 146, 180
Freedom of the Press v. Public Access, 89, 187

Gannett Co., Inc. v. Pasquale, 34, 85, 175
Gertz v. Robert Welch, Inc., 4-7, 13, 57, 58, 62-66, 68, 83, 186
Gilbert v. Allied Chem. Corp., 57

Harris v. McRae, 22

Herbert v. Lando, 25, 53, 54, 56-74, 83-85, 179
Houchins v. KQED, 188

Jacron Sales Co. v. Sindorf, 65

Kissinger v. Reporters Comm. for Freedom of the Press, 173
Kunz v. New York, 8

Lee v. Bd. of Regents, 41, 42, 46
Lehman v. City of Shaker Heights, 91-98
Lorain Journal Co. v. United States, 110

Maryland v. Baltimore Radio Show, 72
Miami Herald Publishing Co. v. Tornillo, 1-8, 12, 13, 40, 42, 43, 54-56, 58-61, 63-65, 69, 70, 73, 74, 94, 97-104, 109-112, 115, 116, 146-148, 177, 186-189
Miami Herald Publishing Co. v. Tornillo, Brief for appellant, 186, 187
Miami Herald Publishing Co. v. Tornillo, Brief for appellee, 15, 187
Midwest Video v. FCC, 141
Mississippi Gay Alliance v. Goudelock, 41-51, 93, 95

N.B.C., Inc. v. FCC, 122, 124, 125, 127, 129, 144
N.C.C.B. v. FCC, 3, 17, 18, 124-126, 137-143
Nebraska Press Assoc. v. Stuart, 31-34, 59, 60
Nebraska Press Assoc., State ex rel., v. Stuart, 32
New York Times Co. v. Jascalevich, 57

New York Times Co. v. Sullivan, 2, 3, 5-7, 11, 12, 54, 56-74, 104, 114, 115, 125, 178, 179, 186, 189
Nixon v. Warner Communications, 188

Packer v. Utah, 92
Pennekamp v. Florida, 190
Police Dept. of Chicago v. Mosley, 47
Pittsburgh Press Co. v. Pittsburgh Commn. on Human Relations, 100-103

Radical Lawyers Caucus v. Pool, 40, 42
Red Lion Broadcasting v. FCC, 1, 5, 59, 66, 85, 123, 131, 139, 141, 146, 147
Regents of the Univ. of Calif., 187, 188
Richmond Newspapers, Inc. v. Virginia, 34, 85, 175
Rosenbloom v. Metromedia, 3, 4, 7

St. Amant v. Thompson, 63
Silkwood v. Kerr-McGee Corp., 57
Stanley v. Georgia, 174
State v. Peter, 57

Time, Inc. v. Firestone, 10, 86, 87
Time, Inc. v. Hill, 61
Tornillo v. Miami Herald Publishing Co., 3, 59

Valentine v. Chrestensen, 89, 90
Virginia State Bd. of Pharmacy v. Virginia Citizens Consumer Council, Inc., 16, 93-96, 99, 103, 106, 107, 109

Warner-Lambert Co. v. FTC, 60, 106-112, 115-117

Wolston v. Readers Digest Assoc., Inc., 86
Wooley v. Maynard, 44, 45
Writers Guild v. A.B.C., 30

Writers Guild v. FCC, 30

Zucker v. Panitz, 41, 42, 46
Zurcher v. Stanford Daily, 83

Index

Note: References are to page numbers. References followed by the letter "n" are to notes to the text introduced on the page bearing that number. Notes to each chapter follow that chapter.

Abortion
  positive government obligation, 22
Absolute privilege, denial of, 57, 61
Access
  broadcast media
    denial of, 2
    methods, 17, 18
  development, trends, in 175-178
  electronic media, methods, 17, 18
  ethical solution, problems, 31-35
  First Amendment. See First Amendment
  grace, by
    development of, 16
    methods, 23-29
    voluntary press code, 23-29
  information, to development of, 173-175
  issue, nature, of 35
  legal solution, necessity for, 31-35
  nature of claims
    commercial advertising, 15, 16
    right of reply, 15
    paid, television, for, 128, 129, 132
  political support for, development, 1, 2
  right of. See Right of access
  subsidies for, proposals, 22
  theory, nature of, 183
  Tornillo case, effects, 1-8
Accountability
  council, to, code proposal for, 29, 30

development of, trends in, 178-180
Advertising
  categorisation of, effect, 97, 98
  censorship
    media, by, 101-103
    state, by, 100, 101
  commercial speech. See Commercial speech
  media censorship, 101-103
  political, commercial speech doctrine restricting, 91-93
  professional, commercial speech protection, 96
  right of access
    consumer interest basis, 112, 113
    evolution, 89
    voluntary code proposal, 24, 25
    state restrictions, 99
Balanced presentation of ideas, fairness doctrine effecting, 3
Bazelon
  access rights, limited, 156n
  change of view, effects, 154
  diversification of ownership support, 137
  fairness doctrine, retreat from, 137
Britain
  open government, reduced importance, 163, 171
  press
    freedom, vulnerability, 160
    influence of, 160, 161
    right of access, 162
    subsidies, 162

197

press law
  constitution, 159
  contempt, 160, 165
  differences, reason for, 169, 170
  libel, 160, 164-171
  national security, 160
  structural differences, 159
  substantive differences, 160
Broadcast media
  access to
    denial of, 2
    methods, 17, 18
  diversity of ownership, effects, 18
  fairness doctrine, 18
  ownership, concentration, 144
  press ownership. See Cross-ownership
  regulatory jurisdiction, 149, 150
Cable television, diversity from, 140, 180, 181
Campus press. See Student press
Censorship, advertising control as, 102
Citizen critic, protection to, 74, 80n
Commercial information, right to, 116
Commercial speech
  access for, nature of claim, 15, 16
  constitutional status, 95
  corrective requirements
    compulsory print order, 77n
    constitutionality, 103, 104
    counter-commercials, 104
    extent of, 105, 106
    media subject to, 100
    product disclaimers, 106-112
    public deception test, 109, 110
  doctrine
    content, 90
    effect, 90, 91
    political advertising, effect on, 91-93
    survival of, 112
  editorial discretion
    effect, 94
    relationship, 101
  equality of access, 95
  meaning, 89-91
  political speech distinguished, 93, 94, 115
  professional advertising, 96
  public interest factors, 94, 95
  right of access for, evolution of, 89
  state involvement, 116, 117
Compelling publication
  corrective requirements. See Commercial speech
  public information test, 111
Complaints, mechanism, code proposal for, 30, 31
Consumer perspective, right of reply based on, 97
Contempt, British law, 160, 165
Corrective advertising. See Commercial speech
Council, accountability to, code proposal for, 29, 30
Criminal trials
  openness principle, 85
Cross-ownership
  constitutional issue, 152
  divestiture
    constitutionality, 152
    requirement, 138
  meaning, 137
  public interest exception, 142
  renewal considerations, 142, 150
  restriction on, 86, 152, 153
  rules, significance, 137-139
Discovery
  editorial privilege at, assertion, 53, 54

Diversification of ownership. *See* Ownership
Diversity of opinion
cable television function, 180, 181
methods of achieving, 141
regulatory promotion, 149, 150
Editorial advisory boards, code proposal for, 27-29
Editorial autonomy. *See* Editorial discretion
Editorial discretion
accountability, relationship, 58, 59
commercial speech, relationship, 101
editor, nature of, significance, 44, 46
fairness doctrine, exception to, 44
freedom of press, as, 6
inquiry into, actual malice cases, 62-64
justification of, 115
political speech, effect on, 116
privilege. *See* Editorial privilege
protection of, necessity for, 15
public media, in, 41-44
restraints on, voluntary code proposal, 26, 27
special status claim, as, 114
unfettered, requirement for, 6
Editorial privilege
accountability, relationship, 58, 59, 64, 65
actual malice rule, relationship, 61, 62
assertion of, 53, 54, 73
denial of, 54, 61, 62
editorial discussion, for, 67
equality of defendants, 65
evidentiary, denial of, 71, 72
Lando case, effects of, 62-66

mental processes, exclusion of, 69
neutral reportage, 64
published material test, 73
qualified, proposal for, 67, 68, 71
recognition of
actual malice test precluding, 57, 58
example, 54
source of, 54-57
special media status, as, 57
surrogate for public basis, 66
Equal time rule, 143
Ethics
law contrasted, access cases, 31-35
solution to access problems, shortcomings of, 31-35
Evidentiary privilege, denial of, 71, 72
Fair trial
press restraints, court imposition, 31-35
Fairness doctrine
broadcast media, 18
editorial discretion exception, 44
efficacy, Bazelon retreat, 137
function, 18
implementation
balanced presentation from, 3
trends in, 9
public television, 44
structural model of press, relationship, 88n
television, application to. *See* Television
Federal Communications Commission
cross-ownership rules, 137
divestiture rule, restriction on, 151, 152
jurisdiction, diversification of ownership, 150

First Amendment
  absolute privilege, restriction on, 12
  access based on, 2, 3
  broadcast media, applicability, 147
  commercial speech doctrine. See Commercial speech
  conflicting claims
    power test, 112
    resolution of, 187, 188
  corrective advertising. See Commercial speech
  discovery process, application to, 70
  economic regulation by, 98
  effectiveness, government obligation to secure, 22
  fairness doctrine. See Fairness doctrine
  market place of ideas theory, 99, 183, 185
  ownership
    public, by, 84, 85, 190
    struggle for, 183
  private conflicts, application to, 60
  protection
    citizen critic, 74, 80n
    commercial emphasis, 117
    effects of, 12
    individual beliefs, 44, 45
    public figures, libel suits, 11
    trends in, 83
    truth as basis, 108
    universal, 74
  public, belonging to, 84, 85
  public forum requirement, 92
  purpose, 12, 13, 74, 181, 190
  qualified privilege, limits of, 11, 12
  special meaning for press, theory, 57, 75n
  television. See Television
  theories, 183-188
  Watergate, effect of, 185
Fourteenth Amendment
  economic regulations, replacement by First Amendment, 98
Fourth Amendment
  application, press, to, 83
Freedom of expression
  Britain, in, 163
  diversity, voluntary code proposal, 23, 24
  freedom for journalism contrasted, 14
  freedom of press contrasted, 21
  process, nature of, 13
  proprietary basis, 98
Freedom of information, 173
Freedom of press
  beneficiaries of, 21
  concept, 13
  criminal trial coverage, 85
  editorial discretion as, 6
  extent of, 14
  fair trial situations, conflicts, 31-35
  freedom of expression contrasted, 14, 21
  government obligtions, 21
  immunity from law distinguished, 84
  proprietary rights, effects, 15
  purpose, 21
  responsibility, correlative to, 190
  speech model, 85
  structural model, 85, 86, 88n
  traditional basis, 83
  Watergate justification, 148
Gag orders, jurisdiction, 32, 34
Government
  counterweight to, press as, 147-149, 184
  intervention, constitutionality, 13, 14

obligations
  abortion subsidies, 22
  First Amendment effectiveness, 22
  freedom of speech, 21
  positive financial aid, 22
  open. See Open government
  public media provision. See Public media
Grace, access by. See Access
Grand jury
  journalists immunity from assertion of, 11, 12, 14
  desirability, 12
Individual beliefs
  First Amendment protection, 44, 45
Information
  access to, development of, 173-175
  freedom of, 173
Investigative television. See also Television
  problems of, 121
Law
  ethics contrasted, access cases, 31-35
Libel
  absolute privilege, denial of, 57, 61
  British law
    differences, reason for, 169, 170
    power of, 164
    voluntary corrections, 166
  damages, restrictions on, 79n
  defences, British law, 168
  editorial privilege. See Editorial privilege
  laws
    function of, 17, 179, 180
    punitive nature, 59
    right of reply contrasted, 17
    trends in, 178, 179

public figures
  British law, 165, 167
  New York Times case
    extensions of, 11, 12
    test, 3, 5-7
    remedies, 4
  right of reply. See Right of reply
Marketplace of ideas theory, 99, 183, 185
Media
  access to. See Access
  access to information, development of, 173-175
  accountability, development of, trends in, 178-180
  broadcast. See Broadcast media
  press. See Press
Mental process, privilege for, denial of, 69, 70, 72
Minority groups, access by. See Access
National security, British law, 160
Neutral reportage, privilege for, 64
Ombudsman, code proposal for, 30, 31
Open government
  importance of
    Britain, in, 163, 171
    United States, in, 163, 171, 173-175
  public records, 173, 174
Outside writers, editorial space for, code proposal, 27-29
Ownership
  concentration
    access rights, 117n
    anti-trust position, 118n, 119n
    breaking of, 18
    Britain, in, 161, 162
    broadcast media, 144
    counterweight to government, as, 147-149, 184
    effects, 18, 19

First Amendment relationship, 84, 146, 147
  problems of, 6
  trends, 16, 17, 84
  Watergate justification, 148
cross. *See* Cross-ownership
diversification
  effect, content, on, 18, 141, 144, 152, 153
  government role, 141
  limited advantages, 154, 155
  proposal for, 137
  voluntary, 145
rights deriving from, plantation theory, 15, 21, 36n
Plantation, ownership rights as, 15, 21, 36n
Political advertising, commercial speech doctrine restricting, 91-93
Political information, right to, 116
Political speech
  commercial speech distinguished, 93, 94, 115
  editorial discretion, effect of, 116
Press
  freedom of. *See* Freedom of press
  access to information, development of, 173-175
  accountability, development of, trends in, 178-180
  Britain. *See* Britain
  government, counterweight to, 147-149, 184
  Marxist view of, 14
  nature of
    Marxist nations, 14
    Western democratic nations, 15
  public surrogate, as, 34, 35
  role
    speech model, 84
    structural model, 85, 86, 88n

special status
  denial of, 189
  theory, 184
student. *See* Student press
subsidy, Britain, in, 162
surrogate for public, privilege based on, 66
United Kingdom. *See* Britain
voluntary code. *See* Voluntary press code
voluntary restraints, ineffectiveness, 31-35
Privilege, editorial. *See* Editorial privilege
Professionals, advertising by, commercial speech protection, 96
Public figures
  libel
    New York Times case
      extensions of, 11, 12
      test, 3, 5-7
    right of reply, 4, 5, 7
Public issues, right of reply where, 7
Public media
  dangers of, 39
  function of, 39, 49-51
  right of access
    erosion of, 50, 51
    fundamental principle, 49, 50
  student press. *See* Student press
Public press
  obligations of, 46-49
  right of access, financial considerations, 49
Public records
  access to, development of, 173-175
Public television, fairness doctrine, 44
Reply, right of. *See* Right of reply
Retraction
  statutory provisions
    constitutionality, 4, 5

right of reply contrasted, 5, 7, 8
Right of access
  advertising
    consumer interest basis, 112, 113
    evolution, 89
    voluntary code proposal, 24, 25
  British press, 162
  broadcast media, denial of, 2
  commercial speech, evolution, 89
  demands for
    development, 2
    origins, 1
  development, trends in, 175-178
  illegality of advertised content, 43
  nature of claims, 16
  public interest factors, 96-101
  reply, for. See Right of reply
  state laws, constitutional questions, 1-7
  state restriction, 99
  student press. See Student press
Right of reply
  See also Access
  basis for, 13
  consumer perspective, 97
  demands for
    development of, 2
    nature of, 15
    origins, 1, 2
  libel cases, remedy, as, 4-7
  libel laws contrasted, 17
  public figures, 4, 5, 7
  public issues test, 7
  retraction statutes contrasted, 5, 7, 8
  state laws, constitutionality questions, 1-7
  television documentaries, 122-124, 134
  Tornillo case effects, 1-8
  voluntary provisions, code proposal, 25, 26
Speech, freedom of. See Freedom of speech
State university student press. See Student press
Student press
  access, right of. See right of access, *infra*
  compulsory support, effect, 44
  function of, 49-51
  nature of, 39
  obligations of, 46-49
  official view test, 44-46
  right of access
    constitutional basis, 47
    court enforcement, 40, 41
    editorial discretion, 41-44
    erosion of, 50, 51
    financial considerations, 49
    fundamental principle, 49, 50
    illegality exception, 41, 43
    right to edit conflicting, 47, 48
    state action test, 41, 42
  Tornillo case, effect, 41-44
Television
  absolute autonomy, effect, 122, 131
  cable, diversity from, 140, 180, 181
  equal time rule, 143
  fairness doctrine
    absolute autonomy solution, 122, 131
    application, approaches, 121, 131-134
    documentary fairness, 129-131, 132
    enforcement, 131-134
    license renewal method, 124-127, 133, 134
    paid access solution, 128, 129, 132

right of response, 122-124, 134
internal fairness, 129-131, 132
investigative, problems of, 121
license renewal
  cross-ownership, effect, 142, 150
  regulation by, 124-127, 133, 134
paid access, 128, 129, 132
Tornillo case
effects, right of reply, 1-8
Trial, openness principle, 85
Voluntary press code
  consent
    advertising access, 24, 25
    complaints mechanism, 30, 31
    council, accountability to, 29, 30
    diversity of expression, 23, 24
    editorial advisory boards, 27-29
    editorial restraint, 26, 27
    ombudsman, 30, 31
    outside writers space, 27-29
    right of reply, 25, 26
  implementation, practical problems, 31-35
  problems of, 31-35
  proposal for, 23
Voluntary restraint
  ineffectiveness, 31-35
  Nebraska Press Association case, 31-35
  press code, by. *See* Voluntary press code
Watergate, effect of
  First Amendment theory, 185
  press role, 148

MAY 4 1983

KF
2750
.B37

002609628 3/9

16.G   0692877   1996 05 16